Backgrounds
to
British Romantic
Literature

Chandler Publications in
BACKGROUNDS TO LITERATURE
RICHARD A. LEVINE, EDITOR

Backgrounds
to
British Romantic
Literature

~

KARL KROEBER
University of Wisconsin

CHANDLER PUBLISHING COMPANY
124 Spear Street, San Francisco, California 94105

S R A Science Research Associates, Inc., 259 East Erie Street, Chicago, Illinois 60611
A Subsidiary of IBM   Distributors

Previously published and copyrighted materials are reprinted with the permission of authors, publishers, or copyright owners as listed below:

From Bernard Smith, *European Vision and the South Pacific, 1768–1850,* pp. 1–7. © Oxford University Press 1960. Reprinted by permission of The Clarendon Press, Oxford.

From Georges Lefebvre, "Revolutionary Expansion and its Effects," pp. 318–324, and "The Results of the War," pp. 347–355, of *The French Revolution from 1793 to 1799,* tr. John Hall Stewart and James Friguglietti; New York: Columbia University Press, 1964. © 1964 Columbia University Press. Reprinted by permission of the publisher.

From G. M. Trevelyan, *History of England,* 3rd ed., Book V, Chapter 5. London: Longmans, Green & Co. Ltd., 1952. Reprinted by permission of the publisher.

From *The Industrial Revolution, 1760–1830* by T. S. Ashton, published by Oxford University Press, 1964. Reprinted by permission of the publisher.

R. J. Forbes, "Power to 1850," pp. 148–164, reprinted from Charles Singer et al., *A History of Technology,* Vol. IV, 1958, by permission of The Clarendon Press, Oxford.

From *English Thought in the 19th Century,* by D. C. Somervell, copyright 1947 by D. C. Somervell (New York). Used by permission of David McKay Company, Inc., and Methuen & Co. Ltd., London.

From Walter Graham, *English Literary Periodicals,* pp. 230–237 and 238–245. Reprinted by kind permission of Mary W. Graham. The book is currently published by Octagon Books, Inc.

From Élie Halévy, *England in 1815,* tr. E. I. Watkin, 2nd rev. ed. London: Ernest Benn Ltd., 1960. English translation © Ernest Benn Ltd., 1960. Reprinted by permission of Ernest Benn Ltd. and Barnes & Noble, Inc.

From *The Rise of Modern Industry,* 7th ed., by J. L. Hammond and Barbara Hammond; London: Methuen & Co. Ltd., 1947. Reprinted by permission of the publisher.

From *Waterloo to Peterloo* by R. J. White; New York: The Macmillan Company. Copyright 1957 by R. J. White. Reprinted by Permission of Heinemann Educational Books Ltd., London.

From *English Country Life, 1780–1830* by E. W. Bovill, published by Oxford University Press, 1962. © E. W. Bovill 1962. Reprinted by permission of the publisher.

From *The Regency Style, 1800–1830* by Donald Pilcher; London: B. T. Batsford Ltd., 1947. Reprinted by permission of the publisher.

From *Turner: Imagination and Reality* by Lawrence Gowing. New York: The Museum of Modern Art, 1966. Reprinted by permission of the publisher.

Contents

Backgrounds
to
British Romantic
Literature

Introduction

~

The Romantic Period is usually defined as including the forty years between the outbreak of the French Revolution and the passage of the first Reform Bill, 1789–1832. Such limits are as sensible as any, although the period so defined possesses two distinct phases.[1] The earlier, ending with the Battle of Waterloo in 1815, is dominated by the impact of the French Revolution, which within four years brought England and France to war. The war, which with the rise of Napoleon severely threatened British sovereignty, lasted for twenty-two years. On Napoleon's fall Britain's position as the chief nation of Europe was established, and the next seventeen years of her history were characterized by increasingly effective agitation for internal political reform to match the social and economic transformations the nation had undergone. "Peterloo" in 1819 became a major symbol of the striving toward more representative government which culminated in the Reform Bill of 1832, the parliamentary act which launched Britain as a democracy in the modern sense.

There is significant continuity between the phases. The French Revolution was a serious matter to Britain because revolutionary aspirations were shared by many Britons. The war was an artificial check on these impulses toward social and political reform, but they reemerged as soon as the threat of Napoleon disappeared. Political power was controlled by the Tory party during the entire epoch, but Pitt, the dominating leader of the first phase, was relatively progressive in domestic affairs, and Lord Liverpool, Prime Minister from 1812 through 1826, was a

---

[1] The two phases are sharply marked in literary history. Burns, Blake, Wordsworth, Coleridge, Scott, and Southey all were born before 1775 and produced poetry before 1800. Byron, Shelley, Keats, and Hunt were born after 1785 and their important work appears only after 1810, by which time the chief poetic contribution of the first group was completed. Virtually all Romantic prose of value was published in the second phase.

stiff but moderate man under whom, as Asa Briggs has pointed out, the government (as well as the opposition) began to respond to the pressure of public sentiment in a fashion foreshadowing the attitude of more democratically elected, post-Reform administrations.

There is continuity, too, in the steady expansion and acceleration of industrialism throughout the period.[2] This "revolution" had begun before the Romantic age, but only in this epoch did the significance of the transformations wrought in human life by industrialism become manifest. For example, one origin of the industrial revolution is the shift during the seventeenth and eighteenth centuries in trading routes, from the Mediterranean to the Atlantic—a shift which contributed to Britain's rise in importance. But the shift in routes involved a shift in what was traded and to what purpose. Eastern trade centered on luxuries, such as silk, for a limited number of wealthy consumers. Western trade centered on commodities, for example, cotton, for mass consumption. In the Romantic period consciousness of the "mass" culture associated with industrialism (with which we are so familiar) began to develop. In the beginning of the epoch "popular" war based on national armies came into being; in the middle the modern concept of "class" began to take shape; toward the close of the era the multitude of professions, from engineering to civil service, which have since characterized all developed, industrialized, "mass" societies, began to become articulated and institutionalized in Britain.

One of the backgrounds to the Romantic period slighted in this collection of essays is the internationalism of the age. To understand fully British Romanticism one must see it in a European, even a global, context. Thus the most important figure of the Romantic era was a Corsican, often to the English, *the* Corsican, Napoleon—yet his name appears but rarely in this

---

[2] Because of its gradualistic nature the "industrial revolution" might better be called the evolution of industrialism. The essay by Forbes in this collection makes clear how late the practical effects of new sources of power were felt in Britain. The steam engine had little direct effect on the Napoleonic wars. However, the Romantic age is a decisive stage in the development of industrialism because it was then that *awareness* of the *potentialities* of industrialism (for good or ill) emerged.

collection after Trevelyan's chapter. Napoleon's rise, however, resulted from the French Revolution, and I have included a selection from Georges Lefebvre's masterful study of that event to suggest the worldwide repercussions of the upheavals in France between 1789 and 1799.

The dates are important. The French Revolution initiates the Romantic epoch (and the American Revolution precedes it). Romantic literature is a reaction to a completed event, insofar at least as Napoleon's seizure of power marked the end of the purely revolutionary phase. The dominating tone of Romantic works dealing with the Revolution is disillusion. Poets who had supported the Revolution or who, too young to have participated in it, sympathized with its original ideals, express disappointment at the defeat or betrayal of these ideals. The most significant British literary work emerging directly from the Revolution is Words-worth's *Prelude,* which shows how the poet's initial enthusiasm for the Revolution was transformed into despairing disillusion-ment that led, finally, to a hopeful but not enthusiastic serenity of mind attained through reaffirmation of values derived from private experiences. Though the dramatic fulcrum of *The Prelude* is the disappointment of youthful idealism for a public cause, the poem is not pessimistic—nor are most works deriving from the Revolution. Just as Napoleon consolidated and codified into lasting form many of the principles of the Revolution, so, in the main, poets enshrined in enduring art the exhilarating sense of creativity released by the Revolution. There are dark aspects and shadowed undercurrents in Romantic literature, but—in Britain at least—the total thrust of the Romantic era was progressive, expansive, liberating; and the tone of Romantic literature as a whole is hopeful, energetic, experimental, and forward-looking, although founded on an experience of the fail-ure of a political ideal.

Although the dark side of Romantic literature comes into being in part through explorations into the depths of the individ-ual psyche, at least as important is the Romantic writers' aware-ness of the social injustices which accompanied Britain's rise to world preeminence during the first years of the last century. On balance, Romanticism emphasizes the evils of the industrial revolution more than its benefits. The opposition of the poets to the course of industrialism is not, however, the simpleminded hostility of bird-watchers and flower-pickers. Nor are the Romantics really nostalgic. I cannot think of an occasion in the Waverley Novels (though there must be some) where Scott contrasts specific contemporary conditions unfavorably with those of the past. Sometimes no doubt he presents the past as prettier than it was, but there is remarkably little "good old days" sentiment in Scott and much about the dangers, discomforts, and disagreeableness of life before industrialization.

Wordsworth, a revolutionary in his youth, later became politically conservative, not to say reactionary, and from the beginning of his career he lamented the destruction of the virtues of the simpler times he associated with his earliest years. Yet little of his poetry is sentimentally nostalgic. Frequently he emphasizes the *inevitability* of social changes he resents, just as he stresses the inevitability of growing old. Indeed, much of his best poetry dramatizes the conflict between his recognition of these inevitabilities and his instinctive, emotional resistance to them.

The Romantics are too involved in the intensity of immediate experience simply to lament the vanished past. Often their experience is of the natural world, and they protest against the destruction of nature by the advance of increasingly mechanized civilization. It is characteristic of them to set up nature as an ideal against which to contrast the iniquities of burgeoning industrialism. They are the first poets to do so persistently, and their art is special testimony to the reality of the social disorientations commented upon by Ashton, the Hammonds, White, and others in this collection. Romantic writers, by and large, speak more for the sufferers of early industrialization than for those who benefitted from it. Yet they are less new spokesmen for the disadvantaged than they are the first artists to be alienated from their culture. Earlier poets had of course criticized social and political conditions, but usually with reference to Christian ideals. The Romantics are alienated in the modern sense, that is, condemnatory of their culture as a culture rather than critical of it as deviating from an abstract pattern provided by the sanctions of traditional religion. Insofar as they set forth social ideals, these are predominantly secular. The most characteristic Romantic protest against civilization is that it carries us away from nature rather than away from God, from the wisdom of instinctive pleasures rather than from divine grace. Yet "naturalism" plays a small role in their art. They praise nature for nurturing the purely human capacity to imagine something beyond and out of nature, for the gift of imagination by which they transcend "nature" and the limitations of "natural man."

The Romantics (like many of their successors) believe the chief shortcoming of modern society to be its tendency to dehumanize. The underlying irony of the Romantic vision lies in its perception that man's creations which should raise him above nature too often turn against their creator and reduce him to something worse than a natural creature. Frankenstein and his monster are Romantic inventions. Insofar as Romanticism expresses a philosophy of organicism, it celebrates vital processes, life; and Romantic criticism of modern civilization is that it diminishes instead of increasing the multiple potentialities of human life, although human life as distinct from purely biological life is seen as dependent upon the artifices created by civilization.

To understand this paradox of Romantic art, one may look at Pilcher's study of the style of building characteristic of early nineteenth-century Britain. Pilcher observes that the style is more impressive for its diversity than for its uniformity, that it comprehends a variety of motifs and aims and functions. But he sees that never far from any variation is the relevance of the "picturesque."

Too much ink has been wasted over this term, but for our purposes, which are general rather than detailed, picturesqueness may be regarded as referring to an interplay between man and nature to the benefit of both. A picturesque landscape is a natural scene observed or drawn or even shaped so as to bring out those qualities which are painterly, that is, evocative of the pleasure arising from artifice. On the other side, a picture, an artifact, an edifice, even a town is picturesque when it partakes of the natural (the "natural" often appearing at one remove through the "naive" artifice of an earlier artistry, one close to the processes of the natural world). Pilcher focuses on this creative intermediariness of the picturesque to show that the Romantic paper war over the definition of the term is a symptom of its significance, not a sign of its relevance only to a trivial skirmish between long-forgotten aestheticians. As he points out, extensive and varied technological innovations play a major role in developing Romantic architectural style. But the style aimed not at isolation from but engagement with nature. The country house served as the model for upper-middle-class housing in the cities, and the ideal country estate of a "man of taste" neither unduly regularized nature nor unduly subordinated artificial structures to the natural situation. Elizabeth Bennett's way of seeing and of judging Pemberley in *Pride and Prejudice* illustrates this interplay.

It was a large, handsome stone building, standing well on rising ground, and backed by a ridge of high woody hills; and in front, a stream of some natural importance was swelled into greater, but without any artificial appearance. Its banks were neither formal nor falsely adorned. Elizabeth was delighted. She had never seen a place for which nature had done more, or where natural beauty had been so little counteracted by an awkward taste.

Picturesqueness is one response to the encroachment of civilization upon nature. As canals, cities, roads spread across the countryside of Britain, and as commons were enclosed, more and more of nature literally could be seen only in relation to the artifices of civilization. Yet the Romantic genius was to make this process two-way. As man extended his domain into nature's, the Romantics deliberately brought nature back into man's artifices. Just as Wordsworth, Coleridge, Byron, Shelley, and Keats extolled the spiritual strengthening to be derived from appreciation of nature, so the best Regency architects and planners strove to mitigate the dehumanizing effects of expanding urbanization by reintroducing into their cities not merely formalized gardens but something of the wildness and irregularity of nature. The authentically Romantic part of London is Regent's Park. But it is not parks which most significantly express the Romantic countermovement to the spread of urbanization. The variety and diversity of Romantic forms, as contrasted to Neo-classic uniformity, is itself an effort to embody *in* artifice the fecund vitality of nature. And, although the poor suffered in the unplanned, all too "natural" squalor of massed slums, Regency architects planned for their well-to-do clients, and even groups of clients, edifices which stressed personal privacy. Picturesqueness is not monumental, not really public: at root picturesqueness is inseparable from private experience. The diversity characteristic of Romantic architecture reflects the celebration of individual experience, which is the subject of so much Romantic literature.

The central feature of life in England during the Romantic period, perhaps, is the intensified interpenetration of town and country life. Yet this picturesqueness casts its penumbra, illuminated by Bovill's essay on poaching. The early nineteenth-century's love of hunting was partly based on technological improvements in firearms (the influence of the war is obvious) and partly on the sudden war wealth of a relatively small segment of British society accompanying the impoverishment of many in the lower classes. Poaching flourished through the sale to city *nouveaux riches* of game obtained by poor men in the country. The realities of poaching are not aesthetically picturesque; they are, nonetheless, a part of Romanticism and demonstrate how pervasive were the increasingly complicated interactions of the rural and urban during the epoch. Entangled in these interactions is a dislocation of traditional balances between sanctions for individual enterprise and social moralities—a dislocation which serves as the inspiration and theme of many Romantic works of literature.

In some such way, it appears to me, one must go about establishing the connections between literary Romanticism and the history of the Romantic era. D. C. Somervell has summarized the hazards in making such connections.

In the last fifteen years of the nineteenth century there was a marked development of pride in the British Empire and also a continuous output of stories by Rudyard Kipling; in the first fourteen years of the twentieth century there was a marked increase of socialistic opinion and a continuous output of stories by H. G. Wells. There can be no doubt, of course, that the imperialist movement contributed to the formation of the mind of Kipling, and the socialist movement to the formation of the mind of Wells. Both are products and exponents of phases of public opinion. How far, if at all, can they also be regarded as creators of opinion?[3]

The question is even more difficult to answer when applied to a group of writers such as the Romantics. Even the existence of such a literary "class" has been challenged by A. O. Lovejoy, a distinguished historian of ideas, who argued that there was no one "Romanticism" in literature but only diverse, smaller "romanticisms." Later scholars have disagreed with Lovejoy but have failed to agree as to the proper definition of Romanticism. A guide to some of the principal schools of definition is supplied in the bibliography. In the following paragraphs I do not intend to provide a new theory. Instead, by looking at literary Romanticism in terms of the sociopolitical context illustrated by selections in this volume, I hope to highlight some features of the cultural thrust of the 1789–1832 period which ordinarily are slighted by purely literary analyses.

The first three essays in this volume touch on the internationalism of the Romantic age. Explorations of the later eighteenth century acted as a major precipitant of Romanticism.[4] Fascination with the exotic is a profound, not a superficial, attribute of Romanticism, and it possesses a temporal as well as a geographical orientation. Eighteen years before the establishment of the Royal Academy, which did much, incidentally, to encourage historical painting, the Society of Antiquaries received a charter, which may be taken as marking the coming of age of scientific history. Romanticism is inseparable from intensified historical consciousness. The fondness for medieval themes and subjects exhibited by many Romantic writers reflects the growing awareness of the importance of history. At the close of the eighteenth century all intellectual disciplines began to become historically oriented. Not only did already established sciences (biology is the

[3] D. C. Somervell, *English Thought in the Nineteenth Century* (London, 1929), p. 9.

[4] The eighteenth century was one of the great eras of discovery and exploration and the first of *scientific* exploration and discovery. Besides the voyages of Cook (discussed by Bernard Smith), one should remember the travels of William Bartram, Mungo Park, and James Bruce, among others. Probably the most important scientist-explorer of the Romantic age was Alexander Von Humbolt.

obvious example) assume historical dimensions that gave them new importance, but with the rise of a systematized sense of history the social sciences were born. The economics, political science, and sociology discussed in Halévy's chapter in this collection all derive from new considerations of historical factors in human societies.[5]

Literary medievalism, in fact, is a relatively superficial expression of this new consciousness. The Romantics are notable as the first poets to explore deeply the conception of human experience as predominantly a temporal process. Again and again their lyrics represent evolution of experience, dynamic experience. With this goes a revolution in positive and negative values. Unlike their predecessors, the Romantics seek authentication of values not in the permanent, which transcends or exists apart from the mutable and transitory, but *in* the processes of mutability, in dynamism as such. Repeatedly the poets define the humanly precious as inseparable from process, transformation, evolution: embodiments of temporal change and movement.[6]

Or, to look at a different feature of the period, one sees that the Hammonds are right to assert that much Romantic poetry is a protest against "The Curse of Midas." However much they differed in other matters, great poets from Blake to Keats agreed in opposing as an immediate evil, not as an abstract iniquity, the dedication of their society to financial profits and its consequent diminution of sensory, emotional, and spiritual qualities of human life. In the work of all the poets can be found noble pronouncements against the misery inflicted by a growing greed for profit. Keats has the reputation of being something of an aesthete, yet of his youthful narrative *Isabella*, which retells a story from Boccaccio, Shaw could write that it anticipates Marx.

[5] Twentieth-century anthropology and psychology originate in Romanticism. Freud's debt to Romantic literature and philosophy is well known, and the anthropological concept of culture has been shown to have begun taking shape at the end of the eighteenth century.

[6] The concern with process and change explains why one finds in the Romantic period the forerunners of later formal developments in art, most significantly, perhaps, the exploitation of a limited point of view as the structurally organizing principle of a work of art, the principle common to the dramatic monologue, impressionism, and so forth.

But one must observe that Romantic poetry probably could not have flourished as it did without the Curse of Midas. There were in the Romantic age people with money to spend on litera- ture—Byron and Scott, who struck the popular taste, who first tapped the rewards of something like a mass market, made for- tunes with their pens. Shelley renounced his claims to most of the wealth he might have inherited, but was left with a thousand pounds a year. Wordsworth's relatives provided him with a good education, and at a critical point in his career he was enabled by a friend's legacy to devote himself to poetry. Coleridge was subsi- dized in various ways by a variety of patrons. Had Keats had the benefit of the inheritance to which he was morally entitled, his life would have been easier and perhaps longer. Yet Keats had little difficulty in getting his poetry printed. In part, certainly, this was due to the singular charm of his personality, which attracted staunch friends. Taylor and Hessey (his publishers) admired Keats, but, to use Wordsworth's phrase, they "could *afford* to suffer" bad reviews and poor sales. Wordsworth and Coleridge found a publisher for the "unpopular" *Lyrical Ballads* and were able to issue a second edition within two years. Byron helped to have Coleridge's none-too-dramatic play *Osorio* pro- duced and so earned the author four hundred pounds. There was enough surplus wealth in Britain at the beginning of the nine- teenth century to enable even innovating poets to survive and to have their works circulated. Without denying the restrictions which Keats's relative poverty imposed on him, nor losing sight of the hack work men like Southey and Hunt were driven to, one notes that the two major Romantics who suffered the worst poverty were born more than a decade before Wordsworth— Robert Burns and William Blake. Chatterton, their contempo- rary, became for the later Romantics a symbol of the neglected, impoverished genius: yet *Endymion,* dedicated by Keats to Chat- terton's memory, was not neglected but was viciously reviewed.

Romanticism initiates modern political activity in that during the period an increasing role was played by a widening range of citizenry in many political processes. Wilberforce's successful an- tislavery campaign has been cited as the prototype for all later pressure groups. Walter Graham indicates in his description of the early years of the *Edinburgh* and *Quarterly* reviews that these important intellectual journals could hardly escape mingling literary criticism with political partisanship. The Romantic poets could scarcely have had the sensitivity to be poets without being affected by the political events of their time. But these events were not local and limited—their reverberations at least were worldwide. The politics of Romantic poets are generally less practical than philosophical, and the fullest political significance of their poetry is often expressed indirectly in nonpolitical verse.[7]

The Romantics, for example, are responsible for a democratization of literature. Before the Romantic epoch poets had been regarded as persons with special gifts and special training who wrote for limited audiences. No one extolled the poet more than the Romantics, but they denied his traditionally specialized attributes. Wordsworth characterizes the Romantics in defining the poet simply as "a man speaking to men" and in emphasizing that the capacities for creating poetry are those which the poet shares with other men, not those which set him apart. Simultaneously, the Romantics argued that the proper subjects for poetry were the sensations, feelings, ideas open, at least potentially, to all men, not merely to those specially educated and of a particular cultivation. The French and American revolutions have been called the first large-scale popular uprisings: in the same sense the Romantics might be called the first consciously popular poets.

This popularization is obscured by the intense personalization of Romantic lyricism. Halévy points out that British scientists were resistive to specialized vocabularies which would cut off their work from a general audience, but he observes also that both natural and social scientists operated individualistically. British poets, analogously, wanted to appeal to a general audience yet were highly individualistic. Poetic individualism, however, was bound up with explorations into new psychological frontiers. In this realm the poets do not so much reflect the impact of intellectual change as act as pioneers of such change. Elsewhere I have suggested that outbursts of lyricism can serve to

[7] It is nevertheless true that a great many Romantic poems cannot be fully understood without reference to the specific contemporary events which inspired them.

initiate major expansions of cultural and social energy through articulating new dimensions of consciousness and self-awareness.[8] Whether or not the generalization holds, Romantic poetry indisputably exposed its readers to new ranges of awareness.

Many Romantic poems deal with subjects which had never before been treated in serious literature. Because subsequent poetry has continued to be original in this way, we sometimes fail today to appreciate the Romantics' innovations. To cite a trivial example, I did not fully appreciate the originality of Wordsworth's minor poem "The Last of the Flock" until I encountered, in Greece, shepherds who own nothing but a small flock, whose lives are necessarily bound to their sheep, and for whom the diminution of their flock must be both economically and emotionally a death in life. The extension of my awareness does not, of course, improve Wordsworth's poem, but it makes me recognize how truly his verses treat of a reality which, although common enough in earlier times, had never before him appeared in sophisticated literature.[9]

But more impressive are Romantic adventurings into uncharted territories of the psyche. As has been well said, when one plunges to the depths of the mind one encounters familiar figures—Cain or Oedipus, for example. Psychological self-exploration seems almost inevitably to lead to the revelation of archetypes. But discovery of the archetypal within oneself is a very different matter from accepting ready-made the traditional archetypes of a cultural heritage. The Romantics rejected the public and official traditions which had dominated the immediately

[8] In *The Artifice of Reality* (Madison, 1964). I have since found support for this view in Ernst Cassirer's discussion in *The Logic of the Humanities* of how few themes there are in lyric poetry. Originality in lyricism must be associated with extensions of the psychic experiences in which the themes are embodied.

[9] Wordsworth has frequently been criticized for claiming in his theoretical writing that poetry should be written in the language used by simple and humble people but at the same time writing poetry in a language simple and humble people could not understand. But Wordsworth did not want to debase poetry; he wanted to enrich and extend it. Like all the Romantics, he wished to deny neither the most refined and subtle nor the most trivial and unsophisticated experiences of mankind their role in both the form and substance of art.

preceding literature and instead probed their own psyches. In so doing they did not so much invent new myths as create new *forms* of mythological art which were scarcely recognizable to most of their contemporaries. All educated Englishmen knew about Prometheus, but few were able to see any meaningful relation between the figure of traditional mythology and the protagonist of Shelley's *Prometheus Unbound.* The most notable victim of this kind of misunderstanding was Blake, who seemed insane to some of his contemporaries, even though much of his "private" allegory is derived from familiar sources such as the Bible and *Paradise Lost.*

The similarity between the difficulties of Blake's art and that of the other Romantics is often obscured by the *apparent* conventionality of their writing. Modern criticism of Romantic poetry, however, has shown how important is the complete meaning which lies beneath the superficial simplicity. Within Keats's odes, in some respects the supreme attainment of British Romantic poetry, are to be found a personal, experiential mythology and system of symbols growing out of conventional, not exotic, literary preoccupations such as contemplation of classical art, listening to the song of the nightingale, looking with observant eyes at an autumnal landscape.

Recently it has become fashionable to discover in Romantic poems apocalyptic elements. The term does justice to the originality of vision and the more-than-rational significance of the Romantic imagination, the psychic power to utilize the subconscious and to transcend the limits of rationalism. But "apocalyptic" misleads us if we associate it too directly with its original religious meaning. As religious poets the Romantics make a rather weak showing—and the essays by Ashton, Somervell, and Halévy in this collection make clear how surprisingly minor was the role of formal religion in the Romantic age.[10]

Science and technology, however, played a large part in the

---

[10] One should not, however, underestimate the influence of Romantic thought and art on subsequent religious developments. Coleridge's influence as a religious thinker has long been recognized, and Wordsworth's poetry undoubtedly did something to shape the tone and direction of many nineteenth-century sermons.

drama of Romanticism, as the poetry of the time shows.[11] Alfred
North Whitehead thought that had Shelley not been a great poet
he could well have been a great scientist, and others have called
attention to the foundation in the science of their day of many
Romantic poems, although only rarely can one equate specific
discoveries with specific poems. The relation is to be found where
Bernard Smith puts it, in a basic attitude of mind which finds
both satisfaction and excitement in the conscientiously accurate
observation of the actual world. As Smith points out in the first
essay in this collection, *scientific* exploration contributed to the
destruction of neoclassical ideals of landscape *art*. Each of the
great Romantics contributed to the literary revolution of his
epoch through conscientiously accurate representation of details
of actual life. The Romantics, odd as it may seem, are in a special
sense realists. They reject the tyranny of literary tradition and
convention. The most obvious evidence of this rejection is their
freedom in handling traditional literary forms, modifying them,
putting them to new uses, sometimes abandoning them altogether. The source and substance of their poetry is actual experience, what is actually seen, or felt, or thought.

Accuracy in representing the details of actuality makes all the
Romantics, regardless of their official politics, revolutionists. For,
as Blake never tired of insisting, what most people see and feel
and think most of the time is not actuality but illusion—
"abstraction," he called it—arising from habits and conventions
of social training. Just as natural scientists showed that the
natural world is different from what it was conventionally believed to be, so the Romantic poets showed that actual human
experience is in fact different, often quite different, from its
traditional representations in art. As a result, much Romantic
poetry is surprising and bewildering, as is so much of the science
of the past century and a half. Some Romantic poetry seems to
have little relevance to our ordinary world. This is why I put at

---

[11] ". . . it is not unfair to describe the nineteenth century as the first age in
which the accumulation of scientific knowledge was more important than law,
religion, art, and letters in determining the direction of ideas and attitudes of
the public at large towards accepted values." Woodward, *The Age of Reform*
(London, 1962), p. 562.

the end of this collection a commentary on Turner's painting, which provides visual illustration of how the Romantics, in manifesting the surge of the scientific spirit of their age, appear at first acquaintance to have separated themselves from it. A fundamental paradox of Romanticism is that the poets managed to establish the primary connotation of "Romantic" as "escapist," when their abiding aim was to reveal the actuality of living processes here and now on this earth.

The conventional opinion of Turner's art from his own day until the present is summed up by Hazlitt's comment: "Pictures of nothing; and very like, too." Vagueness, blurriness, failure to represent actuality, again and again these criticisms of Turner's pictures recur. John Ruskin did not agree. The foundation of his defense of Turner in *Modern Painters* is an absolute denial of the conventional judgment. According to Ruskin, Turner differs from other painters in that he paints things as they actually appear, not as they are conventionally supposed to look. Ruskin argues that Turner is baffling because he is precise in rendering visual impressions. The accurate delineation of topography and meteorological conditions sought by the artists who accompanied Cook on his South Pacific voyages is, if we follow Ruskin, thus fully realized in Turner's pictures. This view is revolutionary, for it means that we do not see as we think we see.[12]

So far as I know Ruskin's lengthy proof of Turner's accuracy has never been seriously challenged. In the few cases where my observations have permitted me to test the validity of Ruskin's evidence, I have found him to be correct. A single point that falls in the range of most people's experience: Ruskin argues that to understand many of Turner's sea scenes we must recognize his point of view to be from the sea, not the shore, and that the waves of the sea look entirely different from the sea than they do from the shore. This is manifestly true, as is Ruskin's claim that

---

[12] At this point one can make a connection between Blake's graphic art and Turner's, which are in some ways antithetical. Blake believed the artist should represent the truth seen, as he phrased it, *through* the eye, not *with* the eye. Ordinary descriptions of visual impressions are in fact representations of delusions (abstractions) sustained by convention. Only by exercise of imagination can we break through distortions fostered by tradition and perceive, truly *see,* actuality.

condemnation of these pictures is off the mark when it faults the artist for not representing the sea as it appears from the shore, the most conventional viewpoint for seascapes.

Much Romantic poetry is easily misunderstood in the way Ruskin shows Turner's pictures to be misunderstood. The poets' insistence on dealing with actual experience led them frequently to the representation of that which seems to a conventional view wild, baffling, unreal. Probably the clearest examples of this kind of representation are provided by poems of magic, myth, dream, and vision, in which the poet celebrates inner experiences which either transcend reason or find expression for subrational psychic energies. As literal narration of travel *The Ancient Mariner* is childish.[13] Its haunting power stems from its giving meaningful design to subtle psychological actualities. Yet much of the poem derives from Coleridge's reading of reports of actual travels, as Lowes proved in his famous study, *The Road to Xanadu*. If *The Ancient Mariner* represents accurately the psychological configuration of an experience of guilt and expiation, it does so in words and images which owe much to the literalistic descriptions of travelers and scientists. *The Ancient Mariner* is often rightly treated as a typical Romantic work because its imaginativeness consists in this unifying of disparate realities, of experiences which had, in the art of the preceding century and a half, been disassociated.

Almost more baffling than Romantic visionary art is the prosaic art that accompanies it, Wordsworth's meditations among the mountains of the Lake Country, Byron's skeptical satirizations of Regency high life, Jane Austen's realistic portrayals of the mundane occurrences of bourgeois daily life, Walter Scott's reconstructions of past history, and, in the visual arts, John Constable's pictures of East Anglian scenes. These last are certainly "accurate." Yet Constable's accuracy goes beyond verisimilitude. A critic must avoid being overimpressed by the artist's superficial realism. If we praise Constable, as too many of his admirers have, for his literal correctness, Ruskin's objections to

[13] This is why the "primitive" ballad form is appropriate, although there is nothing simple or crude about Coleridge's metrics: as so often in Romantic poems, the surface, the apparent form, is used to conceal deeper artifice.

his paintings have weight: *The Hay Wain* is only an early example of calendar art, a forerunner of *Saturday Evening Post* covers. But the literal accuracy of *The Hay Wain* (and other pictures by Constable) is not an end but a means, a means of representing the imaginative vision of a unified life of man and nature which transcends particular times and circumstances. Insight into that unity, however, is possible only through perception of its specific, momentary embodiments.[14] The aesthetic power of *The Hay Wain* is analogous to that of *The Solitary Reaper,* as to most of Wordsworth's better poems. As a recorder of natural phenomena Wordsworth is inferior, for example, to Tennyson. Description *per se* is almost never Wordsworth's central purpose, and his career exhibits progress away from an art of verisimilitude to an art of imaginative emblemizing.

There is much reliable history in Scott's narrative poems and novels, but in notes to these works he frequently draws attention to his deliberate departures from literal correctness. His goal as an artist is an imaginative truth which is inseparable from actuality yet not confined to a literal representation of it. Analogously, if one reads Jane Austen as a realist, one is almost driven to accept Charlotte Brontë's negative judgment of her as an artist. It is the imaginative vision which is contained within her fidelity to mundane truth that makes her novels so rereadable. Likewise it is in an interplay between satire and melodrama that the genius of Byron realizes itself. *Don Juan* is his masterpiece because there the interplay is simultaneously most dense and most quick-moving. And *Don Juan* is properly thought to be a representative Romantic poem because, in Byron's idiosyncratic fashion, it succeeds in being true to the diverse, paradoxical, and serious actualities of life while risking the superficial appearance of triviality and extravagance.

Imagination, the capacity to unify diverse realities and seem-

---

[14] It is, perhaps, the specific instantaneousness, the visual representation of a "spot of time," which renders Constable's sketches so impressive. They capture, more obviously than his formal canvases, the importance of the moment. It is worth noticing that Constable was deeply interested in scientific investigations of nature; his paintings of clouds (like Goethe's and Shelley's poems) are based not merely on accurate observation but also upon an understanding of the principles of meteorological phenomena.

ingly incompatible experiences in order to represent the paradoxical actuality of life concealed within conventionalized orderings
of it, is the special power which animates all great literature of
early nineteenth-century Britain. To appreciate the personal
qualities of the Romantic writers one must read their poems and
novels. The selections in this volume are intended to enrich such
reading by providing an introduction to the principal social and
intellectual circumstances which shaped, and were shaped by, the
poets and novelists of the Romantic age.

1.

Discovery and Exploration:
The European and the Pacific

~

BERNARD SMITH

In the year 1768 the Royal Academy was established and the Royal Society promoted Cook's first voyage to the South Seas. The two events fittingly represent two influential attitudes to nature current in English eighteenth-century thought. The formation of the Academy constituted the official recognition in England of those neo-classical theories of Italian origin which had been transmitted to Britain through French theorists like de Chambray and de Piles. Nature, it was said, was to be rendered by the artist not with her imperfections clinging to her but in her perfect forms; what those perfect forms were the artist could only learn by a close study of the masterpieces of the ancients and their Renaissance disciples. The Royal Society, on the other hand, approached nature in a different way, appealing to travellers, virtuosi, and scientists to observe carefully, record accurately, and to experiment.

Now the opening of the Pacific provided a new world for the philosophers of nature. But it was the empirical approach of the Society and not the neo-classical approach of the Academy which flourished under the impact of the new knowledge won from the

From Bernard Smith, European Vision and the South Pacific, 1768–1850 (Oxford: The Clarendon Press, 1960), Chapter 1, "Introductory: The European and the Pacific," pp. 1–7. Selected footnotes renumbered.

Pacific. For though the discovery of the Society Islands gave initial support to the belief that a kind of tropical Arcadia inhabited by ‚men like Greek gods existed in the South Seas, increasing knowledge not only destroyed the illusion but also became a most enduring challenge to the supremacy of neo-classical values in art and thought. The effect of this challenge is to be observed in painting, in poetry, in the theatre, and even in ideas concerning the nature of the universe. The opening of the Pacific is therefore to be numbered among those factors contributing to the triumph of romanticism and science in the nineteenth-century world of values. Whilst it will be shown how the discovery of the Pacific contributed to the challenge to neo-classicism in several fields, more particular attention will be given to the impact of Pacific exploration upon the theory and practice of landscape painting and upon biological thought. For these two fields provide convenient and yet distinct grounds in which to observe how the world of the Pacific stimulated European thought concerning the world of nature as a whole; in the case of the former as the object of imitation and expression, in the case of the latter as the object of philosophical speculation.

The empirical observation of nature, exemplified in the keeping of ships' logs and seamen's journals, was an established part of British maritime practice a great many years before the foundation of the Royal Society in 1660. And from its inception the Society placed a high value upon the information to be gained from such logs and journals. The information they contained included not only verbal and numerical data but also graphic records in the form of maps and profiles of coasts. Now both Captain Cook and Joseph Banks inherited the traditions of empirical observation derived from maritime practice and the precepts of the Society. Banks, too, was subjected to the influence of the Society of Antiquaries which had received a charter in 1750 and sought to bring habits of close observation, description, and explication to the study of the past, especially as revealed by its material remains, in order to place the writing of history upon a firmer and more objective footing. On Cook's *Endeavour* an important step was taken to advance the techniques of objective observation and recording employed on far voyages by the use of trained scientific observers and professional artists. Also the voyage was, it must be remembered, the first large scientific maritime expedition in whose promotion the Society played a major role. Partly for this reason the Pacific, although the last great ocean to be explored by Europeans, was, curiously enough, the first large region beyond Europe that modern scientific method came fully to grips with. But there are two other closely associated reasons. Firstly, sea travel over great distances was considerably safer than land travel in the last decades of the eighteenth century. Secondly, the scientific examination of the Pacific, by its very nature, depended upon the level reached by the art of navigation. As soon as it was possible to control scurvy and to construct reliable chronometers the archipelagos of the Pacific yielded information of value to the ocean-going scientist far more readily than did the continental masses of Asia, Africa, and America to their land-travelling colleagues. A vessel like Cook's *Resolution,* despite her deficiencies, combined the values of a fortress and a travelling laboratory. Land-travelling scientists had no hope of competing with the results of a Cook, a Flinders, or a Dumont d'Urville. In this regard the case of John Ledyard is illuminating. Ledyard, a marine on the *Resolution* during Cook's third voyage, attempted an overland expedition across Siberia in 1786 for Banks, after returning from the Pacific. He was arrested at Yakutsk, thrust across the Polish frontier to arrive penniless and ragged at Regensburg begging a few guineas in the name of Sir Joseph. In 1789 Ledyard died of fever in Cairo while about to set out in search of the source of the Niger.[1] The interiors of the great continents remained virtually unknown while the islands of the Pacific were visited by one scientific voyage after another.

Indeed so well known did the islands of the South Seas become following the publicity given to Cook's voyages that the natural productions and native peoples of the Pacific became better known to European scientists than the natural productions and

---

[1] And the famous journey of Pallas into Siberia (1768–74), entered upon like the *Endeavour*'s voyage to observe the 1769 transit of Venus, did not foreshadow the opening up of northern Asia to Europeans in the way that Cook's entry into the Pacific foreshadowed its speedy penetration by scientists, missionaries, and merchants.

peoples of many less distant regions. The plan of operations adopted by Banks and Cook on the *Endeavour* became standard practice for many later expeditions. It is not unlikely that Gilbert White had the achievements of his friend Banks in mind when he recommended to Thomas Pennant (a friend both of Banks and White) a programme for a naturalist's tour of Ireland. The programme suggested was virtually identical with that employed so successfully by Banks in the Pacific some six years before:

Some future faunist, a man of fortune, will, I hope, extend his visits to the Kingdom of Ireland; a new field, and a country little known to the naturalist. He will not, it is to be wished, undertake that tour unaccompanied by a botanist, because the mountains have scarcely been sufficiently examined; and the southerly counties of so mild an island may possibly afford some plants little to be expected within the British Dominions. . . . The manners of the wild natives, their superstitions, their prejudices, their sordid way of life, will extort many useful reflections. He should also take with him an able draughtsman.

Now the empirical approach to nature, despite its standing in philosophy and science, played little part in the theory and practice of landscape-painting in England at the time of the establishment of the Royal Academy. Claude was the model held up by Reynolds to those who sought to perfect the art of landscape. When the empirical approach to nature did begin to influence English landscape-painting during the later decades of the eighteenth century, it began to influence the art, naturally enough, through those scientific disciplines concerned with the description and analysis of the structure, vegetation, and atmosphere of the earth's surface. For the landscape-painter shared with the botanist, geologist, and meteorologist certain common fields of interest and, in a sense, similar materials of study, however different the purposes of scientist and artist.

During the second half of the eighteenth century the sciences of botany, geology, and meteorology, in company with a number of other sciences based on exacting empirical research, were beginning to perfect their techniques and modes of classification. An essential condition for the progress of these new sciences was the collection of evidence from all parts of the world. Consequently, the scientific voyages to the Pacific played an important part in their programmes and did much to stimulate an interest in them. Now such sciences as botany, zoology, and the nascent science of ethnology, made extensive use of draughtsmen to assist in the description of material observed or collected. It was the business of the botanical and zoological draughtsmen to depict with great care and accuracy the appearance and structure of type specimens upon which new species might be erected. A great deal of artistic talent was absorbed between 1750 and 1850 in thus serving the biological sciences as they sought to perfect the descriptive and systematic phases of their respective disciplines.

On scientific voyages, however, professional artists trained in art schools and academies worked side by side with nautical and scientific draughtsmen. Frequently they were called upon to do similar work. At all times they were exposed to the influence of scientists and naval officers trained in the empirical habits of observation championed by the Royal Society and the Navy. In consequence their mode of perception became increasingly less dominated by neo-classical theories of art and increasingly more influenced by empirical habits of vision.

The mode of perception and expression which artists thus tended to acquire as a result of the conditions imposed upon them on scientific voyages is not to be equated with a naïve and unselective naturalism. Neo-classical theory had stressed the supreme importance of the unity of mood and expression in the highest forms of landscape art. Analytical and empirical observation, however, tended toward the disruption of such unity, forcing the artist to look at the world as a world of disparate things. But these 'things', the rocks, plants, animals, people, and atmospheric conditions perceived by the painter acquired a new significance under the pressure of scientific inquiry. As scientists came to question the teleological position implicit in the view of nature as a great chain of being, they tended to seek an explanation for the origin and nature of life in the material evidence provided by the earth's surface. The intense study of rocks, plants, animals, people, and the laws governing climatic conditions acquired a new significance even for the landscape-painter. For such things held the clue to the meaning of nature and the origin of life. It was most desirable, therefore, that the artist should depict them accurately, for it was only by the closest scrutiny and the most careful description that they could be made to yield their meaning. Furthermore, it became increasingly clear that certain essential relationships existed in the world of nature between certain types of rocks, plants, animals, and climates. These ecological relationships were quite different from the relationships imposed by the neo-classical landscape-painter in the search for a unity of mood or expression. They were only to be revealed by a careful empirical study of nature and were the object of scientific inquiry. Under the influence of science, however, ecological principles began to determine increasingly the forms of unity which the landscape-painter imposed upon his material.

An early example of the type of relationship which art began to take over from science at this time is to be found in botanical and zoological illustration. One of the important features of the description of a new species was the description of its habitat. Consequently, illustrators of animals usually placed them in their appropriate environmental setting. During the period under discussion this became a more frequent practice in the illustration of plants also. The relationship which existed between a species and its habitat could, however, be extended to all the species peculiar to a particular habitat. The placing of plants, animals, and primitive peoples in their appropriate environmental situation became a matter of increasing importance for the landscape-painter. In this tendency lay the implicit recognition of the intimate connexion between the objects in a landscape and the environmental and climatic situation of which the landscape as a whole was both a representation and a symbol. Thus landscapes came to be painted in which the rocks, plants, animals, peoples, and atmospheric conditions depicted were selected and organized to characterize the *type* of landscape painted. In this practice is to be observed a further expression of that interest in types which had gained such impetus in the scientific world from the work of Carl von Linné.[2] His work in the classification of plants and

[2] Better known as Linnaeus.

animals was extended to the classification of clouds by meteorologists and the classification of climates by geographers. In this situation there arose the desire to represent in works of art what may best be called typical landscape, a form of landscape the component parts of which were carefully selected in order to express the essential qualities of a particular kind of geographical environment. Landscape-painters became fully conscious of the fact that the world contained distinct types of scenery with their own forms of visual unity. Such unity was only to be achieved by an appreciation of the essential character and beauty of each scenic type. ..

In this study the emergence of the idea of typical landscape is traced from the appearance of scientific illustrations used by geologists and natural historians, and the interests of a circle of virtuosi centred upon Sir Joseph Banks. The idea was given more complete expression in the practice and writings of William Hodges in whose work it begins to impinge upon the world of taste and neo-classical values. Through Alexander von Humboldt the typical landscape was given a theoretical justification and championed as an artistic programme for painters. Humboldt's writings were very widely read and influenced the thoughts of such men as Karl Gustav Carus and John Ruskin. Through the work of such men the idea of typical landscape was elaborated and became the common property of nineteenth-century artistic thought. Now although the factors which united to produce this new approach to landscape were by no means confined to European experience in the Pacific, it will be shown that Pacific exploration played a significant part both in its emergence as an art and in its theoretical formulation.

Typical landscape is one aspect of the growing influence of the biological sciences which Pacific exploration did so much to stimulate. The stimulus operated with great effect at the empirical level, for the Pacific, naturally enough, provided scientists with a vast amount of new data. Concerning Matthew Flinders's voyage, for instance, Joseph Dalton Hooker wrote, 'the botanical results . . . have been . . . incomparably greater, not merely than those of any previous voyage, but than those of all similar voyages put together'. The stimulus, however, was also felt at the level of theory. Despite their empirical methods most eighteenth-century biologists sought to relate their findings to a cosmology Platonic in its origins. 'If we consider the generation of Animals', wrote von Linné, 'we find that each produces an offspring after its own kind . . . and that from each proceeds a germ of the same nature with its parent; so that all living things, plants, animals, and even mankind themselves, form one "chain of universal Being", from the beginning to the end of the world.' Scientists working in the Pacific, however, found it increasingly difficult to classify their material according to the presuppositions of this cosmology. Sir James Edward Smith, the first President of the Linnean Society, put the difficulty in this way:

When a botanist first enters on the investigation of so remote a country as New Holland, he finds himself as it were in a new world. He can scarcely meet with any fixed points from whence to draw his analogies; and even those that appear most promising, are frequently in danger of misleading, instead of informing him. The whole tribes of plants, which at first sight seem familiar to his acquaintance, as occupying links in Nature's chain, on which he is accustomed to depend, prove, on a nearer examination, total strangers, with other configurations, other œconomy, and other qualities; not only the species themselves are new, but most of the genera, and even natural orders.

Confronted with such problems natural philosophers not infrequently suggest novel solutions. Indeed, interest in the formation of coral islands, and in the plants, animals, and native peoples of the Pacific may be said, in general, to have promoted thought along evolutionary lines. Pacific voyages stimulated the reflections of Erasmus Darwin, Lord Monboddo, and a number of minor writers. And during the first half of the nineteenth century, three scientists, Charles Darwin, Joseph Dalton Hooker, and Thomas Henry Huxley, whose joint efforts did so much to establish organic evolution as an acceptable scientific explanation of the nature of the universe, spent the crucial formative years of their lives as naturalists on scientific voyages to the Pacific region.

European experience of the Pacific by thus helping to promote thought along evolutionary lines challenged the supremacy of neo-classical values in cosmological theory as it had helped to challenge those values in the theory and practice of landscape-painting. For these reasons alone European experience of the Pacific is not without significance for the history of European art and ideas. Even so, it is to be stressed that the impact of Pacific experience upon European art and thought is only to be observed operating within an intricate interplay of ideas in which, for the most part, European observers sought to come to grips with the realities of the Pacific by interpreting them in familiar terms. Both classical antiquity and the traditions of Christian thought provided a stock of attitudes and preconceptions which Europeans continually brought to bear upon their experience of the Pacific.

European attitudes to Pacific peoples provide an illuminating example. The first European visitors to Polynesia tended to view the natives as noble savages, an attitude with its roots deep in the thought of classical antiquity. It is possible to distinguish two forms of this primitivistic approach to Pacific peoples: a soft primitivism, applied mainly to the inhabitants of the Society Islands, and a hard primitivism, applied to such peoples as the Fuegians, the Maoris, and the Australian aborigines. The primitivistic interpretation of Pacific peoples was, however, severely challenged by evangelical thought during the last decade of the eighteenth century. Soft primitivism, more closely associated with deistic thought and neo-classical values, was singled out for the most severe attacks by evangelical critics; the notions of austerity and fortitude associated with hard primitivism being somewhat more congenial both to Calvinistic Christianity and to the romantic interest in the historical origins of the northern nations of Europe. Nevertheless, Christian thought, with the decline of deism, found any kind of belief in the natural virtue of pagan savages repugnant and did much to spread the belief that the native peoples of the Pacific in their natural state were depraved and ignoble.

Such preconceptions both as to the nobility and to the ignobility of Pacific peoples exhibited considerable vigour in popular thought despite the objective investigations of scientists, educated missionaries, and travellers. Nevertheless, Europeans gradually became aware of the physical and social factors which differentiated one people from another. In the end scientific method triumphed in the description both of nature and man.

Historians of Pacific exploration have tended to neglect the importance of other fields of investigation undertaken by the scientific explorers of the Pacific. As a result of Banks's decision to sail with Cook there was added to research in the physical sciences, of direct interest to the Admiralty and the Royal Society, the interests of a virtuoso specializing in the biological sciences. Banks's success set the organizational pattern for the later exploratory work in the Pacific by England, France, Russia, and America; research in the biological sciences being undertaken along with research in the physical sciences. And to these inquiries there came to be added the objective and comparative study of native peoples, a study greatly promoted by the work of the Forsters, father and son, during Cook's second voyage, and officially written into La Pérouse's instructions. Furthermore, it must be stressed that the scientists of these great voyages inherited the rational enthusiasm of the Enlightenment and went to the South Seas ambitious to discover man and the world. As John Reinhold Forster put it: 'My object was nature in its greatest extent; the Earth, the Sea, the Air, the Organic and Animated Creation, and more particularly that class of Beings to which we ourselves belong.' Their enthusiasm was not altogether misplaced; for in the hundred years after 1768 the Pacific Ocean became one of the finest schools for scientists in the world and stimulated European thought concerning man and nature both in art and in science.

2.

Effects of
the French Revolution

~

GEORGES LEFEBVRE

Stimulated by the hostilities, the ambitions of the powers obscured the essential nature of the struggle between the Revolution and the Europe of the Old Regime. Yet contemporaries were by no means unaware of this. Above all, it was a social conflict, between the aristocracy and the bourgeoisie supported by the rest of the Third Estate, particularly the peasants. It was also a political conflict. The kings felt that their despotism was threatened, while they themselves, by taking the aristocracy under their protection, were in danger of perishing along with it. Finally, it was an intellectual conflict. The enemies of the Revolution portrayed it as the daughter of rationalism, whose impious criticism dispelled the mysteries and destroyed the traditional supports of the old order.

It has been wrongly maintained that the rulers fought merely to increase their power. Selfishness might divide them, but Burke's crusade, which their publicists—most notably Mallet du Pan and Friedrich von Gentz—continued to promote, was never a matter of indifference to them. Besides, the aristocracy would have reminded them, if necessary, that they were fighting an

From Georges Lefebvre, The French Revolution from 1793 to 1799 *(New York: Columbia University Press, 1964)* ; Chapter 15, "Revolutionary Expansion and its Effects," pp. 318–324, and Chapter 17, "The Results of the War," pp. 347–355.

'ideological' war, in defence of society and civilization. Even as Pitt and Grenville declared that they would negotiate only when the European equilibrium had been re-established and the interests of Great Britain safeguarded, they never failed to stigmatize the spectacle of destruction presented by France, and to invite the enemy to restore the monarchy, which would re-establish the indispensable foundations of the social hierarchy. Already the spirit of the Holy Alliance was guiding the Coalition, just as it was to unite it against Napoleon.

The Old Regime no longer existed in Belgium or in the territory of Liége, which had been annexed to France, divided into departments, and subjected to all the laws of the Republic. It was not quite the same in the Rhineland. Although the cession of the left bank by the Empire was incomplete, it remained in abeyance, and administrative assimilation was only beginning. Nevertheless the aristocracy there had vanished. In the new Batavian and Helvetian republics, founded under the protection of the French armies, change was taking place. It had gone quite far in the Cisalpine Republic, but in reconquering Italy, the Austrians and Russians had neutralized its effects, had checked it in the Ligurian Republic, and had prevented it at Rome and Naples.

It was by arms, however, at the cost of even more unparalleled efforts and tragic convulsions, that the Revolution extended its sway. In the conquered countries the sympathy it might have aroused was impaired by the ravages of war, the burdens of occupation, and the arbitrary authority of soldiers and officials who too frequently were unscrupulous. In addition, events spread fear among the population, and sadness and discouragement among the partisans of the new order. Not all of these disavowed its principles: in Germany, Kant and Fichte remained faithful, and in England, the Whigs, led by Fox, continued to plead their cause. But the number of those who took refuge in silence, or who admitted their disillusionment, was increasing, even if they did not change sides.

Moreover, there were very few persons who believed that kings could be dispensed with, and the Republic was seen only as a short-lived monster. Its interpretation of equal rights and its popular character roused indignation. Democracy horrified the bourgeoisie everywhere, even more than in France; and in Great Britain and the United States, where a constitutional regime satisfied this class and, in any case, seemed to permit peaceful reforms, the bogy played particularly into the hands of the oligarchy. Washington and the Federalists used it against Jefferson and the republicans, all the more since Genet's activities had had their impact on the people. On the Continent, however, the argument was still valid.

The advent of the Directory and its military and diplomatic successes restored some confidence among the partisans of the new France. The Republic, with its bourgeois Constitution of the Year III, once more became acceptable. Its victories and conquests proved that a state did not necessarily collapse when it repudiated monarchy. Bourgeoisie and liberal nobles in the annexed regions co-operated in their assimilation; and those in the vassal republics aided in the inauguration of regimes similar to that of France.

If the Revolution thus regained some prestige, it should not be credited entirely with the diffusion of liberal ideas. British influence did not diminish, for many followers of the principles of 1789 still remained Anglophiles. To them the government of Great Britain seemed to moderate the application of democracy so well that it need not be feared. Even more, the nobles and functionaries persisted in turning their gaze complacently towards a country where the former saw a pre-eminent aristocracy and the latter a model for the renovation of the economy. Nor did the example of the United States lose its prestige. The Creoles of Latin America were inspired by it as well as by that of France. The development and consequences of the war, above all, were responsible for currents of opinion in which revolutionary infiltration undoubtedly appeared occasionally; but this cannot be said to have been the guiding principle, even though the Old Regime governments naturally held it responsible.

In Prussia the Treaty of Basel encouraged among leaders of the Enlightenment an understanding with France. Pastor Riem, for example, expressed it openly. This opinion persisted among office-holders, and even at the court, but its appeal was to the interests of the kingdom. In 1796 the Directory momentarily hoped that agitation in South Germany would increase. The prospect of an invasion aroused discontent. The Bavarian nobility and the upper class of Württemberg continued their opposition, but the thought of renouncing their privileges never occurred to them. Hamburg remained a centre of French influence, because businessmen were annoyed at seeing the war continue if there were no government contracts for them.

Petitions in favour of peace increased in England for the same reason. In January, 1797, Erskine published his *Summary of the Causes and Consequences of the Present War With France,* which enjoyed an extraordinary success. The burden of taxes, economic difficulties, and especially scarcity also aroused the common people. The revolt of the Silesian weavers in 1794 and the serious outbreaks that occurred in London during the autumn of 1795 have already been mentioned, and they had some bearing on Pitt's decision to negotiate. We should not be misled by the war effort that the latter imposed on the country, beginning in 1797, when the danger reached its height. His unpopularity grew, and he deemed it prudent to send Malmesbury to France again.

In England, unlike the Continent, the influence of the French Revolution could lead only to democracy. So the British government, in contrast to the others, was disturbed by the discontent of the artisans and the sporadic agitation that high prices provoked among the working class. These circumstances favoured propaganda hostile to the oligarchy. At a London banquet on May 18, 1797, toasts were drunk to electoral reform, Irish freedom, and the French alliance. The societies continued, secretly or otherwise, and a pamphlet claimed to be the voice of 80,000 indomitable Jacobins. Even assuming that this assertion was not exaggerated, it does not follow that an insurrection was imminent; and the alarming reports that flooded the Home Office do not agree in their evidence. But the government exaggerated its fears in order to justify repression.

No longer could anyone doubt that the rise of the bourgeoisie constituted a dominant feature of European civilization. The English revolutions were proof of it. Their advent in France had demonstrated the power of this class in a far more radical way, since they had eliminated the nobility. Thus endless repercussions of the French Revolution were ensured for the future. On the eve of 18 Brumaire, however, nothing remained of the hopes cherished by the Girondins, for no other people had yet followed the example of the French. Everywhere the selfish partisans of the Old Regime held a tight grip on the machinery of repression, and they had long given adequate proof of this fact.

Sovereigns and publicists vilified the revolutionary government for invoking the relativity of individual rights, in order to justify their suspension in case of revolution or civil and foreign war. The British governments seemed particularly justified in becoming indignant, because eighteenth-century England was one of the few countries where the individual was respected. Actually, in practice the individual was disregarded when public safety required it, and the reaction proved this again. With habeas corpus suspended, the arbitrary power of the police was unlimited. The loyalists and their associations, through surveillance and denunciations, assumed a mission similar to that of the clubs and revolutionary committees. In 1799, measures against assemblies and seditious publications were intensified, and printers were subjected to declarations. Since Great Britain had no Vendée, the repression was limited to what was known in France under the Directory as the 'dry guillotine'. By use of the press gang suspects were shipped aboard His Majesty's vessels, and their leaders were condemned to transportation to Australia; but no special courts were created. The terror became bloody only in Ireland, where insurrection led to massacres and executions.

The Continental despots were not hampered by constitutional scruples. Their arsenal of coercion was always ready, and it sufficed for them to use it with the severity that circumstances demanded. In the Iberian states and the papal domain the Inquisition had only to open new trials. In Latin America, Nariño was sentenced to ten years in prison, and following a conspiracy that cost numerous lives, Rodríguez deemed it prudent to flee his country in 1797. His disciple Bolívar followed his example two years later. Tsar Paul I acted in a similar manner. At first he liberated Novikov, Radishchev, and Kosciusko; but nourishing his mother's hatred of the Revolution, he was not long in restoring the harshness of the oppressive regime when he took over the army of Condé and installed Louis XVIII at Mitau. In the Hapsburg Empire, Colloredo, the secretary of state, improved the police methods of Joseph II, and perfected the system for which Metternich later claimed credit: the all-powerful police, the 'black cabinet' and censorship, widespread espionage, particularly at the expense of the functionaries, and arbitrary imprisonment. After the executions in Hungary, silence prevailed in the hereditary domains.

The other states of the Holy Roman Empire copied this system more or less closely, depending upon the inclinations of their rulers. Even at Jena, Fichte, accused of atheism, had to abandon his professorship in 1799. The most stubborn liberals emigrated—thus Rebmann reached Paris in 1796. In Prussia, to be sure, the leaders of the Enlightenment continued to resist. Frederick William II died in 1797, and his son Frederick William III put an end to the persecution of Wöllner, who was dismissed. Kant nonetheless was extremely prudent. It goes without saying that once the French were driven from Italy, the White Terror knew no bounds at Rome, and especially at Naples, where it was witnessed by Nelson.

The maintenance of authority did not necessarily mean that all reforms had to be renounced. Pitt could not deny that the improvements advocated by the Whigs had formerly won his approval. On the Continent the renovation of agriculture on the English model commended itself to the attention of the governing classes and the intelligent nobles, with its natural consequences—abolition of serfdom, redemption of manorial rights, redistribution of lands, and suppression of collective rights. Some elements in the constructive work of the Constituent Assembly, even of the Committee of Public Safety, were suited to enlightened despotism, and the war pointed up the defects of an administrative apparatus inherited from the past.

The great majority of the privileged few, however, detested any change as a Jacobin contamination that would lead to others. The common people, declared the Anglican bishop Horsley in

1795, had nothing to do with the laws except to obey them. The governing classes were of the same opinion. Pitt believed that any reform would encourage the popular movement, and even had he felt differently, his pact with George III would have tied his hands. Little or no improvement was made in the agencies and methods of government, because the bureaucrats and their superiors secretly opposed it.

As always, the war altered the course of international trade. It also interfered with the rise of capitalism on the Continent. Nevertheless England derived appreciable profit from the conflict, and extended her empire. European expansion, however, was hindered. The shock to the colonial system increased as Latin America moved towards emancipation, and France even abolished slavery.

Deprived of the markets that France controlled, but rid of French competition, Great Britain compensated herself at the expense of her allies and the neutrals. Through the Hanseatic ports she rushed into the conquest of Germany. In 1800 she cleared 500 vessels for Hamburg, as contrasted with 49 in 1789. At the fairs of Frankfurt and Leipzig she came into contact with the Swiss, the Austrians, the Poles, and the Russians. Her cotton goods, and particularly her threads, drove out Swiss and Saxon products. Her trade with Germany rose from £2 million in 1789 to £13.5 million in 1801. Since Amsterdam had fallen into the hands of the republicans, finance turned towards London. The elector of Hesse invested his funds there, and it was in helping him that Meyer Amschel Rothschild of Frankfurt developed his business; in 1798 his son Nathan settled in England, and soon became rich.

The Baltic became increasingly important in British commerce. At the beginning of the nineteenth century 72 per cent of British imports came from Prussia and Russia—three-fourths of the grain from the port of Danzig alone. The vessels of the Hanseatic towns and the Scandinavian lands entered her service, and with or without licences, continued to touch at French ports so long as the Directory did not break with the neutrals. On the other hand, Holland was declining rapidly, and Amsterdam yielded its pre-eminence to Hamburg; the reserves of its bank, which had risen to 13 million florins in 1793, fell to 1.5 million in 1799.

In the Atlantic the preponderance of the British navy became more pronounced each year. Joining with the navies of the neutrals, it took over the triangular trade of Europe, the African coasts (from which Negro slaves were drawn), and tropical America. Still, the expansion of the United States to some extent counterbalanced this ascendancy; her vessels also developed a triangular route between her own ports, the West Indies or Latin America, and Europe. Having secured the Jay Treaty, the British accommodated themselves to this, especially since the attitude of the Directory led John Adams to break with the French. In the South Atlantic the alliance of Spain with France enabled the English to reduce relations with her colonies to almost nothing, and the Cape route saw hardly anything but British convoys. In Asian waters they no longer encountered anyone but a few Americans. The French East India Company disappeared in 1791, the Dutch Company in 1798. In the Mediterranean, France's position was better. Genoa, Leghorn, the Barbary States, and the Greeks came to her aid. Conquering Italy, she hindered her enemy without eliminating her; but she lost it in 1799, and as early as 1798 was driven from the Levant.

The naval war increased the importance of the Continental link between the Mediterranean and the northern seas. Heretofore largely assured across France, Italy, Switzerland, and Holland, it was compromised by the closing of the Rhenish route. Since 1790 France interrupted traffic along the left bank by extending her customs offices to the river, and the occupation of the Rhineland and Holland affected this route still further. In 1798 the Directory applied its tariff to the crossing of the Rhine. With the closing of the mouth of the river the trade of Cologne had already declined, and by 1800 it was reduced to less than a third. Only a part of the traffic slipped through Emden to Frankfurt to supply contraband or reach Switzerland. Moreover, the latter was separated from Genoa. The route across Europe thus retreated to the East, as in the time of Louis XIV, and henceforth it passed through Hamburg and Leipzig to Venice and preferably Trieste.

In 1800, English commerce exceeded £30 million in imports and £38 million in exports.[1] This was 53 per cent more than in 1792, and the balance of payments was almost double. The tonnage of outgoing ships had increased by a third, and rose to almost two million tons. It was during the war that the docks of London were built and endowed with the bonded-warehouse system. The expansion of markets partly explains this progress, especially as shipments to France and her satellites did not diminish greatly, thanks to the neutrals and contraband. This was to hasten the advance of England in the direction of rationalized or mechanized production and of capitalist concentration.

The price rise also remained a favourable factor. The war accentuated it everywhere, and contributed to it indirectly by the increase in the issue of paper money in almost every country. France was not alone in suffering from it. In Spain the Bank of St. Charles staved off bankruptcy only with great difficulty in 1799. In England, on the contrary, it seemed that the monetary crisis and the extension of banking organization would benefit business. Foreign capital flowed in. In 1794 the Bank of England bought £3.75 million of precious metals. After the occupation of Holland it became the safest refuge, and the favourable balance of foreign trade had the same result. Coining of gold could be resumed: £2 million in 1797, almost £3 million in 1798.

After the crisis of 1793 the county banks again increased. In 1800 their number is said to have risen to 386; they continued to issue notes without controls, and probably added some credit inflation to the paper inflation. The Bank of England gradually extended its operations; it dealt with 1,340 clients in 1800. The suspension of convertibility of bank notes in 1797 might have struck the economy a terrible blow, but as has been seen, it did not precipitate a panic. Inflation remained sufficiently moderate

[1] These are 'official' figures. The research of A. H. Imlah has shown that the true figures are £66.5 million in imports, £52.3 million in exports, with a deficit of £14 million.

that it did not ruin the currency, and it spared the English the deflation that the Directory suffered. Moreover, a fall in the pound favoured exports, since the leading businessmen took in specie, but paid their workers in notes. In its empiricism the financial policy of Great Britain attested a mastery of which no other country was then capable.

Prices increased almost continuously; taking those of 1790 as a base of 100, they rose to 109 in 1793, and reached 156 in 1799. A quarter of wheat, which was worth an average of 45 shillings from 1780 to 1789, jumped to 55 during the following decade. According to Lord Beveridge, however, the index of industrial activity, which had been in the midst of an upsurge until the war (112 in 1792 in relation to a base of 100 in 1785), appears to have dipped thereafter to 85 in 1797, eventually to recover to 107 only in 1802. It must be recognized that the expansion of exports resulted in large part from the resale of colonial products. The war assured Great Britain a virtual monopoly of these, to such an extent that the planters lamented the fall in sugar prices, although home consumption was increasing uninterruptedly. Nevertheless the needs of the army and navy sustained the demand. The disappearance of German steel was also an advantage to the metal industry (which expanded the use of coal in smelting), and mining developed. In 1800, England exported, in addition, two million tons of coal and one-and-one-half million tons of wrought and cast iron. The cotton industry prospered more than any other. Its exports rose from £1.5 million to £6 million in 1800. Even in 1797, England imported £734,000 worth of cotton; and three years later it had risen to £1,663,000 worth.

In any case, there is no doubt that the Industrial Revolution was continuing to advance. Yet it must be emphasized that it was not progressing as quickly as is sometimes believed. Cotton spinning held the lead, but weaving was still done by hand. Cartwright's loom was first adopted only in 1801, at Glasgow, and its use became widespread only after Radcliffe invented the dressing machine about 1804. The woollen industry remained in an experimental state. Even the spinning jenny was used very little, and Cartwright's frame for the spinning of cardings was perfected only in 1803. Coal mining remained backward, despite the growing use of the rail and the introduction of the steam engine. This last did not penetrate industry except in some cotton mills, the others being content with water frames.

As for communications, the canals remained the centre of attention, and there were few good roads. Owing to the slowness of transport and the increasingly low wages, the traditional industries defended themselves energetically, and capital continued to be concentrated in trade rather than in the creation of factories. Of the captains of industry of the time, Robert Owen's father-in-law, David Dale, and Radcliffe of Stockport began by 'putting out'. Even though the spinning mule was not adopted everywhere, it gave cotton spinning an irresistible superiority. Hosiery and lace made by looms prospered. Metallurgy became largely modernized, and engineers, the most famous being Bramah, inventor of the hydraulic press, increased the number of machine tools.

The rise in prices also benefited agriculture. England no longer produced enough grain to feed herself, and the war made purchases costly. Wheat had become so expensive that the Corn Laws no longer operated; and it was so much more profitable than stock raising that more was planted. Hence enclosure was further extended; so this was a golden age for landlords as well as for farmers. Techniques continued to improve, and in 1793, John Sinclair and Arthur Young were placed at the head of a Board of Agriculture. The agrarian revolution spread in Scotland. There the heads of the clans (recognized as landlords), in order to devote themselves to stock raising, evicted their tenants, who were reduced to emigration. This agricultural prosperity reinforced the might of the country, because it rendered it less vulnerable in its food supply. It also aided the small landowners to maintain themselves, and even to increase in numbers in some counties. Actually very few remained; at least they felt satisfied with their lot, and, with the farmers, they constituted an element of stability.

Despite its advances, English capitalism still did not think in terms of free trade. Far from renouncing the Corn Laws, landowners and farmers demanded that they be reinforced. Industrialists remained faithful to mercantilism to the extent of forbidding the exportation of machinery. At home, however, they increasingly evaded regulations that limited the number of apprentices and authorized the setting of a minimum wage. The workers, on the contrary, continued to invoke the Statutes of Labourers, and backed up their demands through the use of blacklists and strikes. These were forbidden in principle, but justices of the peace hesitated to condemn them when employers themselves set the example of violating the law. Also, it is worth remembering the Combination Act of July 12, 1799, which renewed penalties against strikers and workers' associations, at the same time that the authorities allowed the regulations favourable to the wage earners to fall into disuse. Depressed by the influx of foundlings, women, and uprooted farmers, wages lagged far behind the rise in the price of goods. They were further reduced by the truck system, or payment in kind, and by arbitrary fines; but since 1795 they had been complemented, at the expense of the poor tax, by assistance based on the price of bread. This was the reason for the relative resignation of the common people.

The economic supremacy of Great Britain asserted itself all the more as the war retarded the development of industry elsewhere on the Continent even more than in France. To meet competition Switzerland and Saxony considered modifying their cotton machinery. The knitting machine appeared at Chemnitz in 1797, and the water frame in 1798; and the concentration of spinning there became obvious. In general, capitalism remained in its commercial form. Moreover, traditional products suffered from unfavourable circumstances; in Silesia the cloth industry was ruined. In agriculture, Denmark alone seriously imitated England, which could not but congratulate itself, since it imported grain.

England took a similar view of the progress of the United States, particularly in sea-island cotton, brought from the Bahamas in 1786, offered in Glasgow for the first time in 1792, and immediately appreciated by the spinners. When the difficulties of ginning had been resolved by Whitney's machine in 1793, exports soon attained a level of 8 million pounds and rose to almost 20 million in 1800, worth about $5 million. It was an event of great significance for the United States, because from that time on, slavery became a fundamental institution for the South, and the planters began to covet Florida and Louisiana. For the moment, however, the North saw in it only an occasion for using its capital and ships. English machines were just beginning to be introduced there. In 1790, Slater established the first spinning mill using Arkwright's system. The country remained primarily agricultural, and British industry doubled its shipments to it. The great fortunes of the Astors and the Girards were built on commerce and speculation in land.

At the moment of the advent of Bonaparte, however, the situation in England was critical. The war was raging on the Continent, and scarcity made the purchase of grain necessary at a cost of almost £3.5 million. The reserves of the Bank of England declined, and the exchange rate fell: the pound sterling lost 8 per cent of its value at Hamburg, and 5 per cent at Cadiz. At home the small bank notes of one or two pounds became widespread. By year's end they represented a tenth of the issue. Specie became scarce and was at a premium. The illicit practice of double prices became commonplace. Pitt realized that he would have to increase taxes. The evil had worsened, because London suffered the repercussions of the catastrophe that struck Hamburg.

The conditions of international commerce were not entirely healthy, because of the war. London, Hamburg, and Amsterdam speculated in colonial goods by conceding each other credits, and by immobilizing their capital in order to constitute stocks. During the winter of 1799 the rise was staggering at Hamburg, because the Elbe was frozen and navigation was suspended. When the ice broke up before the spring fairs, ships poured in, and a tremendous decline ensued; the price of sugar fell 72 per cent just as the war resumed, and in August, on the eve of the Anglo-Russian invasion, the bankers of Amsterdam cut off their advances. One hundred and thirty-six houses of Hamburg failed, and the Parish family lost more than a million marks. Every financial centre in Europe was affected, but especially London. The cotton industry dismissed workers or reduced wages, while the price of bread soared. A quarter of wheat, which had been 49 shillings at the beginning of 1799, reached 101 shillings in February, 1800. This crisis was soon to weaken the morale of the nation. It strengthened the French in their conviction that the British economy was artificial and fragile.

As mistress of the seas, England alone was capable of imposing the authority of the white man throughout the world; but she did not seem greatly inclined to do so. Mercantile opinion did not adopt Bentham's hostility towards colonies, but the emancipation of the United States did not encourage her to multiply them. True, Canada had remained undisturbed since the Act of 1791, which (except for Nova Scotia, New Brunswick, and Prince Edward Island) had organized two provinces, one French, the other English, each provided with an elected assembly, but without parliamentary government. The Catholic clergy, moreover, had displayed no sympathy for revolutionary France. Yet this country did not interest British merchants. They were concerned only with the sugar islands, and thinking of profit alone, valued the expansion of trade most of all. Their imperialism therefore assumed a commercial character.

Yet the empire grew. The French West Indies were ripe for the taking, as were Curaçao and Trinidad. Enormous amounts of capital were invested in Dutch Guiana, which was occupied from 1796 to 1800, and production there multiplied tenfold. The navy needed ports of call, like the Cape of Good Hope, which it seized in 1795. The colonial leaders, sons of the aristocracy, satisfied their taste for action by pressing for conquest on their own. In Africa the colony of Sierra Leone had been founded in 1792. Mungo Park explored the Niger as far as Timbuktu. In Australia, Phillip landed the first convoy of convicts at Sydney in 1788.

The English expanded particularly in India. Cornwallis was not enterprising, but he had to support the Nizam against Tippoo, who reopened the campaign at the end of 1789. In 1791 the governor finally took charge of these operations, and the next year imposed on his adversary the cession of a third of his domain and the payment of an indemnity of £3 million. Then the European war permitted the occupation of the remaining French territory. It encumbered the East India Company with debts. With a revenue that rose to £8 million in 1797, it sustained itself only through loans; and its debt, which had mounted to £10

million, was doubled by 1805. Cornwallis applied himself chiefly
to making reforms. He provided Bengal with courts composed of
English judges and Hindu assistants. In 1793 the 'permanent
settlement' of Bengal still remained the most familiar feature of
its government, and constituted a good example of colonial exploitation. It was assured at the expense of the native population
by the collusion of the conquerors with its own dominant class.
The zamindars, who traditionally farmed out the collection of
dues from their estates and taxes, were recognized as the landowners, so that the peasants were reduced to holding their lands
on lease.

Cornwallis left India in 1793, and his successor remained at
peace; but the situation darkened. Tippoo maintained relations
with the Île de France and the presence of Bonaparte in Egypt
provided cause for concern. India and the Mahrattas became
restless, and the Nizam could not be trusted. But in 1798, Richard Colley, earl of Mornington (later Marquis Wellesley), arrived. He imposed his alliance on the Nizam, and occupied
Hyderabad. Then in 1799, he attacked the ruler of Mysore, who
perished in his capital, Seringapatam, which was captured on
May 4. Colley partitioned his conquest between the East India
Company and the Nizam. Afterwards he attacked the Mahrattas.
He also watched Punjab, where Ranjit Singh had been ceded
Lahore by the Afghans in 1794. In Persia, in 1801, Malcolm was
to obtain a treaty that opened the coast of the Persian Gulf to
English commerce. Perim in the Red Sea was occupied in 1798.
To the east, Malacca and the Muluccas likewise succumbed.

3.

The Napoleonic Wars

~

G. M. TREVELYAN

The Napoleonic wars stand half-way between the Marlborough wars and the Great War of our own day, in time, in size and in character. The resemblance to the Marlborough wars is the most obvious, because the weapons employed by sea and land were very similar in the two periods, and the enemy was France. The geography and strategy, therefore, of the naval and military operations which quelled Napoleon resemble those which quelled Louis XIV. Again, in the days of Pitt and Castlereagh, as in the days of William and Marlborough, the two props of the alliance against France were British sea-power and British subsidies, applied along all the coasts and in half the Treasuries of Europe. The huge British sailing ships whose broadsides conquered at Trafalgar were of the same general character as those which had conquered at La Hogue, while the 'thin red line' and the British cavalry charge won Waterloo by tactics not so very different from those of Blenheim and Ramillies. Again a British General of genius, commanding a small but excellent British army, played a decisive part among the larger military establishments of the continent. Again British troops were landed in the Netherlands and in Spain, in Mediterranean islands and on American coasts. And again, in 1815 as in 1713, the war ended for

From G. M. Trevelyan, History of England, *3rd ed.* (*London: Longmans, Green and Co., 1952*); *Book V, Chapter 5, pp. 571–587. Selected footnotes renumbered.*

England with the establishment in the Netherlands of a Power from which she had nothing to fear, and by great additions to her colonial Empire and her maritime prestige.

But the Napoleonic wars not only repeated the past but rehearsed the future. The issue of the campaigns against Louis had indeed been affected by the course of trade competition between England and France, but a hundred years later the commercial struggle was more formal and more decisive as a weapon of war. The British blockade of Napoleon's Europe, and his attempt to starve England by the Berlin and Milan Decrees, were warlike operations of the same general character as the British blockade of the Central Powers in our own day and the German submarine campaign; they disturbed the economy of the whole world and had serious consequences for the combatants in their relations with the United States and other would-be neutrals.

Furthermore there is a political element of a distinctively modern type in the wars that originated from the French Revolution. The new regime in France, whatever its defects or crimes, filled the humblest French peasant and bourgeois with pride as a citizen and zeal as a patriot, opened military and civil careers to talent without distinction of birth, and, under the Consulate of Bonaparte, supplied the new nation with the administrative system of a wholly new type of efficiency. The other peoples of the continent were marched into the field as mercenaries or serfs, not as citizen soldiers. Britain alone could match the new spirit of France with a national patriotism of yet older date. But the Englishman's 'will to conquer' could be fully aroused only in defence of sea-power and commerce. After our expulsion from the Netherlands in 1794, it is true that we stayed in the war when others submitted to France, but we kept our armies out of Europe for a dozen years together, safe behind the shield of the Navy. We took no serious part, except naval and financial, in the wars of the two Coalitions that suffered defeat at Marengo and Austerlitz. Nor, until the Peninsular War in 1808, did we begin to fight on land as a principal, and even then with armies of not more than 30,000 British at a time.

Success only began to shine on the allies when the popular sense of nationhood was aroused in Spain, Russia and Germany, by indignation against French tyranny at length outweighing in Europe the sense of the benefits of French reform. Only in its last phase did the war become a contest between self-conscious nationalities, not altogether unlike those which fought the Great War of our own day. The horror and the slaughter increased in proportion as the peoples were aroused to fight willingly, to some extent on their own behalf and not merely as the obe-1812– dient vassals of Emperors and Kings. The Moscow and 1813. Leipzig campaigns adumbrated the bloody future of nationalist Europe armed with the machinery of modern science and locomotion.

During the greater part of twenty years of war, the immense superiority of the new French national spirit and organization over the lifeless and old-fashioned machinery of the 1793– continental States of the *ancien régime,* ensured the de-1805. feat of each successive Coalition that England encouraged and financed against France. Until the Peninsular 1808– War and the popular movements in Russia and Ger-1815. many made possible the grand operations of Wellington and Castlereagh, England's effective action was limited to the sea. It was much that she maintained her hold over all the waters of the world, when all the lands of Europe had passed into the orbit of French vassalage. Because the border of England's power reached to the enemy's coastline, she was able to refuse for years together to recognise the accomplished fact of the abrogation of Europe's independence. The double bent of the national purpose, successful naval enterprise and dogged resistance to French hegemony, were embodied in Nelson and in Pitt. The complete and hearty co-operation of the two men saved the British Empire.

Nelson, born in a fortunate hour for himself and for his country, was always in his element and always on his element. Pitt, on the other hand, was a great peace Minister, compelled against his will to take up the burden of war and bear it till he died under it. He had prepared the country and the Empire for this supreme test by ten years of sound government at home, and by his Canadian and Indian legislation. But it was certainly not his expectation or his wish that Britain should be subjected to a fresh ordeal within so short a time of the loss of the American colonies. Pitt had refused to join in the original attack of the reactionary powers on revolutionary France in 1792; indeed, at the beginning of that year he had prophesied a long peace and reduced the numbers of our fighting forces. But the French attack on the Netherlands drew him into the war early in 1793.

By that time he had become a violent Anti-Jacobin, living in a state of panic about the activities of Reformers at home. But he never satisfied Burke by regarding the war as a crusade, nor did he consider it our business to dictate a form of government to France. His objects were to protect the State system of Europe from the aggression of France, in particular to prevent the annexation of the Austrian Netherlands and Holland, and incidentally to recoup the British tax-payer by seizing some French colonies in the West Indies.

For good and for evil Pitt had not Burke's imagination. He regarded the world crisis as a repetition, under changed political conditions, of the Seven Years' War, and he accordingly hoped to fight, as his father had done before him, for naval supremacy and colonial conquest, while sending over a few British troops and much British money to enable our allies to maintain themselves in Europe. But he had not his father's genius for war; it was a very different France with which he had to deal; and there was no Frederic the Great—at least not upon our side. In 1793 a vigorous advance on Paris from the Netherlands might have changed the course of history, before Carnot had time to create the new democratic army of France out of the mutinous welter of the old royal army, deserted by its aristocratic officers. But the chance was let slip, and the Revolution had time to organize its latent energies. Neither the Austrian nor the British armies then in Flanders had the training or the leadership for such an enterprise, which Wellington or even Sir John Moore might have ventured upon with the reconstituted army that we afterwards sent to Spain.

Pitt, moreover, in 1793, sent a large part of the available British forces to the West Indies. He was imitating the war plans not of Marlborough but of Chatham: the French West Indian

Islands should be his Canada, which he would win for the Empire. In his generation the wealth of the sugar islands, where great fortunes were made by English planters, caused them to be much more highly regarded than Canada, and the sacrifices which Pitt made to preserve and to acquire such islands for the Empire, though severely criticized by modern historians, seemed very natural at the time. But he had no knowledge of the local conditions of warfare in the West Indies comparable to the knowledge his father had acquired of how Canada and the Ohio valley were to be won. Disease swept off the British soldiers by thousands. The slaves in the French and English islands rose, adding fresh horror and difficulty to the undertaking, and rendering it impossible to withdraw the troops and allow the whole Archipelago to sink like Haiti into black savagery. The affair, which added little to the British Empire, was only liquidated after the death of 40,000 British soldiers in three years, a number roughly answering to that with which Wellington in six years drove Napoleon's troops out of Spain.

1793–
1796.

These fearful losses in the tropical world, and the inefficient army system of the day, crippled England's efforts in Europe. The selfish preoccupation of Prussia and Russia in sharing up the corpse of murdered Poland, prevented them from playing the part against France assigned to them in Pitt's scheme. The British and Austrian armies were driven out of the Low Countries to the sound of the Marseillaise. Holland and the Rhine lands were revolutionized by the French, the inhabitants half sympathizing. Finally, Bonaparte's conquest of Italy, and his establishment there of vassal Republics, introduced a new ear of French conquest and of world politics. In 1797 Austria, beaten to her knees by this astonishing young genius, crept out of the war, leaving England alone against France.

1793–
1794–

1796–
1797.

'The Grand Nation,' more formidable than even the 'Grand Monarch' whom William and Marlborough had tamed, was now in the hands of the Directorate, a set of energetic ruffians, the survivors of the guillotine, the fathers of modern war and conquest, who were determined to re-establish the finances of France by plundering the rest of Europe. And the ablest servant of these men, soon to be their master, was already learning from his Italian experience how a French European Empire might be founded, on the basis of uniting the social benefits of the Revolution to religious toleration and political order, which the Directorate were incapable of restoring.

England meanwhile was in a sorry plight. Her ships were excluded from the Mediterranean waters, where the Spaniards had joined the war on her enemies' side; her   1797. home fleets at Spithead and the Nore were in mutiny against the neglect and harsh treatment which had always been the lot of the sailors who won her battles; on land her military reputation was at its lowest ebb; it seemed unlikely that she could, without an ally, hold out against all Western Europe united for her destruction.

In this evil hour she was saved by the high quality of Pitt's courage, and by his instinct for naval affairs. The mutinies were pacified and quelled, and somewhat better conditions of life on board were established. The late mutineers   1797. sallied out under Duncan and destroyed the Dutch fleet at Camperdown. Pitt was clumsy and unsuccessful in diplomatic operations, which he conducted through Grenville, and in military operations, which he conducted through Dundas. But to call him a bad war Minister is to overlook the sea affair, which for English statesmen comprises half the conduct of war. He chose, in Spencer and Jervis, the right men through whom to act; he helped them to pick out Nelson, one of the youngest flag-officers on the list; and he insisted on sending him back to recover our hold of the Mediterranean, which had been a French lake for more than a year. The result was the battle of the Nile.

The battle of the Nile [Aug. 1, 1798] was indeed one of the cardinal events of the whole war. It restored British naval power at the moment when it was wavering, and in the region whence it had been withdrawn; whereas Trafalgar only put the crown of glory on a campaign already decided and on a life whose work was done.

Bonaparte had been safely carried to Egypt by the French fleet, and had seized Malta on the way from the Knights of St. John. The path to Constantinople and India seemed open to the most

ambitious spirit since Alexander the Great. But when Nelson
        annihilated his fleet, at anchor at the mouth of the Nile,
1799.   these Oriental visions soon faded. Next year Bonaparte
        was fain to leave his army locked up in Egpyt, and slip
back to France. There he rebuilt the structure of his ambitions on
a Western basis, and only after many years attempted to cut a
path back to the East by the route of Russian conquest. Nelson's
cannonade that summer evening off the Egyptian shore secured
the full establishment of British supremacy in the Indian Peninsula, in the difficult days of 'Tippoo Sahib' of Mysore and of the
Maratha Wars conducted by the Wellesley brothers.

Another consequence of the Nile was the restored dominance
of Britain in Mediterranean waters. The power of our fleet was
firmly based on Malta, which we took from the French in 1800
and never relinquished, and on Sicily, where the royal family,
exiled from Naples, became Nelson's friends, and remained
England's *protégés*.

But the Nile evoked other and more formidable allies than the
South-Italian Bourbons. Austria and Russia felt encouraged to
        form the Second Coalition, which after a sudden and
1799.   brief day of success in North Italy under Suvoroff,
1800.   perished on the field of Marengo at the hands of Bona-
        parte. As First Consul he now had at his command all
the civil and military resources of France, which he reorganized
in the four best years of his life as the resources of no nation had
ever been organized before, giving to France the modern administrative institutions by which she has lived ever since.

Next followed the episode of the 'armed neutrality' formed
by Russia and the Scandinavian Powers against England, partly
on grounds of neutrals' complaints of the right of search as
exercised by the lords of the sea, partly as admirers and would-be
        allies of Bonaparte, for whose friendship the Czar Paul
1801.   had half-crazy yearnings. The assassination of the Czar
        and Nelson's destruction of the Danish fleet under the
guns of the Copenhagen forts, put an end to the peril in that
quarter. In northern as in southern seas, the arm of Britain was
omnipotent. French and Spanish, Dutch and Danish fleets had
been shattered, and Britain helped herself at will to the colonies

of the unhappy allies of France. The Cape of Good Hope and Ceylon were taken from the Dutch to secure the sea route to India.

But on land no one could make head against Bonaparte. The two victorious enemies recognized their respective limits by the Treaty of Amiens. But though hailed with joy   1802. in England, the long-expected peace proved only a hollow truce. For it soon appeared that Bonaparte interpreted the Treaty of Amiens to mean the retirement of Britain behind the sea curtain, while he remained free to annex every State of Europe to which he had a mind. It was not so that British statesmen interpreted the peace they had signed, which in their eyes set an agreed limit to French expansion. So the two weary nations turned again to war.   1803.

England was once more matched alone against France. For the moment, Bonaparte had no other use for his incomparable army than to threaten 'perfidious Albion' from   1804. the camp of Boulogne. His vigorous but crude and unprofessional schemes for securing the mastery of the Channel, appointing an elaborate *rendez-vous* for the Brest and Toulon fleets in the West Indies, were baffled by the vigilance and energy of Nelson and his 'band of brothers.' Our ships hunted the French across the Atlantic and back, sometimes at fault, sometimes in full cry. The pursued ran breathless to earth in the ports of France and Spain, and no more was heard of the invasion of England. Then, when all seemed over, the anger of Napoleon against Villeneuve, his unfortunate Admiral, caused the main French and Spanish fleet to come out of harbour for the last time, to the final sacrifice off Cape Trafalgar. [Oct. 21, 1805.] It saved the British much rope and timber in blockading work during the remaining ten years of the war, and it stamped on the mind of Europe an indelible impression that England's naval power was invincible. That belief helped to make the Nineteenth Century a time of peace and security for the British, and stood them in good stead when that long period of prosperity and high civilization was at length broken by another great war on land and sea.

Nelson is the best loved name in English ears. There is more in our relation to him than can be accounted for by his genius and our obligation. For Marlborough was unpopular, and there was an element of fear in the respect and admiration felt for the Iron Duke. Indeed, Wellington's complete devotion to the public service was rooted in a noble but not very lovable aristocratic pride, which made him live reserved as a man apart, saving him indeed from mistakes and loss of dignity into which Nelson sometimes fell on shore. But Nelson entered straight into the common heart of humanity. As he lay expecting the Trafalgar fight, he chanced to discover that a coxswain, one of the best men on board the *Victory*, had been so busy preparing the mail bags that he had forgotten to drop into them his own letter to his wife, till after the despatch vessel was under full sail for England: 'Hoist a signal to bring her back,' said Nelson; 'who knows but that he may fall in action to-morrow? His letter shall go with the rest.' And the vessel was brought back for that alone.

Dec.   Meanwhile Napoleon, now Emperor, had turned from
             the useless camp at Boulogne to conquer Eastern Europe
1805.   at Austerlitz. His success matched Nelson's, and men
             could not then see that it would be more ephemeral
Jan.   than the dead man's empire over the waves. It was an
1806.   hour of gloom and glory for England. Pitt, worn out
             with care and disappointment and illness, died at his
post. His death and Nelson's, rather than the fruitless Treaty of Amiens, marked the close of the first half of the war of twenty years.

The great French war,—alike in its first phase in the time of Pitt and Nelson, and its last in the time of Castlereagh and Wellington,—was fought by the House of Commons. The comparison of the Roman Senate fighting Hannibal was in the mind of every educated man. The persons whom the House trusted could wield the nation's power and purse, on condition of explaining their plans to the benches of country gentlemen, and winning their approval. For this reason Parliamentary eloquence was at its zenith; popular oratory was not yet of importance, except at the hustings in the few open constituencies at election time. Public meetings there were none. So long as the war lasted, and longer, there was little freedom of press or speech for Reformers. When Cobbett denounced the flogging of British militiamen by German mercenaries, he got two years. The restrictions on popular liberty and propaganda were partly a measure of precaution in war time, but they did not end with the war, because they were also designed to prevent the revival of the movement for domestic Reform, which the Anti-Jacobin mind identified with sedition.

But though liberty was in partial abeyance, no one was tempted to abridge the power of Parliament, or to restore the rule of the King who had lost the American colonies. George III was not, indeed, entirely without power. Even in the intervals of the lunacy that closed gradually on his old age, he was able to prevent Pitt from emancipating the Irish   1801. Catholics, and he exerted a certain influence in the struggle for Cabinet office between the groups and personages of Parliament.

The temporary revival of the group system in place of the two-party system was indeed a feature of the period, which tended to a certain limited extent to revive the influence of the Crown as arbitrator. The two-party system was no longer in full working order, because the split in the Whig party over Reform and the French Revolution reduced the Foxites to about a hundred members, and left them for a generation without hope of power. The hibernation of the Whig party between 1793 and 1830 may be compared to the hibernation of the Tory party from 1714 to 1760, and it had the same result in the revival of a group system on the floor of the House of Commons. Just as the long weakness of the Tories caused the Whigs to divide into Walpole and anti-Walpole factions, so the Tories in the first year of the Nineteenth Century broke up into Pittites, Addingtonians and Whig-Tory followers of the Grenville family. These groups, personal rather than political in their differences, combined each in turn with the Foxite remnant to form the governments and oppositions of the remaining years of war.

In these circumstances, a certain power of selection rested with the old King, and, when his insanity was pro-
1811.   nounced incurable, with the Regent Prince George.

They both used it heavily against any combination that included the Foxite Whigs. Immediately after Pitt's death
George III was, indeed, compelled to submit for a
1806–   year to the coalition Ministry of 'All the Talents,' in-
1807.   cluding the dying Fox, with the result that the slave
trade was at last abolished. But the King managed speed-
ily to rid himself of servants whom he so much disliked, and
though the ground on which he dismissed them was indefensible,
it was, perhaps, no real misfortune. For the Whig chiefs and their
Grenvillite colleagues did not make good war Ministers. Ever
since the camp at Boulogne the Foxites had, indeed, accepted the
necessity of war with France, and their leader in his few months at
the Foreign Office was converted on his death-bed to the view
which he had so often denounced, that peace with Napoleon was
impossible. Yet his successors in the Whig hierarchy, like Lords
Holland and Grey, too easily despaired, and had neither the
phlegm nor the *flair* necessary for those who conduct a long and
doubtful war.[1]

The pure Tory groups combined after 1807 to govern the
country and fight Napoleon through the agency of the House of
Commons. The prestige of Waterloo and the final victory re-
dounded most to the credit of the nation that had never submitted and always hoped. And, in the secure judgment of the world,
the victory of the stubborn islanders was due, not to King or
Regent, but to British Parliamentary institutions, to the British
aristocracy, and to the steady character and rapidly increasing
wealth of the British middle class.

Napoleon signalized his coronation as Emperor by conquering
Eastern Europe up to the Russian border—a three years' task:
each year there was

> another deadly blow!
> Another mighty Empire overthrown,

---

[1] After a moment of first enthusiasm for the cause of the Spanish people
risen against Napoleon, most of the Whigs took fright about the Peninsular
War after Moore's retreat, and thought Wellington's campaigns there fore-
doomed to failure.

Austria at Austerlitz, Prussia at Jena, Russia at Friedland. The work was crowned in the summer of 1807 by   1805,
the Treaty of Tilsit, made on a raft in the Niemen, where   1806,
Napoleon embraced the Czar Alexander, an impres-   1807.
sionable young man, destined to play many different
parts in Europe's tragedy, each with the same conscientious
solemnity as the last. For four years it flattered him to be Napoleon's ally and half-sharer in the rule of the continent. From the
Urals to the Pyrenees the civilized world was banded against
England, and closed to her shipping and her goods. But in that
vast hostile camp she had many secret friends, whom it was the
chief task of her statesmanship to rouse into mutiny. The prospect
of British subsidies if they should take up arms, was one inducement offered; while another and harsher was the deprivation of
tea and coffee, sugar and cotton, so long as they remained French
vassals.

England and France now organized the world-warfare of
blockade and starvation, on a scale never before witnessed,
because never in the history of war had there been sea-power
like that of England after Trafalgar, or land-power like that of
Napoleon after Tilsit. By Napoleon's Berlin and Milan
Decrees, neutrals and French allies were forbidden to   1806,
trade with Great Britain or her colonies. Britain replied   1807.
by the Orders in Council, a series of measures of ever-
increasing stringency, of which the general drift was   1807,
that all Napoleonic Europe was subjected to blockade.   1812.

Of three sets of victims, which would rebel the first? Napoleon's German vassals and Muscovite allies, deprived of their
luxuries and comforts for his sake? Or the United States, the one
great neutral carrier, angry with England because her ships effec-
tually barred the Yankee skippers from European ports, whereas
Napoleon, having no submarines, could not by mere proclama-
tion exclude them from trading with Britain? Or, finally, as
Napoleon had in 1811 some reason to hope, would the strain
prove too much for the English middle and lower orders, whose
business, employment and real wages were subject during these
terrible years to the vagaries of war prices and war markets?

In fact, by 1812, Russia had rebelled against Napoleon's

decrees, and the United States against the British Orders in Council and the right of search as exercised by her captains. But the classes on the British 'home front' who suffered from the war, stood firm. The mercantile community refused to submit to Napoleon, but strongly urged the Perceval Ministry to relax the Orders in Council enough to prevent war with our largest remaining customer, the United States. But the middle classes were still for the most part unenfranchised, and stood outside the close ring of the Tory governing class. Their advice was heeded too late and war broke out between England and America, causing

1812–
1814.
great momentary suffering to Britain by commercial stoppage. But neither that nor the distraction of naval and military bickering on the Canadian frontier and along the American coast, proved fatal to Britain's victory in Europe, because in the same years Russia and Germany rebelled against France. The next generation of Englishmen forgot the American war as an unpleasant and unnecessary episode in the greater Napoleonic struggle; but Americans remembered it only too well, as a patriotic landmark in their early growth as a nation. From the point of view of future Anglo-American relations, it was most unfortunate that the first foreign war of the young Republic should have been waged with the motherland, against whom also her War of Independence had been fought.

The Napoleonic struggle, though as dangerous at times to Britain as the Great War of our own day, affected the life of the community at fewer points; above all it made a much smaller

1795–
1807.
drain upon the manhood of the country. For a dozen years we had practically no troops on the continent, except for very small and very occasional raids. The total death-roll in the whole twenty-two years was probably about 100,000, nearly half lost in the West Indies in Pitt's time and 40,000 more in the six years' fighting in the Peninsula. It was in economic suffering that England paid. The course of the Industrial Revolution, during two critical decades, was warped and diverted by the exigencies of the war.

But the economic suffering was by no means evenly divided among the whole people. The upper class throve on enhanced rents, and paid too small a proportion of the war taxes; for revenue was raised largely by duties on articles of consumption, of which the effect was felt by the poor in the rise of prices. Pitt's useful new device of the income-tax, which was continued till the end of the war, did something, but not enough, to redress the balance. In 1815 twenty-five millions were raised by direct, and sixty-seven millions by indirect taxation. Those who enjoyed rent and tithe, composing a single governing class of the well-born, knew little of the hardships of war time.

It was, indeed, a notable period in the higher civilization of the island, where all through the war great landscape painters, poets and novelists were working for a large and eager class with the wealth and leisure to enjoy their works. Never was countryhouse life more thriving or jovial, with its fox-hunting, shooting, and leisure in spacious and well-stocked libraries. Never was sporting life more attractive, with its coaching on the newly improved roads, and its boxing matches patronized by the nobility. In the mirror that Miss Austen held up to nature in the drawing-room, it is hard to detect any trace of concern or trouble arising from the war.

The middle classes suffered more. Many merchants, like poor old Mr. Sedley in *Vanity Fair*, were broken by the sudden opening and shutting of markets, or the rise and fall of war prices. But many also made their fortunes in new factories, and in commerce with the black and brown peoples of the world, whom England was learning to clothe, wholesale, as yet without a rival in that profitable business.

The chief sufferers by the war were the working classes, for whom little was done except the general adoption of the policy originated by the Berkshire magistrates at Speenhamland, for granting rates in aid of wages to prevent families from positively dying of starvation. But the better policy of an enforced minimum wage, though discussed, was unfortunately rejected as old-fashioned and unscientific. Meanwhile, Pitt's Act made Trade Unions illegal, so that the workmen found it difficult, in the face of hostile authority, to keep up wages in their proper relation to prices.

That sense of the brotherhood of classes in the Great War which was so marked in our own more democratic day, had no place in the Anti-Jacobin mentality. Wellington's remarks about the soldiers who won his battles, as 'the scum of the earth,' enlisted 'for drink,'[2] represent the common limitations of upper-class sympathy at that period, though Nelson and his coxswain's letter strike another note. Harshness often appeared, not only in the treatment of the much flogged soldiers and sailors, but in the attitude to Luddites and the 'labouring poor' in general. While engaged in beating Napoleon, the authorities recognized a double duty in relation to starving men,—to keep them alive and to keep them in due subordination.

Napoleon's endeavor to enforce his 'continental system' for excluding British goods from Europe,—his only available means of chastising the insolent islanders,—drew him into the two most fatal errors of his career, the attempt to annex
1808.   Spain against the will of its people, and the invasion of
1812.   the vastness of Russia. Those two acts let loose upon him
         the rising of the peoples, after he had dealt successfully
         with the Kings. The earlier and more criminal of these
1808.   enterprises gave England the opportunity to commence
         the Peninsular War. Our operations there began very
humbly in an attempt to maintain according to precedent the independence of our ancient ally, Portugal. Throughout the next six years Portugal continued to be the base, and sea-power the condition of the whole affair, as in the less lucky operations of the British armies in Spain during the Marlborough wars.

The Portuguese consented to be drilled and commanded by British officers, with the result that in this war they made very respectable troops of the line. The Spaniards, on the other hand, seldom made even tolerable regulars, but seldom failed to act with amazing efficiency in guerrilla warfare. The more primitive nature of Spanish character and society rendered the land which Napoleon had despised more formidable to the armies of French occupation than any of the more civilized nations of modern

---

[2] We must do the Duke the justice of remembering that he added words not always quoted: 'it really is wonderful that we should have made them the fine fellows they are.'

Europe, upon which they had so long trampled. For this reason the 300,000 French in Spain were mostly engaged in guarding communications, and could never concentrate enough force to destroy the persistent British army of some 30,000 men under Moore or Wellington. Issuing from Portugal in well-planned raids across Spain, Wellington year after year carried off the victory in an ascending scale of the decisive,—Tala-   1809, vera, Salamanca, Vitoria,—as Napoleon's increasing   1812, commitments in Russia and Germany gradually reduced   1813. the pressure of France upon the Peninsula. The military power and reputation of Britain, that had sunk so low at the beginning of the Revolutionary Wars, were raised to the height where they had stood under Cromwell and Marlborough. The Peninsular battles and sieges, recorded in such numbers on our flags, confirmed and perpetuated the regimental traditions which remained the true life of the British Army during the next hundred years.

The victories in Spain, though due largely to the previous work of the Duke of York and Sir John Moore in reforming the Army, and to Wellington's own strategical and tactical genius, were facilitated by the superiority of the British line over the French column. The history of that difference of formation is very curious. The dynastic wars of the Eighteenth Century, from Marlborough to Frederic the Great, had been fought in line, —three deep, reduced towards the end of the century to two. But this method of war, then universal in civilized armies, implied the perfect drill of highly professional troops. When, therefore, the first armies of the French Republic took the field with their high-spirited but ill-disciplined hosts straight from the counter and the plough, they could only be led into action in compact masses with a cloud of skirmishers flung out in front. But so great were their zeal and numbers, that in this crude formation they again and again chased off the field the well-ordered lines of the Austrian infantry. Thus defeated, the ancient monarchies of Europe imitated their conquerors by adopting their faulty tactics and formation, without the spirit that had been the true cause of the French successes. Only the British Army, guided by a combination of conservatism and good sense, con-

1801,   tinued to fight and manœuvre in line. On the rare occa-
1806.   sions, therefore, when they had met the French in Egypt
           and in South Italy they had an advantage over them
shared by no other nation. And now, in the more continuous
campaigns of the Peninsula, again and again the narrow head of
the French column was mowed down by the concentrated fire of
the long red line. It is indeed remarkable that the greatest military genius of modern times never attempted to reform the retro-
gressive tactics of his infantry.

The Peninsular War was finally won because the French disasters in Russia and Germany continually reduced the number
           of their troops in Spain. Similarly, the decisive victory
1813.   of our allies over Napoleon in person at Leipzig, was
           rendered possible by the number of French engaged by
Wellington in the South. Early in 1814 France was entered by
Wellington from across the Pyrenees, and by the Austrians, Prussians and Russians across the Rhine. The final success had been
rendered possible by the wisdom and energy of Castlereagh's
diplomacy in mid-Europe in 1813–14, which held together the
alliance of jealous Princes until the common object was attained.

The first fall of Napoleon was followed by his return from
Elba, the rally of the veterans of the army to his standard,
           while the French people looked on with divided feelings.
Ju. 18,   His Hundred Days' adventure ended at Waterloo. The
1815.   fortunate brevity of this last war was due to the prompt
           and courageous action of the British Government in de-
claring war at once, and sending over Wellington to defend Holland and Belgium in alliance with Blucher and his Prussians, till
the allied armies from the East could arrive in overwhelming
numbers. The decisive character of the great battle put a sudden
end to the war, because France was half-hearted in her desire that
it should be renewed.

The reputation of Great Britain, as the most consistent and
formidable antagonist of Napoleon, reached its height as a result
of Waterloo. At the peace conference, Castlereagh and Wellington spoke with a voice of unrivalled authority among the Emperors and Kings. To the influence of these two Anglo-Irish aristocrats the merits of the Treaties of Vienna were largely due.

The most striking merit of the Settlement of 1815 lay in

securing at the outset a long period of quiet for Europe by justice
and even leniency to the conquered, a point on which Wellington
and Castlereagh both insisted, with the aid of the Czar Alexander,
against the very natural desire for vengeance on the part of
Blucher and the Germans and a large part of the British public.
France,—with the Bourbons restored but the social arrangements
of the Revolution left intact,—was allowed her old boundaries of
1792, was not compelled to give up Alsace or Lorraine, and received back from England most of her possessions in Africa and
the two Indies seized during the war. The indemnity which she
had to pay was fixed from the first at a moderate sum, and in
three years her territory was completely evacuated by the allied
armies. Revenge was eschewed, but security was gained by an alliance to prevent, in arms, the return of Napoleon, whom meanwhile the English kept out of harm's way on remote St. Helena.

The defect of the Settlement was that nationality and popular
liberty were both disregarded on the continent, outside the
boundaries of France herself. Except England, the Great Powers
who had triumphed were Powers of reaction and despotism, and
even Castlereagh cared nothing for Parliaments outside England.
The rulers of Russia, Prussia and Austria divided up Poland,
Germany and Italy as if inhabitants were so many head of population to be bartered among royal hagglers. The Temporal
Power of the Pope over Central Italy was restored. The hopes of
national and popular self-expression, which in Spain and Germany had partly inspired the late patriotic uprising against
France, were crushed to the earth.

The merits of the Settlement of Vienna gave Europe forty years
of peace. Its faults rendered war certain in the end,—war to assert
national and popular aspirations which Metternich's system could
not for ever keep in check.[3]

One of the points in the Treaties of 1815 in which Britain was

[3] Professor Webster, Castlereagh's distinguished biographer, writes: 'More
worthy of reprobation is the discouragement of the idea of self-government,
which had already come to a fuller consciousness than that of nationality.
Alexander alone, with some of his advisers, showed any sympathy with it; and
it was he who secured the "Charte" for the French with the assistance of
Talleyrand, who was also aware of the fundamental importance of this aspect
of the French Revolution. To almost all the other statesmen democracy meant
nothing but anarchy and revolution; and among these must be included the

specially interested was the restoration of the Anglophil House
of Orange to Holland, and the addition of Belgium to their
Kingdom of the Netherlands. The Delta of the Rhine was again
            in hands from which England had nothing to fear, but
1830–   another sharp crisis was necessary fifteen years later, be-
1831.   fore a permanent settlement was reached by the separa-
            tion of Belgium from Holland on a basis of two separate
and independent States.

But the greatest interests of Britain lay beyond the ocean, and
there she was supreme arbiter. It was for her alone to decide how
many she would give back of the colonies which she had seized in
the war. On the whole she was not ungenerous in her restorations.
While keeping Ceylon and the Cape of Good Hope and Singa-
pore, and purchasing a part of Guiana for three million pounds,
Britain gave back to the Dutch their old possessions of Java and
the other East Indian islands which have ever since remained the
chief source of Holland's external wealth. France and Denmark
got back their most valuable islands. But England kept Mauritius
and Heligoland, and the Mediterranean vantage points of the
Ionian Islands and Malta. The network of British naval, maritime and commercial posts, soon to be used also as coaling
stations, had already begun to spread over the globe. Australia,
peacefully acquired by Captain Cook's voyages (1769–1775), was
in process of colonization. Upper Canada was filling with English
and Scots. A Second Empire was arising to replace that which had
been lost, based like the first on sea-power, commerce and
liberty.

Tory Ministers of Great Britain, who even secretly encouraged the attacks on
the constitutions which had been set up with the direct connivance of British
representatives. It was this policy that made the subsequent national movements take strange paths, instead of being an expression of the people's
desires.'—*Congress of Vienna*, p. 147.

4.

The Industrial Revolution

~

T. S. ASHTON

In the short span of years between the accession of George III
and that of his son, William IV, the face of England changed.
Areas that for centuries had been cultivated as open fields, or had
laid untended as common pasture, were hedged or fenced; ham-
lets grew into populous towns; and chimney stacks rose to dwarf
the ancient spires. Highroads were made—straighter, stronger,
and wider than those evil communications that had corrupted
the good manners of travellers in the days of Defoe. The North
and Irish Seas, and the navigable reaches of the Mersey, Ouse,
Trent, Severn, Thames, Forth, and Clyde were joined together by
threads of still water. In the North the first iron rails were laid
down for the new locomotives, and steam packets began to ply on
the estuaries and the narrow seas.

Parallel changes took place in the structure of society. The
number of people increased vastly, and the proportion of children and young people probably rose. The growth of new communities shifted the balance of population from the South and
East to the North and Midlands; enterprising Scots headed a
procession the end of which is not yet in sight; and a flood of
unskilled, but vigorous, Irish poured in, not without effect on the
health and ways of life of Englishmen. Men and women born and
bred on the countryside came to live crowded together, earning

From *T. S. Ashton,* The Industrial Revolution, 1760–1830 *(New York: Oxford
University Press, 1964)* ; *Chapter 1, "Introduction," pp. 3–17.*

their bread, no longer as families or groups of neighbours, but as units in the labour force of factories; work grew to be more specialized; new forms of skill were developed, and some old forms lost. Labour became more mobile, and higher standards of comfort were offered to those able and willing to move to centres of opportunity.

At the same time fresh sources of raw material were exploited, new markets were opened, and new methods of trade devised. Capital increased in volume and fluidity; the currency was set on a gold base; a banking system came into being. Many old privileges and monopolies were swept away, and legislative impediments to enterprise removed. The State came to play a less active, the individual and the voluntary association a more active, part in affairs. Ideas of innovation and progress undermined traditional sanctions: men began to look forward, rather than backward, and their thoughts as to the nature and purpose of social life were transformed.

Whether or not such a series of changes should be spoken of as 'The Industrial Revolution' might be debated at length. The changes were not merely 'industrial', but also social and intellectual. The word 'revolution' implies a suddenness of change that is not, in fact, characteristic of economic processes. The system of human relationships that is sometimes called capitalism had its origins long before 1760, and attained its full development long after 1830: there is a danger of overlooking the essential fact of continuity. But the phrase 'Industrial Revolution' has been used by a long line of historians and has become so firmly embedded in common speech that it would be pedantic to offer a substitute.

The outstanding feature of the social history of the period—the thing that above all others distinguishes the age from its predecessors—is the rapid growth of population. Careful estimates, based on figures of burials and christenings, put the number of people in England and Wales at about five and a half millions in 1700, and six and a half millions in 1750: when the first census was taken in 1801 it was a round nine millions, and by 1831 had reached fourteen millions. In the second half of the eighteenth century population had thus increased by 40 per cent., and in the first three decades of the nineteenth century by more than 50 per cent. For Great Britain the figures are approximately eleven millions in 1801, and sixteen and a half millions in 1831.

The growth of population was not the result of any marked change in the birth rate. During the first four decades of the eighteenth century, it is true, the number of births per thousand people seems to have risen a little. Farm labourers tended to set up households of their own instead of boarding with their employers, and a decline of the system of apprenticeship in industry also led to earlier marriage and larger families. But from 1740 to 1830 the birth rate appears to have fluctuated only very slightly: for no decade does the estimate rise above 37.7, or fall below 36.6. Throughout the industrial revolution fertility was high but steady.

Nor can the increase of people be attributed to an influx from other countries. In every decade men and women took ship from Ireland to England and Scotland, and at times of dearth the trickle became a stream. But there was no such torrent of Irish immigration as was to come in the last five years of the eighteen-forties. On the other hand, during the eighteenth century perhaps a million people left Britain to seek a living overseas, mainly in the colonies. Among them were some 50,000 criminals transported to Maryland or Botany Bay, and a number of artisans who defied the law by carrying their technical knowledge and skill to Europe—not in the long run, it may be guessed, to the disadvantage of their native land. On balance, Britain was not a receiving centre but a breeding-ground for new communities across the seas.

It was a fall of mortality that led to the increase of numbers. In the first four decades of the eighteenth century excessive indulgence in cheap gin and intermittent periods of famine took a heavy toll of lives; but between 1740 and 1820 the death rate fell almost continuously—from an estimated 35.8 for the ten years ending in 1740 to one of 21.1 for those ending in 1821. Many influences were operating to reduce the incidence of death. The introduction of root crops made it possible to feed more cattle in the winter months, and so to supply fresh meat throughout the year. The substitution of wheat for inferior cereals, and an increased consumption of vegetables, strengthened resistance to disease. Higher standards of personal cleanliness, associated with more soap and cheaper cotton underwear, lessened the dangers of infection. The use of brick in place of timber in the walls, and of slate or stone instead of thatch in the roofs of cottages reduced the number of pests; and the removal of many noxious processes of manufacture from the homes of the workers brought greater domestic comfort. The larger towns were paved, drained, and supplied with running water; knowledge of medicine and surgery developed; hospitals and dispensaries increased; and more attention was paid to such things as the disposal of refuse and the proper burial of the dead.

Since there are no reliable statistics it is not possible to say which age groups of the population benefited most from these improvements. In a well-known passage of his *Autobiography* Edward Gibbon says:

'The death of a new-born child before that of its parents may seem an unnatural, but it is strictly a probable event; since of any given number, the greater part are extinguished before their ninth year, before they possess the faculties of mind or body. Without accusing the profuse waste or imperfect workmanship of Nature, I shall only observe that this unfavourable chance was multiplied against my infant existence. So feeble was my constitution, so precarious my life, that in the baptism of each of my brothers, my father's prudence repeated my Christian name of Edward, that in case of the departure of the eldest son, this patronymic appellation might be still perpetuated in the family.'

This was written in 1792–3. By that time it is probable that the profuse waste of infant life was a little less than at the date of Gibbon's birth, and, if so, there would be a higher percentage of children and young people in the population. It is a matter to be borne in mind in considering the constitution of the labour force of the early factories.

The increase of the population of Britain occurred at a time when the output of commodities was also increasing at a rapid rate, and this coincidence has led to hasty generalizations. Some writers have drawn the inference that it was the growth of industry that led to the growth of numbers. If this were true the growth of industry must have exerted its influence, not through the birth rate (which, as we have seen, remained steady), but through the death rate. Some of the improvements in the arts of living mentioned above certainly depended on a development of industry, but it would be rash to assign to this a major part in the reduction of mortality. For population was growing rapidly, not only in Britain, but also in most other countries of western and northern Europe, where nothing in the nature of an industrial revolution occurred.

Other writers, reversing the causal sequence, have declared that the growth of population, through its effect on the demand for commodities, stimulated the expansion of industry. An increase of people, however, does not necessarily mean either a greater effective demand for manufactured goods or an increased production of these in the country concerned. (If it did we should expect to find a rapid economic development of Ireland in the eighteenth, and of Egypt, India, and China in the nineteenth century.) It may just as well lead to a lower standard of life for all. The spectre of the pressure of population on the means of subsistence which oppressed the mind of Malthus in 1798 was no chimera. It is true that the immediate pressure was less than Malthus supposed. But if, after the middle of the nineteenth century, there had been no railways in America, no opening up of the prairies, and no steamships, Britain might have learnt from bitter experience the fallacy of the view that, because with every pair of hands there is a mouth, therefore every expansion of numbers must lead to an increase of consumption and so of output. In Britain, in the eighteenth century and later, it so happened that, alongside the increase of population, there was taking place an increase of the other factors of production, and hence it was possible for the standard of life of the people—or of most of them—to rise.

There was an increase in the acreage of land under cultivation. Much attention was given to the draining of fens and marshes, to the breaking up and turning to arable of the old, rough, common pastures (which were usually spoken of as the waste), and to the hedging of land, so as to make it more productive of both crops and livestock. 'In this manner', wrote an observer of these developments, 'was more useful territory added to the empire, at the expence of individuals, than had been gained by every war since the Revolution.' Several new crops were introduced. The turnip made it possible to increase the size of the herds of cattle, and the potato, which was becoming a popular food in the North, brought substantial economies in the use of land. More will be said later about the agricultural and agrarian changes. It is sufficient here to make the point that land previously outside the system of economic activities was being drawn in, and put to better use. The lines of the moving frontier can be discerned on the hillsides to-day by those with eyes to see.

At the same time there was taking place a rapid increase of capital. The number of people with incomes more than sufficient to cover the primary needs of life was growing: the power to save was increasing. Stable political and social conditions, following the settlement of 1688, encouraged men to look to more distant horizons: what economists call time-preference was favourable to accumulation. The class structure also was favourable to it. It is generally recognized that more saving takes place in communities in which the distribution of wealth is uneven than in those in which it approaches more closely to modern conceptions of what is just. Estimates of statisticians, from Gregory King in 1688 to Colquhoun in 1812, exhibit wide variations in the incomes of different social classes; and the rise of new institutions, including that of the National Debt, intensified the disparities that had been handed down from earlier generations.

The public debt, as we know it to-day, arose out of the exigencies of the wars of William III. It grew steadily—almost entirely as the result of successive wars—until, by 1815, it had reached a figure of £861 millions. Not all of it was held by the British people themselves: in 1776, perhaps a quarter or more of it was in the hands of the Dutch. But, after 1781, when Holland became involved in war with Britain, the great bulk of the debt came to be held in this country—by noblemen, squires, lawyers, retired merchants, and widows and spinsters of the well-to-do classes. In 1815 perhaps about one-eleventh, and in 1827 (according to the estimate of Sir Henry Parnell) one-twelfth, of the money income of the people of the United Kingdom consisted of sums raised from the taxpayers, including the poor, and transferred to the relatively rich holders of government bonds. In this way, increasingly, wealth came into the hands of those whose propensity was to save, rather than to spend.

Accumulation does not of itself, however, lead to the creation of capital goods: it was not only a willingness to save, but also a willingness to employ savings productively, that increased at this time. In the early eighteenth century, landlords had used saved resources to improve their own estates, merchants to extend their markets, and manufacturers to engage more labour; and some of the savings of the retired and leisured classes had been lent on mortgage to local landowners, farmers or tradesmen, or invested in the shares of a turnpike trust. Gradually the market for capital widened, aided by the rise of country bankers (who existed long before they took the name). The offer by the State of a mass of gilt-edged stock accustomed men to the idea of impersonal investment, and so they came to put their savings into enterprises distant in space and speculative in character. That the results might not always be advantageous was made manifest when the South Sea Bubble burst in 1720 and brought ruin to thousands. But, in general, the increased mobility of capital was socially beneficial, leading as it did to a substantial fall in the rate of interest.

For centuries the attitude of the State to the taking of interest had been one of hostility or, at least, of suspicion. The State was an habitual debtor—and laws had been passed prohibiting the making of loans at more than a prescribed rate. In 1625 the legal rate had been lowered from 10 to 8 per cent.; in 1651 it was reduced to 6, and in 1714 to 5—in each case following upon a fall in the 'natural' rate. In the early eighteenth century the abundance of loanable funds made it possible for finance ministers to reduce the interest paid to the creditors of the State. During the wars, the Government of William III had been obliged to offer 7 or 8 per cent. (the Usury Laws did not apply to the State) ; but in 1717 the rate on the perpetual annuities was reduced to 5, and in 1727 to 4 per cent. Finally, in the 1750s, Pelham lowered it once more, and, by converting a number of issues into a single one, brought into being, in 1757, the 3 per cent. Consolidated Stock which, for short, we call Consols. These conversions were not imposed on an unwilling public: they reflected, rather than initiated, a fall of the rate of interest in the community generally. There was, at this period, no single market rate to which reference can be made, but the process can be observed in the rising price of Bank of England stock; and the ledgers of merchants and manufacturers afford further evidence of what was taking place. Much economic activity at this time was controlled by small groups of partners, each of whom was entitled either to receive his share of the annual profits or to leave it, wholly or in part, to earn interest in the concern. During the early part of the eighteenth century the rate allowed on money reinvested in this way was falling steadily. A firm of ironmasters of Worcestershire, Edward Knight and Company, for example, credited each partner with 5 per cent. on the undisturbed profit during the 'twenties and early 'thirties, but in 1735 the rate was reduced to 4, and in 1756 to as little as 3 per cent. If a group of men were considering the investment of their savings in some new, large capital enterprise, such as a turnpike, they would first make an estimate of the number of years it would take for their capital to be restored to them in full. If the current rate of interest were 5 per cent. it would be worth while embarking on an undertaking that would return the capital in twenty years; at 4 per cent. investment might be extended to one that would take twenty-five years, and at 3 per cent. to one that would take up to thirty-three and a third years, to reimburse the initial outlay. The lower the rate at which capital could be obtained—the smaller the advantage foregone in locking it up in a fixed form—the further would capital works be extended.

As early as 1668 Sir Josiah Child remarked that 'all countries are at this day richer or poorer in an exact proportion to what they pay, and have usually paid, for the Interest of Money'. He went on to observe that 'the bringing down of Interest from 6 to 4, or 3 per cent. will necessarily . . . double the Capital Stock of the Nation' and added that 'the Nobility and Gentry, whose estates lie mostly in Land, may presently upon all they have, instead of fifty write one hundred'. In spite of this early exposition of the relation between interest, capital, and well-being, the importance of the lowering of the rate of interest in the half-century before the industrial revolution has never been properly stressed by historians. If we seek—it would be wrong to do so—for a single reason why the pace of economic development quickened about the middle of the eighteenth century, it is to this we must look. The deep mines, solidly built factories, well-constructed canals, and substantial houses of the industrial revolution were the products of relatively cheap capital.

One thing more was necessary: the increasing supplies of labour, land, and capital had to be co-ordinated. The eighteenth and early nineteenth centuries were rich in entrepreneurs, quick to devise new combinations of productive factors, eager to find new markets, receptive to new ideas. 'The age is running mad after innovation', said Dr. Johnson; 'all the business of the world is to be done in a new way; men are to be hanged in a new way; Tyburn itself is not safe from the fury of innovation.' The sentiments and attitudes of mind of the period were propitious. The religious and political differences that had torn society apart in the two preceding centuries had been composed; and if the eighteenth century was not markedly an age of faith, at least it practised the Christian virtue of tolerance. The regulation of industry by gilds, municipalities, and the central government had broken down or had been allowed to sleep, and the field was open for the exercise of initiative and enterprise. It was perhaps no accident that it was in Lancashire and the West Riding, which had been exempted from some of the more restrictive provisions of the Elizabethan code of industrial legislation, that the development was most marked. It was certainly no accident that it was the villages and unincorporated towns—places like Manchester and Birmingham—that grew most rapidly, for industry and trade had long been moving away from the areas where some remnants of public control were still in operation.

During the seventeenth century the attitude of the Law had changed: from the time of Coke judgements in the courts of Common Law had become tender indeed to the rights of property, but hostile to privilege. In 1624 the Statute of Monopolies had swept away many vested interests, and a century and a half later Adam Smith was able to say of Englishmen that they were 'to their great honour of all peoples, the least subject to the wretched spirit of monopoly'. Whether or not the patent system, the lines of which had been laid down by that same Statute, was stimulating to innovation in industrial practice is not easy to determine. It gave security to the inventor, but it allowed some privileged positions to be maintained for an undue length of time, and it was sometimes used to block the way to new contrivance: for nearly a quarter of a century for example, James Watt was able to prevent other engineers from constructing new types of steam engine, even under licence from himself. Many manufacturers—not all from disinterested motives—opposed the application of the law and encouraged piracy. Associations were brought into being in Manchester and other centres of industry to contest the legality of rights claimed by patentees. The Society for the Encouragement of Arts, Manufactures and Commerce, founded in 1754, offered premiums to inventors who were willing to put their devices at the free disposal of all. And Parliament itself made awards (for example, £14,000 to Thomas Lombe when his patent for silk-throwing expired, £30,000 to Jenner for the discovery of vaccine inoculation, £10,000 to Edmund Cartwright for various contrivances, and £5,000 to Samuel Crompton for his invention of the 'mule') in addition to the substantial annual grants it voted for the use of the Board of Agriculture and the Veterinary College. Without any such monetary incentive, one of the outstanding industrialists, Josiah Wedgwood, resolved 'to be released from these degrading slavish chains, these mean, selfish fears of other people copying my works'; and, at a later stage, the inventors of the safety lamps, Sir Humphry Davy, Dr. Clanny, and George Stephenson, all refused, in the interest of the miners, to take out patents for their devices. It is at least possible that without the apparatus of the patent system discovery might have developed quite as rapidly as it did.

Some accounts of the technological revolution begin with the story of a dreamy boy watching the steam raise the lid of the kettle on the domestic hearth, or with that of a poor weaver gazing with stupefaction at his wife's spinning wheel, overturned on the floor but still revolving. These, needless to say, are nothing but romantic fiction. Other accounts leave the impression that the inventions were the work of obscure millwrights, carpenters, or clockmakers, untutored in principles, who stumbled by chance on some device that was destined to bring others to fame and fortune and themselves to penury. It is true that there were inventors—men like Brindley and Murdoch—who were endowed with little learning, but with much native wit. It is true that there were others, such as Crompton and Cort, whose discoveries transformed whole industries, but left them to end their days in relative poverty. It is true that a few new products came into being as the result of accident. But such accounts have done harm by obscuring the fact that systematic thought lay behind most of the innovations in industrial practice, by making it appear that the distribution of rewards and penalties in the economic system was wholly irrational, and, above all, by over-stressing the part played by chance in technical progress. 'Chance', as Pasteur said, 'favours only the mind which is prepared': most discoveries are achieved only after repeated trial and error. Many involve two or more previously independent ideas or processes, which, brought together in the mind of the inventor, issue in a more or less complex and efficient mechanism. In this way, for example, the principle of the jenny was united by Crompton with that of spinning by rollers to produce the mule; and the iron rail, which had long been in use in the coal mine, was joined to the locomotive to create the railway. In such cases of what has been called cross-mutation the part played by chance must have been very small indeed.

Yet other accounts of the industrial revolution are misleading because they present discovery as the achievement of individual genius, and not as a social process. 'Invention', as a distinguished modern scientist, Michael Polanyi, has remarked, 'is a drama enacted on a crowded stage.' The applause tends to be given to those who happen to be on the boards in the final act, but the success of the performance depends on the close co-operation of many players, and of those behind the scenes. The men who,

together, whether as rivals or as associates, created the technique
of the industrial revolution were plain Englishmen or Scots,

Being neither demigods nor heroes,
But ingenious, hard-working descendants of *homo sapiens,*
Who had the luck to plant their seedlings in fine weather,
Not in the frost or storm, but when the slow ripening of time, the
    felicitous crossing of circumstance
Presented unimagined opportunities,
Which they seized. . . .

(The words are those of a master cotton-spinner, Godfrey Armi-
tage, of our own day.)

Invention appears at every stage of human history, but it rarely
thrives in a community of simple peasants or unskilled manual
labourers: only when division of labour has developed, so that
men devote themselves to a single product or process, does it
come to harvest. Such division of labour already existed when the
eighteenth century opened, and the industrial revolution was in
part cause, and in part effect, of a heightening and extension of
the principle of specialization.

Invention, again, is more likely to arise in a community that
sets store by things of the mind than in one that seeks only
material ends. The stream of English scientific thought, issuing
from the teaching of Francis Bacon, and enlarged by the genius
of Boyle and Newton, was one of the main tributaries of the
industrial revolution. Newton, indeed, was too good a philosopher and scholar to care whether or not the ideas he gave to the
world were immediately 'useful'; but the belief in the possibility
of achieving industrial progress by the method of observation
and experiment came to the eighteenth century largely through
him. Natural philosophy was shaking itself free from its association with metaphysics and—again the application of the principle of division of labour—splitting up into the separate systems
of physiology, chemistry, physics, geology and so on. The sciences
were not, however, as yet so specialized as to be out of contact
with the language, thought, and practice of ordinary men. It was
as a result of a visit to Norfolk, where he had gone to study the
new methods of farming, that the Scottish landowner, James

Hutton, became interested in the constitution of soils; and the discoveries that made him the most famous geologist of his day owed something to the navvies who were cutting the clays and blasting the rock to provide England with canals. Physicists and chemists, such as Franklin, Black, Priestley, Dalton, and Davy, were in intimate contact with the leading figures in British industry: there was much coming and going between the laboratory and the workshop, and men like James Watt, Josiah Wedgwood, William Reynolds, and James Keir were at home in the one as in the other. The names of engineers, ironmasters, industrial chemists, and instrument-makers on the list of Fellows of the Royal Society show how close were the relations between science and practice at this time.

Inventors, contrivers, industrialists, and entrepreneurs—it is not easy to distinguish one from another at a period of rapid change—came from every social class and from all parts of the country. Aristocrats, like Lord Lovell, in the early part of the century, and Coke of Holkham in the later, initiated improvements in agriculture; others, such as the Duke of Bridgewater and Earl Gower, created new forms of transport; and yet others were responsible for innovations in the chemical and mining industries. Clergymen and parsons, including Edmund Cartwright and Joseph Dawson, forsook the cure of souls to find out more efficient ways of weaving cloth and smelting iron. Doctors of medicine, among whom were John Roebuck and James Keir, took to chemical research and became captains of large-scale industry. Under the influence of a rationalist philosophy, scholars turned from the humanities to physical science, and some from physical science to technology. Lawyers, soldiers, public servants, and men of humbler station than these found in manufacture possibilities of advancement far greater than those offered in their original callings. A barber, Richard Arkwright, became the wealthiest and most influential of the cotton-spinners; an innkeeper, Peter Stubs, built up a highly esteemed concern in the file trade; a schoolmaster, Samuel Walker, became the leading figure in the north of England iron industry. 'Every man', exclaimed the ebullient William Hutton in 1780, 'has his fortune in his own hands.' That, it is needless to say, has never been true, or even half true; but anyone who looks closely at English society in the mid- and late eighteenth century will understand how it was possible for it to be said, for at this time vertical mobility had reached a degree higher than that of any earlier, or perhaps any succeeding, age.

It has often been observed that the growth of industry was connected historically with the rise of groups which dissented from the Church by law established in England. In the seventeenth century the congregation of Puritans gathered about Richard Baxter at Kidderminister included the Foleys, the Crowleys, and the Hanburys, who were to set up great establishments in places as far afield as Staffordshire, Durham, and South Wales. In the following century members of the Society of Friends played a prominent part in the development of corn-milling, brewing, pharmacy, and banking; and the Quaker families of the Darby's, Reynolds, Lloyds, and Huntsmans came to direct the destinies of the iron and steel industries at a period of rapid change. There were Baptists, like Thomas Newcomen, and Presbyterians, like James Watt, in engineering; Independents, like John Roebuck and Joseph Dawson, alongside the Quakers, in ironsmelting; and Unitarians, including the M'Connels and the Gregs, in cotton-spinning. In cotton, moreover, the greatest inventor, Samuel Crompton, was a disciple of Emmanuel Swedenborg—who himself, it may be recalled, was an authority on metals and the technique of mines. Other industrialists, among whom were the Guests of South Wales, drew strength from the teaching of John Wesley. But Wesley's first appeal was to the poor and unprivileged, and the effects of Methodism are to be seen less in the quickening of enterprise than in the greater sobriety, diligence and self-discipline of the workers who came under its influence.

Many explanations have been offered of this close association between industry and Dissent. It has been suggested that those who sought out new forms of worship would also naturally strike out new paths in secular fields. It has been argued that there is an intimate connexion between the tenets peculiar to Nonconformity and the rules of conduct that lead to success in business. And it has been asserted that the exclusion of Dissenters from the universities, and from office in government and administration, forced many to seek an outlet for their abilities in industry and trade. There may be something in each of these contentions, but a simpler explanation lies in the fact that, broadly speaking, the Nonconformists constituted the better educated section of the middle classes. This view is supported by a consideration of the part played in the economic movement by the stream of energy that poured into England from Presbyterian Scotland after (though not immediately after) the Union of 1707. The greatest inventor of the age, James Watt, came from Scotland, as also did seven of his eight assistants in the business of erecting engines. Sir John Sinclair, Thomas Telford, John Macadam, David Mushet and James Beaumont Neilson brought their Scottish vigour of mind and character to English agriculture, transport, and iron-making. Highlanders and Lowlanders, alike, tramped to the Lancashire cotton area, many of them pausing at the little village of Chowbent, where a fellow-countryman named Cannan directed them to centres which offered scope for their several abilities. Among those who took the southern road to fortune in textiles were James McGuffog, James M'Connel, John Kennedy, George and Adam Murray and—bearers of names that are honoured to-day, not only in Lancashire—John Gladstone and Henry Bannerman. These and other immigrants were not illiterate peasants. Some were sons of the manse, and even those of humbler station had been given at least the rudiments of a sound education in the village or burgh school of their native place.

If the Scottish system of primary education was in advance of that of any other European country at this time, the same was true of the Scottish universities. It was not from Oxford or Cambridge, where the torch burnt dim, but from Glasgow and Edinburgh, that the impulse to scientific inquiry and its practical application came. Many young men, attracted by the learning and personality of Joseph Black, Professor of Chemistry at Glasgow and later at Edinburgh, were trained to methods of thought and experiment which were afterwards directed to industrial ends. Among them was James Keir, a pioneer in the chemical and glass industries, and (if the circle may be extended to those who were not formally students of Black, but owed much to his teaching and friendship) John Roebuck, James Watt, and Alexander Cochrane, the brilliant but unfortunate Earl of Dundonald.

In a humbler way the academies established by nonconformist zeal for education—at Bristol, Manchester, Northampton, Daventry, Warrington and elsewhere—did for England in the eighteenth century something of what the universities did for Scotland. Open to all, irrespective of creed, they provided a curriculum which, weighted, it is true, with Divinity, Rhetoric and Jewish Antiquities, included Mathematics, History, Geography, French, and Bookkeeping. Among their pupils were Daniel Defoe (and a contemporary named Cruso), John Cope, John Howard, Thomas Malthus, and William Hazlitt—to name only a few of those who were to rise to distinction in letters and public life. What is more to our immediate purpose, they were nurseries of scientific thought. Several of them were well equipped with 'philosophical instruments' and offered facilities for experiment: their teachers included men of the quality of Joseph Priestley and John Dalton; and from them proceeded a stream of future industrialists, among whom were John Roebuck (who was trained at Northampton before proceeding to Edinburgh and Leyden), Matthew Boulton, John Wilkinson, Benjamin Gott, and—of a later generation—Joseph Whitworth.

Apart from the dissenting academies, there were in many towns institutions which, like the national Society of Arts, were devoted to the improvement of methods of production. Informal groups of scientists and manufacturers came into being in Lancashire and the Midlands, as well as at Edinburgh and Glasgow. Who can say how much the master cotton-spinners gained from their contact with Thomas Percival and John Dalton in the Literary and Philosophical Society of Manchester; or how much Birmingham and its province owes to the Lunar Society, in which Erasmus Darwin, R. L. Edgeworth, Joseph Priestley, James Watt, Matthew Boulton, and Josiah Wedgwood brought their powerful minds to bear on the problems of life and, no less, on those of getting a living?

The conjuncture of growing supplies of land, labour, and capital made possible the expansion of industry; coal and steam provided the fuel and power for large-scale manufacture; low rates of interest, rising prices, and high expectations of profit offered the incentive. But behind and beyond these material and economic factors lay something more. Trade with foreign parts had widened men's views of the world, and science their conception of the universe: the industrial revolution was also a revolution of ideas. If it registered an advance in understanding of, and control over, Nature, it also saw the beginning of a new attitude to the problems of human society. And here, again, it was from Scotland, and the University of Glasgow in particular, that the clearest beam of light was thrown. It is, no doubt, an academic error to overstress the part played by speculative thought in shaping the lives of ordinary men and women: it is arguable that John Wesley, Tom Paine, William Cobbett, and Orator Hunt were of as much immediate consequence as David Hume, or even Jeremy Bentham. But, at least, there is one product of Scottish moral philosophy that cannot pass without mention in any account of the forces that produced the industrial revolution. The *Enquiry into the Nature and Causes of the Wealth of Nations,* which appeared in 1776, was to serve as a court of appeal on matters of economics and politics for generations to come. Its judgements were the material from which men not given to the study of treatises framed their maxims of conduct for business and government alike. It was under its influence that the idea of a more or less fixed volume of trade and employment, directed and regulated by the State, gave way—gradually and with many setbacks—to thoughts of unlimited progress in a free and expanding economy.

5.

Power Sources in
the Industrial Revolution

~

R. J. FORBES

During the last 250 years five great new prime movers have produced what is often called the Machine Age. The eighteenth century brought the steam-engine; the nineteenth the water-turbine, the internal combustion engine, and the steam-turbine; and the twentieth the gas-turbine. Historians have often coined catch-phrases to denote movements or currents in history. Such is 'The Industrial Revolution', the title for a development often described as starting in the early eighteenth century and extending through much of the nineteenth. It was a slow movement, but wrought changes so profound in their combination of material progress and social dislocation that collectively they may well be described as revolutionary if we consider these extreme dates.

The roots of this revolution stretch back into the sixteenth century, when important technological changes slowly began to take place. These had gained momentum by the middle of the eighteenth century. Outside Britain the revolution was far from complete even by 1880; thus Germany cannot be said even to have entered the industrial stage before the 1870s. In the United States, though it began early in the 1860s, it did not obtain a firm

From Charles Singer et al., eds., A History of Technology, *5 vols. (Oxford: The Clarendon Press, 1958)* ; *R. J. Forbes, Vol. 4, Chapter 5, "Power to 1850," pp. 148–164. Footnotes omitted; figures renumbered.*

grip until the turn of the century. Economically the basic factor in the industrial revolution was the remarkable expansion of overseas trade in the seventeenth and eighteenth centuries. The new markets came first, the inventions followed. Unconsciously, the successful inventors worked within the limits laid down for them by the changing society in which they dwelt and the new materials that were becoming available.

That the industrial revolution first gained momentum in the British Isles and that its results first began to become most clearly visible in Scotland and the midland counties of England may be ascribed to many fortuitous factors. Britain, by conquering the seas, established the largest foreign markets; she had the necessary capital for industrial experiments, a currency firmly based on gold, an efficient banking system, political and social stability, abundance of iron ore and coal, a humid climate suitable for textile manufacture, and social circles interested in scientific knowledge. The economic demands were met by scientific and technological advances of an increasingly high standard. Much of the new science of the seventeenth century had from the beginning stressed the importance of practical aims.

From the days of Stevin (1548–1620) and Galileo (1564–1642) the science of mechanics yielded fresh understanding of machines, particularly when, in the eighteenth century, mathematics came to be constantly applied to the theory and practice of their construction. That century also saw the start of experiment on the strength of materials, and thus notably contributed to practical mechanics and the design of well built engines. Exact measurement, the very basis of science, was becoming ever more important for the design and maintenance of all complex mechanisms. Moreover, practical engineering itself had gained momentum. The classical world had been seriously concerned with the study and control of motion, though several factors, notably slave labour, had kept power resources at a low level. Subsequent developments had involved changes in scale rather than in principle. In the words of Usher, 'these developments may seem to be little more than a diffusion of knowledge already attained. For a long time, no additional theoretical knowledge would have been of much practical use. It would be an error, however, to minimize the magnitude of the technological changes that opened up the first extensive applications of power. It was the beginning of an essentially new stage in mechanical technique'.

By the mid-seventeenth century there were many who saw clearly that cooperation between science and practical engineering formed the essential basis of technical improvements. In this century and the following one there was a notable rise in the number of patents (figure 1). Adam Smith (1723–90) realized

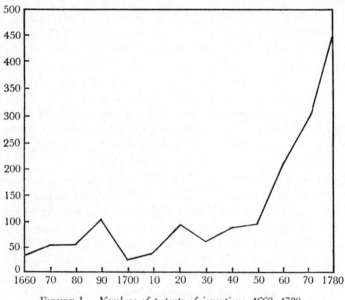

FIGURE 1—*Numbers of patents of inventions, 1660–1780.*

that these improvements were not only the work of practical engineers but that 'some came to be by the ingenuity of those men of speculation, whose trade it is not to do anything, but to observe everything; and who, upon that account, are often capable of combining together the powers of the most distant and dissimilar objects'.

The four basic technical achievements of the industrial revolution were:

1. *Replacement of tools by machines.* Both enable man to perform certain operations more dextrously than with the bare hand. The chief difference is that the tool is set in motion by man's physical strength, the machine by some natural force. The word machine is here used in the eighteenth-century sense, for both then and long afterwards no proper distinction was made between prime movers and other machinery. This is clear from the definition given in 1875 by Reuleaux: 'A machine is a combination of solid parts so contrived that by means of it natural forces can be made to cause certain definite motions.'

2. *The introduction of new prime movers.* The new machines demanded a new prime mover, for the older ones had grave limitations. Wind was cheap but unreliable, water was limited by local conditions, but steam suffers neither disadvantage. It is independent of the weather and the seasons. The invention of the steam-engine is the central fact in the industrial revolution.

3. *The mobile prime mover.* The power of the steam-engine could be created where needed and to the extent desired. This mobility is the most characteristic feature of the Machine Age, and made possible the industrialization of many countries that had no great resources of water-power. Moreover, the steam-engine proved capable of producing much more power than the older prime movers, and thus in time it raised energy-output to a significantly higher level.

4. *The factory as a new form of organization of production.* Factories were built long before the advent of the steam-engine. Thus the early textile mills and ironworks were of this type, rather than of the workshop type so characteristic of medieval and earlier technology. In the eighteenth century, however, the word factory was not used in its present sense. A factory then was merely a shop, a warehouse, or a depot, and only by the end of the century was the word used for mills or machine-factories. The word mill was much more common, for the machine that first caught the eye was usually the great water-wheel. Not only the flour mills but the ironworks and foundries with their hammers and bellows were worked by water-wheels in sixteenth-century England, and so were the first cotton mills. The first legal use of the word factory is in the Textile Factory Act of 1844. The

concentration of machines driven by steam-engines had become a characteristic feature of the industrial revolution by 1800, but certainly not the only one; much of the manufacturing still took place in workshops, and the part of factories in the industrial revolution has been overstressed.

The steam-engine did not rapidly displace the earlier prime movers. It was some time before it had been sufficiently developed as a prime mover with an appreciably higher average energy-output. Mobility alone was not enough to displace the treadmill, the water-wheel, and the windmill. In fact, the earlier phase of the industrial revolution was certainly not characterized by the steam-engine. Windmills still dotted many a landscape. Water was the main source of power in eighteenth-century England, driving fulling-stocks, millstones, saws, bellows, and ore-crushers. The new textile inventions came in an area of hills, valleys, and streams, and the early mills were built on river-banks. The pioneers of the industrial revolution hardly thought in terms of steam-engines. Wyatt pictured the mechanized textile industry as a kind of mill with wheels turned either by horses, by water, or by wind. Lewis Paul (d 1759) and he used two donkeys for their first machines; Cartwright drove his invention with a cow; Arkwright speaks of a 'water-frame'; and the first two power-looms in Scotland (1793) were worked by a Newfoundland dog.

For many industries in the sixteenth and seventeenth centuries, the obstacles to the use of power were cost and physical availability rather than the mechanical difficulty of application. The capital involved was large relative to the amount of power generated, so that power-using devices were not generally preferred to mechanisms actuated by the workman. Much early machinery was concerned with exchanging low intensities exerted through long distances for high intensities exerted through short distances. Many machines were designed so as to make it a simple matter to arrange for them to be driven by any prime mover capable of producing rotary motion. But until power became cheap, reliable, and generally available, there was no purpose in attempting to run them from a specialized power-plant.

In the eighteenth century no factory could be established far from a stream powerful and swift enough to work its machines. Mill-owners therefore crowded in narrow valleys, where an artificial fall could be secured by using dams. Hence the importance of the valleys of the Pennine range for eighteenth-century British industry. This continued as long as water was the driving-power of machinery, but the introduction of steam gradually brought industrial ruin to those districts where no coal was available locally.

In many other parts of England the water was mostly slow-flowing. Even the little water-power that was available was wasted by the clumsy systems of wheels and troughs used to collect and transmit it. The only practicable method was to create artificial waterfalls. The water had then to be raised to the level of a reservoir by a pump. It was for raising water that the first steam-engines came into use. . . .

The coal-mines and the iron industry proved the best promoters of the steam-engine. Scarcity of charcoal and limitation of water-power were economic threats to the iron industry of the eighteenth century. Many attempts were made to break this tyranny of wood and water. In 1757 Isaac Wilkinson took out a patent for a new machine or 'bellows . . . so that a furnace, forge or any other works may be blowed from any waterfall or falls . . . to several miles distant by means of a pipe'. This was never used and, until late in the century, iron-works continued to use direct water-power. Inadequacy in the fall of water caused a tendency to separate the smelting and the finishing of the metal. The adaptation of the steam-engine to crushing ores in iron-works discouraged this separation. More important still, Watt's engine freed the ironmasters from their dependence on constant supplies of running water for their bellows, hammers, and mills. Before its introduction it was estimated that the average period of working in iron-works was about forty weeks a year, but a season of drought might curtail this considerably and bring financial loss to the masters and distress to the workers. Attempts at economy of water had been made with various devices; at Coalbrookdale the water that had passed over the wheel was raised above it again by a Newcomen engine, and at Furness hand-pumps had been used for the same purpose. Steam-power meant that the iron-works could be carried on with cheap mineral fuel, so that there was no reason for the separation of furnace, forge, and mill that had characterized the iron industry in the early years of the century.

By the end of the same century the coal-pits throughout the midlands had also come to rely largely on the steam-engine for their working. This meant heavy capital expenditure, since a Newcomen engine cost about £1500 to install, but the investment was well worth the while of the larger enterprises. The change had come about because Boulton had had the Kinneil steam-engine designed by Watt brought down from Scotland and had turned his Soho (Birmingham) works into the prototype of the modern factory. The first two steam-engines built by the firm of Boulton and Watt were erected at Bloomfield colliery in Staffordshire and at John Wilkinson's new foundry at Broseley, Salop, respectively.

Certain factors, however, prevented the rapid displacement of the earlier prime movers by the steam-engine. The early machine-builders were handicapped by want of skilled engineers. Their engines were built by a miscellaneous collection of blacksmiths, wheel-wrights, and carpenters, as their designs show clearly. Only too often the parts refused to work when put together. Watt found that a cylinder made by the best workmen available in Glasgow varied by three-eighths of an inch in diameter, and Smeaton told him 'that neither tools nor workmen existed that could manufacture so complex a machine with sufficient precision'. John Wilkinson, however, could tool metal with a limit of error not exceeding 'the thickness of a thin sixpence' in a diameter of 72 inches. No wonder that Watt avoided applying high-pressure steam in his engines, even though this was the only way to higher thermal efficiency and energy-output.

The builders of the first engines had therefore both to train the necessary specialists to build their machines, and to devise means of finishing their parts with sufficient precision. Prime movers had hitherto been of wood with few metal parts; steam demanded stronger and more durable material. The way to precision was to clamp the relevant tool and material firmly in a machine; then the tool could be adjusted and guided to do its work of grinding, boring, slotting, drilling, turning, or cutting. Maudslay's slide-rest of 1794 was the first of a series of such fundamentally important machine-tools developed by the new engineers, but the co-operation of science and mechanical engineering was not yet sufficiently close to allow a rapid advance.

When Watt's patent expired in 1800 there were 496 Watt engines at work in Britain in mines, metal plants, textile factories, and breweries. Of these 308 were rotative engines and 164 pumping-engines, while 24 were for producing blast-air. One or two were rated at 40 hp, but the average capacity was only 15 to 16 hp and therefore not significantly higher than that of the windmill and the water-wheel. The steam-engine profited by its relative mobility and its dependence on coal rather than on the fickle elements, but it could have revolutionized technology only very slowly if it had stopped at this point.

The real development of the steam-engine into a new and stronger prime mover came between 1800 and 1850. In the earlier days of Watt the nascent theory of heat had had some influence on the development of the steam-engine, but it was not yet ready to assist in the proper calculation of such engines. The engineers themselves had by trial and error found the means of introducing high pressure, and they made the methods of transmission of energy from engine to machinery less cumbersome. Several branches of science provided new knowledge useful for the building of steam-engines. The science of applied mechanics was gradually extended after the testing of materials by such men as Coulomb and La Hire had yielded practical rules for calculating the proper dimensions of engine parts. The rise of the art of bridge-building contributed much to the calculation of the constructional details of steam-engines. Tools and methods were devised to measure elasticity and the different stresses acting on parts of the engine. The inquiry into friction and its importance in engine and transmission came rather later. Important also was the elaboration of the theory of gases by such men as Mariotte (1620–84), Gay-Lussac (1778–1850), and Regnault (1810–78).

Fundamental, too, was the further development of the theory of heat, not only in calorimetry and temperature measurement, but most of all in the rise of the new science of thermodynamics. The foundation of thermodynamics was laid by Sadi Carnot (1796–1832) in his 'Motive Power of Heat'; he stated that the efficiency of an engine depended on the working substance and the temperature-drop between cylinder and condenser. In 1842 Robert Mayer (1814–78) calculated the work equivalent to a unit of heat. The law of conservation of energy—the first law of thermodynamics—was formulated in 1847 by Helmholtz (1821–94). Joule (1818–89) carefully measured the mechanical equivalent of heat (1843), and his work was later confirmed by Rankine (1820–72). Clausius (1822–88) finally reconciled Carnot's theory of heat and the discovered equivalence of heat and work, and was thus able to formulate the second law of thermodynamics, namely that heat cannot of itself pass from a colder to a hotter body. Only after the elaboration of these laws could real progress be achieved in designing steam-engines.

Earlier engineers found perplexity in expressing the power of their engines and comparing them. For the most part, figures are given expressing the engine's 'duty', the unit being one million ft-lb per bushel (84 lb) of coal. This allows us to calculate the thermal efficiency of the engine, but gives no accurate data on its power. The following data are reported:

RECIPROCATING STEAM ENGINES

Date	Builder	Duty	Percentage thermal efficiency
1718	Newcomen	4.3	0.5
1767	Smeaton	7.4	0.8
1774	Smeaton	12.5	1.4
1775	Watt	24.0	2.7
1792	Watt	39.0	4.5
1816	Woolf compound engine	68	7.5
1828	Improved Cornish engine	104	12.0
1834	" " "	149	17.0
1878	Corliss compound engine	150	17.2
1906	Triple-expansion engine	203	23.0

The rapid rise in thermal efficiency in the early nineteenth century is remarkable.

6.

Orthodoxy and Its Challenges

~

D. C. SOMERVELL

The Tory party came into power, with the vigorous assistance of George III, in 1783, under the leadership of the younger Pitt. It remained in power, with one interval so brief that it can be ignored, until 1830. As a rule the essentials of public opinion can hardly be deduced from the political label of the party that happens to be enjoying a brief spell of office, but here we have a Tory domination of such abnormal length, so utterly unlike anything that has followed it, that we may quite confidently attribute to it some deep significance. It was, in fact, the political response of the governing classes of England to the French Revolution.

Ever since the English Revolution, the 'Glorious Revolution' of 1688 which overthrew James II, ordinary Englishmen of all classes had been proud of their constitution and their national way of life. The French Revolution quickened their pride in what they possessed, for it added a feeling of genuine alarm lest what they possessed should be taken away from them. For a whole generation the word Jacobin came to hold in the public mind the place occupied between the Armada and the Popish Plot by the word Jesuit, the place occupied to-day in many minds by the word Bolshevik. It symbolized the political and spiritual

From D. C. Somervell, English Thought in the Nineteenth Century *(London: Methuen & Co. Ltd., 1929)* ; *Chapter 1, "The Old Tory Orthodoxy," pp. 3–8, and Chapter 2, "Religion and Philanthropy," pp. 16–27. Footnotes omitted.*

enemies of England, a class of continental mischief-makers, with disciples—alas!—in our very midst, who would, if they could, defeat us in war, destroy us by revolution, or transform us into their own likeness by propaganda. For over twenty years Pitt and his disciples had fought revolutionary France; for the first fifteen years of the peace they continued to rule England in face of a hopelessly divided opposition.

Pitt himself had been a man with many enlightened ideas of reform, ideas which he rigorously postponed until the war should be over. Some of Pitt's disciples in the last ten years of the period of Tory domination showed themselves ready to accept, without abandoning their essential Toryism, a variety of reforms dictated by proved practical expediency. But such measures were to be taken as exceptions. The fundamental 'Die-hardism' (to use modern jargon) of the rank and file was hardly affected, and its representative was Lord Eldon, who was Lord Chancellor in a succession of Tory Governments from 1801 to 1827. He was, we are told, a very great lawyer, though he was certainly a very slow one. He made the Court of Chancery a byword for the interminable delays of its procedure, and as such it was long afterwards satirized by Dickens in *Bleak House*. Here we are concerned not with his law but his politics. We may look at him through mid-Victorian eyes. Only thirty years after his death such political ideals as those of Lord Eldon had become quite inconceivable. Walter Bagehot, a mid-Victorian Liberal, wrote in 1855: 'As for Lord Eldon, it is the most difficult thing in the world to believe that there ever was such a man. He believed in everything that it is impossible to believe in,—in the danger of Parliamentary reform, in the danger of Catholic emancipation, in the danger of altering the Court of Chancery, in the danger of abolishing capital punishment for trivial thefts, in the danger of making landowners pay their debts.' The Jacobins had altered everything, from God down to the calendar, and had sought to make a clean slate and a fresh start; the response of Lord Eldon and the section of the public he genuinely represented was to hold fast to everything and alter nothing.

It is easy to present Eldonism as something simply absurd, but to do so is not, perhaps, very helpful. For if there is one thing which, more than another, we must always bear in mind when studying the history of opinion, it is that no opinion ever enjoys prolonged authority over the minds of men outside a lunatic asylum unless there is a certain amount of real good sense behind it. To understand the mind of the old Tory orthodoxy of the first thirty years of the century, we must go behind Eldon and behind Pitt to the great philosopher and prophet of the old Toryism, Edmund Burke. He died in 1797, but his thought dominated the rulers of England for a generation after his death. It is very English thought and its influence is by no means entirely exhausted to-day.

The leading principle of all Burke's thought seems to be distrust of political theory. 'Talk not to me', he seems to say (these are not his own words), 'of schemes which prove by infallible logic how happy man would be if only his affairs were organized on an entirely new pattern. Man is not a logical animal. The present social and political system is no doubt very much open to criticism, but it is the product of past experience. It *works;* who can guarantee as much for any other system that has not yet been tried? Old institutions, like old boots, are more comfortable than new ones, even of the cleverest workmanship, can possibly be, for they have been shaped not by artifice but by use; and, unlike old boots, they can, if properly looked after, be made to last for ever.'

The French Revolution has exalted 'Reason'; Burke rejects 'Reason' as Voltaire and his disciples had understood it, in favour of Tradition, or, as he calls it sometimes, Prescription. 'Truth', he says, 'may be far better than prescription; but as we have scarcely ever that certainty in the one that we have in the other, I would, unless the truth were very evident indeed, hold fast to peace.' Better, in fact, endure those ills we have than fly to others that we know not of. It is more surprising to find Burke exalting against 'Reason' not merely Tradition but Prejudice. Wise men, he says, 'instead of exploding general prejudices will employ their sagacity to discover the latent wisdom that prevails in them. If they find what they seek, and they seldom fail, they will think it more wise to continue the prejudice, with the reason involved, than to cast away the coat of prejudice and to leave nothing but the naked reason'. Prejudice, in fact, is not necessarily mistaken; it is simply opinion held, for which the holder cannot himself find the reasons; it comes near to what we call instinct, the common sense of the plain man. And Burke always had his eye on the plain man, for whose benefit, after all, laws and constitutions exist. 'Burke was essentially a thinker,' writes a modern Tory, Sir John Fortescue, 'and, moreover, one of those rare thinkers who cannot contemplate human institutions apart from human nature. A political constitution, for instance, was not a code of articles, nor a carefully devised machine. It was rather something alive—a concourse of bustling men with more prejudices than principles and more passion than prejudice; fallible men with their pageantries and pedantries, their intrigues and their jobbery, and all the strange appliances that go to the government of mankind. Vast historical knowledge, with long pondering thereupon, wide sympathy and vivid imagination—'. Burke, in fact, was grounded in history. Some people, such as Voltaire and Rousseau, learn from history to despise the past for its crimes and blunders: others, like Burke, learn to respect it for its achievements and to thank it for its heritage.

Such a heritage of the past, such an embodiment of the wholesome prejudices of human nature, Burke found in the old unreformed English constitution, rotten-boroughs and all. He speaks of it in terms of almost superstitious respect. 'Great critics', he says, 'have taught us that if ever we should feel ourselves disposed not to admire those writers and artists whom all the learned had admired, not to follow our own fancies but to study them until we know how and what to admire. It is as good a rule, at least, with regard to this admired constitution. We ought to understand it according to our measure; and to venerate where we are not able presently to comprehend.' Let us, at least, refrain from laying rash reforming hands upon it. 'Our constitution stands on a nice equipoise, with steep precipices and deep waters upon all sides of it. In removing it from a dangerous leaning towards one side there may be a risk of oversetting it upon the other.'

A great man is seldom, perhaps never, faithfully represented by those of the next generation who most fervently proclaim themselves his disciples. The living thought of the living man is

ossified into a scheme of barren dogmas. We cannot tell what
Burke would have been if he had lived through the fifteen years
after Waterloo, but we may be fairly certain that he would not
have contemplated Lord Eldon with unmixed approval. None
the less, he more than any other man was responsible for the Old
Tory orthodoxy. The governing class up to 1830 were, it has been
said, a surviving fragment of the eighteenth century. In 1830 the
Duke of Wellington, the last of the Old Tory Prime Ministers,
made a famous statement which ensured his immediate defeat.
'The English (unreformed) Parliament', he said, 'answers all the
good purposes of legislation, and this to a greater degree than any
legislature has ever answered in any country whatever: *it possesses the full and entire confidence of the people.* I will go
further. If at the present moment I had imposed upon me the
duty of forming a legislature for any country, and particularly for
a country like this, in possession of great property of various
descriptions, I do not mean to assert that I could form such a
legislature as we possess now, for the nature of man is incapable
of reaching such excellence at once, but my great endeavour
would be to form some description of legislature which would
produce the same results.' This statement is pure Burke, except
for one clause which I have placed in italics. That clause might
have been spoken by Burke in 1790, for it would have been
approximately true; it was notoriously untrue in 1830 and Burke,
unlike the Duke, would have refrained from asserting it. The
whole speech from which the words are taken is a last defiance
from the generation soaked in anti-Jacobinism to a new generation which had forgotten the Jacobins and was pressing forward
into new paths. . . .

The most conspicuous fact about the state of religion in England in the first third of the nineteenth century was the entire
insignificance of the official heads of the Established Church as
leaders of religious opinion. That Church was still, as it had been
since the Reformation, a heavily privileged institution, and a
privileged Church will always be tempted to think more of its
privileges than its mission. The State, it was said, paid lip-service
to the Church, and the Church in return paid life-service to the

State. The Church was described as the praying section of the
Tory party. This was too sweeping, for there were, even at the
end of the eighteenth century, many devoutly religious men in
the Church of England, and we shall have something to say of
them later, but they were not its official leaders; they were not
found upon the episcopal bench. Most of the bishops were politi-
cally-minded Tories for the same reason as the judges in the
Ship-money case were royalists; Charles I selected the judges, and
since 1783 a long succession of Tory Prime Ministers had selected
the bishops. Some of them had served the party by political
activity, some had been the college tutors of eminent statesmen,
some were the near relations of noblemen who owned rotten
boroughs. In 1815 eleven of the bishops were of noble family, and
ten had been the tutors or schoolmasters of a prince, a duke, or a
Cabinet minister.

It has been said that those who rise to leadership within the
sheepfold generally exhibit some of the qualities of the wolf; but
the metaphor is too harsh to describe the mild and decorous
rapacity of such a one as Manners-Sutton, Archbishop of Canter-
bury from 1805 to 1828, who distributed sixteen livings as well
as a variety of cathedral appointments among seven members of
his family. Another notable bishop of the age was Watson of
Llandaff, whose long life extended to the year after the battle of
Waterloo. As a very young man he became Professor of Chemistry
at Cambridge, and subsequently Professor of Divinity. His knowledge of both subjects was slight, but his services to chemistry
were the greater, for he secured an endowment for the profes-
sorial chair. In 1782 the Whigs made him Bishop of Llandaff for
his political services in opposing the American war. Shortly afterwards he appointed a deputy to undertake the duties of his professorship, and withdrew to a country house on the shores of
Windermere. He visited his diocese once in the thirty-four years
of his episcopate; he held sixteen livings; he was deservedly popular among his north-country neighbours, and desired to be remembered as an improver of land and a planter of trees. The
possibility of such a career throws a flood of light on one department of English thought at the beginning of the nineteenth century.

Among the rank and file of the parish clergy it would be easy to select examples of notorious impropriety, but such examples would not be typical. The ordinary parish clergymen were entirely respectable, and, as such, respected; they were kindly men who, though they did not do much, did all that was expected of them. Like the House of Lords in *Iolanthe* they 'did nothing in particular and did it very well'. They have left no mark, unless a negative one, on history, but their type is embalmed in current fiction. Jane Austen's novels were written in the first twenty years of the century, and contain a variety of parsons; some of these young men are amiable and some ridiculous, but none of them has anything to do with religion, nor does the novelist ever notice this deficiency in them. The poet Crabbe describes exactly the same type in a more critical spirit:

> Fiddling and fishing were his arts; at times
> He altered sermons and he aimed at rhymes;
> And his fair friends, not yet intent on cards,
> Oft he amused with riddles and charades.

The Church and the Army were the obvious alternatives for young men of good social position and no particular gifts or inclinations. During the French wars the army naturally took first place; after 1815 there was a marked increase of candidates for ordination, but its causes were economic rather than religious. Too many of the new ordinands were of the type of the half-pay officer who figures in an old forgotten book of reminiscences; he secured a substantial benefice 'by which he was enabled to launch again into the gay world'.

This half-pay officer presumably did not reside in the parish from which he drew his stipend. Many others, who drew stipends from several parishes, obviously could not reside in all of them, and sometimes found it less invidious and more convenient to reside in none. Porteus, Bishop of London, in his charge to his clergy in 1790 deals earnestly, if gently, with these evils. 'There are, indeed,' he writes, 'two impediments to constant residence which cannot easily be surmounted; the first is (what unfortunately prevails in some parts of this diocese) unwholesomeness of situation; the other is the possession of a second benefice. Yet

even these will not justify a *total and perpetual* absence from
your cures. The unhealthiness of many places is of late years by
various improvements greatly abated, and there are now few so
circumstanced as not to admit of residence there in *some* part of
the year without any danger to the constitution.'

Such was the old 'High Church' at the beginning of the nineteenth century. It had nothing in common with the ardent and
Anglo-Catholic High Church party which has long since sup-
planted it. It has been called the 'high and dry' Church; it
detested nothing so much as 'enthusiasm', a term used to include
all Methodists and nearly all missionaries. The most notable
exponent of its religious philosophy was Archdeacon Paley,
whose *Evidences of Christianity* were published in 1794, and
continued to be set as a compulsory subject to all candidates for
admission to Cambridge University down to 1921. It is an admirable text-book, a model of lucidity, logic, and well-marshalled
evidence, proving the truth of the dogmas of the Church with the
quiet efficiency of a mathematical demonstration. 'To take it to
pieces and put it together again, noting how each part fits into
the whole, is an education in reasoning and in the art of advocacy.' In fact, it assumes that the truths of religion are akin to
scientific truths and defensible by the same methods. Long afterwards, Charles Darwin, the evolutionist, found it the one item of
his Cambridge curriculum that was of the least use to him. 'I did
not at that time', he says, 'trouble myself about Paley's premises;
and, taking these on trust, I was charmed and convinced by the
long line of argumentation.'

Paley defines virtue as 'doing good to mankind in obedience to
the will of God, and for the sake of everlasting salvation'. An old
hymn at once suggests itself:

> Whatever, Lord, we lend to Thee
> Repaid a thousandfold will be;
> Then gladly will we give to Thee . . .

Christ, says Paley, was quite unlike the Methodists; he was *not*
marked by 'impassioned devotion'; there was no enthusiasm, no
'heat in his piety'; on the contrary, he was a person of 'moderation and soundness of judgement'. Paley was a good writer and a

good man; his work is much less absurd than a brief description, spiced with comical quotations, would suggest; but it is not, in the modern sense, a religious work at all.

Typical in a very different way of the old Church was Sydney Smith, a man of the generation after Paley's; he lived till 1845. Sydney Smith was a man of exuberant energy, intelligence and humour, who went into the Church because his father would not support him while he read for the Bar. He was one of the founders of that great Whig journal, *The Edinburgh Review*, and contributed to it regularly for a quarter of a century, so that, when the Whigs came into power in 1830, most people expected that he would be made a bishop. He also did his duty manfully for many years as the rector of a remote Yorkshire village. There are many worse parish priests to-day than this vigorous journalist who, finding himself saddled with parochial duties, proceeded to constitute himself 'village parson, village doctor, village comforter, village magistrate'. In London he was reckoned an attractive preacher, for in fact the man himself was attractive, but his published sermons are the weakest part of his writings. And the reason is plain. 'The Methodists', he says somewhere, 'are always desirous of making men more religious than it is possible, from the constitution of human nature, to make them.' True perhaps; but all real leaders of real religions have been such because they have devoted their lives to this impossibility. Sydney Smith's sermons, says Bagehot, 'are sensible and well-intentioned, but they have the defect of his school. With misdirected energy these divines have laboured after a plain religion: they have forgotten that religion has its essence in awe, its charm in infinity, its sanction in dread; that its dominion is an inexplicable dominion; that mystery is its power'.

There was indeed abroad in England a religion very different from that of Archbishop Manners-Sutton, Bishop Watson, Archdeacon Paley, and Sydney Smith, a religion which they all condemned as 'enthusiastic', a religion which, among the poor, had established the new sects of the Methodists, and within the Church had created the already powerful party of the Evangelicals. It had many roots far back in the middle of the eighteenth century, but its most powerful apostle had been John Wesley, who died in extreme old age, after half a century of incredible activity, in the first years of the French Revolution.

The eighteenth century was, in the main, an age of clear and limited views, an age of placid optimism. Yet that quiet century was disturbed by two prophets, two experts in the arts of rousing violent and sustained emotions, two men who exercised an influence upon thought which long survived their deaths and is not exhausted to-day—Wesley and Rousseau. It is impossible to imagine two men more unalike—Rousseau, the disreputable dreamer of dreams, writing in a garret books which kindled strange fancies of human perfectibility; Wesley, respectable to the point of unattractiveness, one of the few major prophets of religion who was also a consummate man of business, yet gifted so markedly with the power of kindling in his hearers the sense of sin and the awfulness of divine judgement, that, when he preached, the days of the early Church seemed come again, and sinners exhibited contrition by foaming at the mouth, speaking with tongues, and falling down in convulsions. Rousseau came as near as any literary man can come to being the author of a political and social revolution; Wesley, by his influence on the religious revival in which his was the most important single figure, did more than anything or anyone else to inoculate the English people against the virus of revolutionism. Rousseau impelled a whole society to seek to establish by violence a Kingdom of heaven upon earth; Methodism and Evangelicalism set men's hearts upon a Kingdom which was not of this world, and certainly could not be established by violence.

When the nineteenth century opens, the grosser transports of religious ecstasy, which signalized the early triumphs of the new preachers, were happily over and done with. The new movement had firmly established itself both in the Church and in the world of Nonconformity. The new emotional Nonconformity of the Methodist chapel gave a colour of idealism and romance to the lives of thousands of the victims of the power loom and the steam engine in the new industrial slums of the north. Within the Church of England Evangelicalism was not yet the party in power, but it was already a formidable and active opposition. Its leaders were not clergy, for it was a type of religion which did not exalt its priesthood. The leaders of Evangelicalism were wealthy laymen. Some of the most conspicuous, William Wilberforce for example, lived in pleasant mansions upon the edge of Clapham Common, and Sydney Smith gave them the nickname of 'the Clapham Sect'.

Wilberforce was a man of considerable wealth and remarkable charm of personality. His election to parliament for the County of Yorkshire in 1784 was a singular personal triumph in a constituency normally reserved for members of great county families. As the ablest of the intimate friends of Pitt he had before him, if he had chosen to avail himself of it, a political career of assured brilliance. But accident brought him into contact with Isaac Milner, an Evangelical divine, and immediately afterwards with Thomas Clarkson, a Quaker who was about to devote himself to the cause of the abolition of the Slave trade. From 1787 onwards Wilberforce abandoned the ambitions of an ordinary politician; he remained in parliament as an independent member, devoted to the advocacy of great causes outside party politics. He wrote religious books, promoted religious education and foreign missions, and was one of the founders of an Association for the Better Observance of Sunday. From the beginning of the century until his death in 1833 he was certainly one of the most influential men in the country.

Associated with Wilberforce in many of his activities was Hannah More. In the early part of her long life she made a reputation as a witty and charming young lady in the circle of Johnson, Garrick, and Reynolds, but she too, like Wilberforce, and at about the same date, was claimed by the Evangelical movement. Henceforth she devoted herself to the religious education of destitute children and to the writing of enormous quantities of religious tales and tracts. These had a very large circulation. One of the best known, *The Shepherd of Salisbury Plain,* was translated into several foreign languages, and was sufficiently familiar in the middle of the nineteenth century to be satirized by Thackeray as *The Washerwoman of Hampstead Heath.* Cobbett, who included the Evangelicals among the many objects of his detestation, calls her an 'Old Bishop in petticoats', and offers as a sample of her tracts 'Hannah More's account of the celestial death of an

Evangelical mouse who, *though starving,* would not touch the master's cheese and bacon'.

Another important figure in the movement was Charles Simeon, Fellow of King's College, Cambridge. He made his university a nursing mother of the Evangelicals of the next generation, and it is said that, far on into the nineteenth century, undergraduates of marked piety were known in Cambridge as 'Sims'. One of Gladstone's earliest recollections was being taken as a child of five to Cambridge to see Mr. Simeon. Gladstone's father was a wealthy Evangelical merchant in Liverpool; he had paid for the building of a new church, and went to Cambridge to get Simeon's advice as to the choice of its minister. It would be easy, but unnecessary, to mention many more conspicuous Evangelicals. A characteristic example would be Thomas Bowdler, who produced an edition of Shakespeare in which 'those words and expressions are omitted which cannot with propriety be read aloud in a family'. His name has contributed a verb to the English Dictionary, a verb now generally used with contemptuous intentions; yet there seems to be no doubt that Bowdler did more than many of the subtlest critics to promote the popular reading of Shakespeare. He also produced an expurgated edition of Gibbon's *Decline and Fall of the Roman Empire,* which strikes one as a less useful enterprise.

The Evangelicals accounted nothing of importance in comparison with the human soul and its eternal welfare, yet they were eminently practical, and their energies were poured into all kinds of constructive organizations. Among these was the Bible Society, founded in 1804 'to encourage a wider dispersion of the Holy Scriptures'. It was notable as a completely undenominational society; indeed, the new religious movement, developing simultaneously within and without the Church, was a powerful solvent of the barriers between the Establishment and the Nonconformists. Wesley, in fact, had virtually founded a Nonconformist sect without ever ceasing to be himself a clergyman of the Church of England. The immediate occasion of the foundation of the Bible Society was a shortage of Bibles in the Welsh language, for the Society for the Promotion of Christian Knowledge, whose duty it was to produce Welsh Bibles, had fallen into a comatose condition. From Welsh the Bible Society proceeded to all the languages of the world, and became an indispensable ally of the various Missionary Societies. It need hardly be said that the Bible Society is still very much alive to-day. It so happens that I am writing these words on the day after its hundred and twenty-fourth annual meeting, presided over and addressed by Mr. Baldwin. No Cabinet minister attended the first meeting, though the Bishop of London 'after reasonable delay' gave his approval to the scheme and suggested Lord Teignmouth as its President. Lord Teignmouth is described as 'a fervent Christian and an excellent man of business'; as such he was a typical leader of the Evangelicals.

The Bible Society accidentally inspired one of the minor classics of English literature, George Borrow's *The Bible in Spain,* recording the adventures of the author as a travelling agent of the Society in that country during the years 1835–39. Nothing illustrates the wide ramifications of the Evangelical movement more pointedly than the fact that Borrow, the Bohemian eccentric and associate of gipsies and bruisers, should for a time have taken service in its ranks.

Borrow's principal motive as a distributor of Bibles seems to have been hostility to Popery. 'No popery' had been a potent watchword ever since the Reformation. The Gordon riots of 1780 witnessed its hold on the lowest classes of the London population, and Evangelicalism had strengthened the prejudice. When Louis XVIII left England on a Sunday to resume his throne in France, Wilberforce recorded in his Diary: 'What ingratitude, and without temptation! What folly! Is this the Roman Catholic religion? O shame, shame.' Catholic Emancipation was carried through parliament, it is true, in 1829, but solely to avert a rebellion in Ireland, and the text of the Act reveals the popular prejudice against the persons who were to benefit by it in a curious clause (never enforced) banishing all Jesuits from the British Isles. Walter Scott was not an Evangelical; his religion was entirely conventional, and he might have been expected to sympathize with those who still cherished the Church of the Middle Ages. He did indeed support the Emancipation Act, but for the most singular of reasons. He held that, since we had repealed or ceased to enforce all the rest of the anti-Roman statutes, it was mere pedantry to retain the exclusion from the franchise. He wished that the old statutes had been maintained and enforced with rigour; if they had, he thought we should have long since succeeded in 'smothering the Old Lady of Babylon'.

This age of Tory domination was marked by a number of humanitarian reforms, the abolition of the slave trade in 1806, the partial abolition of the pillory in 1816, the abolition of flogging as a punishment for women in 1820, the first attempt to illegalize various forms of cruelty to animals, e.g., bull-baiting and cock-fighting, in 1822, the prohibition of the use of spring-guns and man-traps to protect property against poachers in 1827. Evangelicals supported all these movements, but it would be a mistake to suppose that they were their only supporters, or that the new religion produced the new philanthropy and humanitarianism. Humanitarianism was a distinctive feature of the age that produced the French Revolution as well as the Evangelical movement. Voltaire was, in his different way, as great a philanthropist as Wilberforce, and the Evangelicals found themselves working as allies with the followers of Bentham and James Mill, who set reason above emotion and regarded religious revelation as moonshine.

Yet it would be true to say that in England the whole movement towards philanthropy was coloured with religious sentiment. The first Factory Act of 1802, a very modest and practically inoperative measure, contained a clause enacting that all pauper apprentices should every Sunday for the space of one hour 'be instructed and examined in the principles of the Christian religion by a qualified person'. After securing the abolition of the slave trade, the energies of Wilberforce and his friends were directed towards the abolition of slavery itself throughout the British colonies. Their first small success was to secure the enactment of an experimental code restricting slavery in the island of Trinidad, and one of its features was that slaves were not to be employed by their owners on Sunday.

The establishment of what came to be called 'the English Sunday' was one of the features of the generation we are concerned with. 'The red skies of Paris', wrote Mr. and Mrs. Hammond in *The Town Labourer,* 'sobered the English Sunday and filled the English churches. *The Annual Register* for 1798 remarks: "It was a wonder to the lower orders throughout all parts of England to see the avenues of the churches filled with carriages. This novel appearance prompted the simple country people to inquire what was the matter." In the merry days of Archbishop Cornwallis (1768–83) the Church had set the fashion in Sunday parties. After the Revolution these dissipations ceased and Sunday became much stricter. Wilberforce, in whose mind the most tremendous problems the nation had ever faced did not overshadow the danger that Parliament reassembling on a Monday might cause many members to travel to London on a Sunday, persuaded Perceval, who spent a good deal of his time in tracing parallels between Napoleon and the Antichrist of the Book of Revelation, to alter the day of meeting to a Tuesday. "House nobly put off by Perceval," he records in his diary.'

7.

The Literary Periodicals

WALTER GRAHAM

In any study of politics and the English press, certain marked tendencies are observed. In the first place, those who wished to oppose the king or attack the government had a ready weapon. In spite of licensing acts and stamp taxes, they used it. And with all their severe repressions and punishments, kings and kings' ministers early learned that the only effective weapon for fighting the press was the press itself. So fire was fought with fire. So, also, for two centuries Tories and conservatives were, in a manner, on the defensive. L'Estrange's *Observator,* designed "to encounter faction and vindicate the government," the distinctly ministerial *Examiner* of Bolingbroke, the Whiggish *Test* of Murphy, offset by the *Con-Test* of Sir Philip Francis, the Tory *Critical Review* rivaling the Whiggish *Monthly*—these are a few notable examples of the deliberate use of English periodicals to oppose those of an attacking party. Thus, it was in a world long accustomed to political warfare, with attacks and counter-attacks carried on in every form of newspaper and periodical, that the two most pretentious organs of this kind, the *Edinburgh* and *Quarterly Reviews,* appeared in the first decade of the nineteenth century.

The *Edinburgh Review* (1802–1929) was not planned prima-

From *Walter Graham,* English Literary Periodicals (*New York: Thomas Nelson & Sons, 1930*); *Chapter 8,* "*The* Edinburgh, Quarterly, *and* Westminster Reviews," *pp. 230–237, 238–245. Some footnotes omitted.*

rily as a party organ, although the politics of its youthful projectors were decidedly Whiggish. In the minds of its founders—Sydney Smith, Francis Jeffrey, and Francis Horner (and later, Henry Brougham), all of whom were between the ages of twenty-three and thirty-one—wit and fun were the first *desiderata*. The idea was not to avoid politics altogether, but to allow them to be handled by the partisans of either camp, as long as they could provide amusement and information for the reader. But it was not long before the seductive tendency toward "witty whiggery" was leading them away from their original plan.

Sydney Smith supervised the publication of the first *Edinburgh,* with the assistance of Francis Horner. Afterwards, Jeffrey was formally appointed editor and conducted the review until 1829. Sydney Smith spoke of the periodical to Constable as "independent," but Jeffrey seems to have tended more and more away from independent principles. On this point, the fall of the Whig government in 1807 caused a change in the views of his colleagues also. Horner, with his more serious turn of mind, saw the danger, and warned Jeffrey more than once against party politics in the articles he published. But in spite of his warnings, the *Edinburgh,* which had commenced on principles of neutrality, became steadily more pronounced in its advocacy of party doctrines, although wide variations of opinion were to be found in the Whig ranks on such questions as Spanish affairs, Catholic Emancipation, and Parliamentary and other reforms. In the early years, Scott and other Tories contributed articles on non-political themes. But the increasing boldness of other writers on national affairs offended this section of its readers and contributors. Flushed by success, the *Edinburgh* reviewers overstepped the bounds of moderation. Inevitable results were the estrangement of readers and that defensive activity of the Tories which led to the establishment of the *Quarterly Review.* When Horner wrote apprehensively to J. A. Murray, December 23, 1809, that the *Edinburgh Review* had gone too far into merely personal and party considerations "in which the Review never engages without a loss of its proper character and usefulness," the mischief had been done. As a matter of fact, the idea of a rival periodical had been in the air for several years before the *Quarterly Review* appeared to dispute the political and critical influence of the *Edinburgh*.

Of Francis Jeffrey, the editor of the *Edinburgh Review* until 1829, much has been written and little may be added here. More than is usual with editors, he contributed essays to his *Review*, on subjects as various as Byron's poetry, jurisprudence, politics, and travels in Egypt. He wrote in October 1802 the first review in the first number, and contributed his last article in 1840. For the most part, however, his interests were literary, and the burden of his essays are reviews of such writers as Swift, Goethe, Alfieri, Southey, Cowper, Campbell, Scott, Crabbe, Wordsworth, Miss Edgeworth, and Washington Irving. Jeffrey's attitude toward literature is now well understood—suggested in his early review of Southey's *Thalaba:* "Poetry has this much, at least, in common with religion, that its standards were fixed long ago, by certain inspired writers, whose authority it is no longer lawful to call in question." With a dogmatism and an obstinacy worthy of a better cause, he valiantly defended his pseudo-classical citadel, long after the battalions of romantics had conquered the field. His was not the classicism of Dryden and Pope, but the degenerate classicism, which found in Campbell and Rogers and Crabbe virtues not recognized by most nineteenth-century critics. For him, there were "only two kinds of great poetry: the pathetic and the sublime." Later *Edinburgh* reviewers, and many of his contemporaries, did not sympathize with Jeffrey's critical position; but he unquestionably put his stamp upon the *Review* for a quarter of a century. The surprising result was that while less liberal in politics, the rival *Quarterly Review* appears today to have been, in its criticism of contemporary literary works, far more hospitable to novelty.

The *Edinburgh Review* from the start wisely abandoned the idea of noticing all the productions of the press. It was hoped it would be "distinguished, rather for the selection, than for the number, of its articles."[1] This, it must be pointed out with care, was a deliberate departure from the practice of the *Monthly* and *Critical Reviews*. The new plan seems to have been a fortunate

[1] See Advertisement to the first number, October 1802.

one. In ten years the *Edinburgh's* circulation had grown to 10,000 copies; by 1818 it had reached its peak of 14,000. The first number consisted of twenty-nine articles in 252 pages. The system adopted in the enthusiasm of the beginning—"all gentlemen and no pay"—was abandoned, after the first two numbers, for the wiser one of generous stipends to editor and contributors. Rapidly, the *Edinburgh* assumed a foremost place among the organs of literary criticism. For although the judgments of Jeffrey and other reviewers, who arrogated to themselves "an authority hardly less than pontifical," have not always been confirmed by the judgments of posterity, on the other hand, they have in many cases been fully vindicated. During the first quarter-century, however, in spite of general impressions, it must be admitted that the rival *Quarterly* contained far more individual criticisms that have stood the test of time.

As the first editor, Jeffrey gathered about him an excellent group of contributors. Walter Scott was an important reviewer, until, in 1808, he became interested in the plans for a rival organ. Between 1802 and 1829, reviews were secured from the pens of Thomas Brown, James Mackintosh, Peter Elmsley, Thomas Campbell, William Hazlitt, John Playfair, George Ellis, T. R. Malthus, Henry Hallam, Thomas Jefferson Hogg, Payne Knight, Francis Palgrave, Thomas Arnold, T. B. Macaulay, and Thomas Carlyle. Macvey Napier (originally Napier Macvey), who had been a contributor to the *Edinburgh* since 1805, in 1829 took the editorial chair, when Jeffrey retired to become Dean of the Faculty of Advocates. Napier brought to his new task the experience acquired as general editor of a supplement of the sixth edition of the *Encyclopedia Britannica,* and carried on the work of Jeffrey with less dogmatism and quite as much energy. . . .

It is worth observing once more that the *Edinburgh Review* gave a new turn to the periodicals of this type, in that, unlike its predecessors, the *Monthly* and *Critical,* it made no pretense of reviewing all the books published. On the contrary, it discussed only those which could be made the texts of articles on subjects of current interest. Rigidly selective in its method, therefore, the *Edinburgh* was the first to acquire certain characteristics which are noticed in all the later reviews of the nineteenth century.

Macaulay writing on Milton, or Jeffrey reviewing "Alison on Taste," seized the opportunity to present their own views of the general subject rather than their reactions on the methods or materials of the author. Pursuing this method, inaugurated more than a century and a quarter ago, the *Edinburgh Review* was never seriously rivaled, except by the conservative *Quarterly Review*. It is remarkable that during its entire career the *Edinburgh* was associated with the house of Longman, just as the *Quarterly* has always been a property of the house of Murray. It is noticeable that in its later years the *Edinburgh*, however, was less of a literary organ than its great rival.

The success of the *Edinburgh Review* spelled the failure of other publishing enterprises. Among these was the *Annual Review* of Arthur Aikin, a chemist and writer on scientific subjects, whose interests naturally were reflected in this periodical. The *Annual* (1803–1808) was very much of a family affair, for it was contributed to by Aikin's father, the Reverend John Aikin, his aunt, Mrs. Barbauld, and his sister Lucy, the biographer of Addison and of her father. Mrs. Barbauld, with Robert Southey and William Taylor of Norwich, gave the *Review* whatever scanty literary values it has today. The *Annual Review*, the *Eclectic Review* (1805–1868), a sectarian religious organ of the Dissenters, and several other periodicals of the type were close imitators of the *Edinburgh*.

The prestige of the *Edinburgh Review* and the influence of its "invisible infallibles" were ineffectively challenged in 1809 by the seventy-seven-year-old Richard Cumberland and his *London Review,* a periodical erected by Tipper, the bookseller—a premature protest against the critical cowardice of anonymity. Hewson Clarke was a partner, and Henry Crabb Robinson had a hand in "getting up" this original enterprise, as he relates in his *Diary.* The *London Review* is distinguished by the fact that each contributor put his name to his review. It was a courageous design, in an age of irresponsible criticism, and one worthy of a better fate than that which overtook it. Except for La Crose's voluntary assumption of responsibility at the beginning of the eighteenth century, there is no other example of such critical frankness in periodicals before the middle of the nineteenth century. Cumberland expresses his convictions rather testily in his Introductory Address:

The Man, who in the genuine spirit of criticism impartially distributes praise or blame to the work he reviews, has no more need to hide his name than the tradesman has, who records himself over his shop-door; for whom has he to fear, or of what to be ashamed? Learning has no truer friend; genius no better counsellor, no safer guide.

Every one must confess, that there is a dangerous temptation, an unmanly security, an unfair advantage in concealment: why then should any man, who seeks not to injure but to benefit his contemporaries, resort to it? . . . a piece of crape may be a convenient mask for a highwayman; but a man, that goes upon an honest errand, does not want it and will disdain to wear it.

It sounds very reasonable, as we read it today, but it did not spell success in 1809. Crabb Robinson wrote one review—that of Wordsworth's Cintra pamphlet. James and Horace Smith, Horace Twiss, G. W. Crowe, and Poet-Laureate Henry Pye, other contributors to this original undertaking, did not give it the brilliance to compete with the *Edinburgh* and *Quarterly,* whose writers "carried on their operations under casemates or by ambuscade." In truth, the *London* was cursed with "original dulness."

If Cumberland and his *London Review* were anticipating what became the almost universal practice of reviewers in the twentieth century, it can have given him little satisfaction. Apparently readers did not yet wish to have the veil of anonymity drawn aside. The bold undertaking languished, and was finally given up, after four half-crown, quarterly numbers had been published. Copies of the Review are now rare curiosities—reminders of a day when men had more faith in the mysterious oracle than in the known critic.

For the origin of the *Quarterly Review* (1809 ff.) three factors may be regarded as responsible—the Administration, represented by George and Stratford Canning; the enterprising and far-sighted young publisher, John Murray (second of the name) ; the reaction of men like Scott and Southey from the politics of the *Edinburgh,* and the harsh criticisms of their own works in the columns of this Scottish *Review.* The complicated plans and activities of the group of Tories who founded the *Quarterly* have more to do with politics than literature. Yet, since they involve one of the greatest literary figures of his generation, they are not out of place in a story of this, the oldest existing and most important Review in the history of English periodicals.

It is hard to determine what individual first conceived the plan of a Review to rival the *Edinburgh*. Only two direct claims were made, one by Southey, which may be dismissed, the other by Stratford Canning, the diplomatist, a cousin of George Canning. While walking along Pall Mall one day, early in 1808, Stratford Canning made a plan for a Tory organ, conducted along the lines of the *Edinburgh*. He proposed the idea to George Canning, who referred him, with evident satisfaction, to William Gifford. Stratford Canning declared that the name as well as the idea originated with him and his friends, and that he drew up the sketch of a prospectus. Later he introduced John Murray to William Gifford. This may have been the initial step toward the establishment of the *Quarterly*. Stratford Canning's part in originating this *Review* was at least an important one, for John Murray sent him a complimentary copy of the first number on March 12, 1809, and referred to it as "a work which owes its birth to your obliging countenance and introduction of me to Mr. Gifford."

It is possible, however, that Stratford Canning's suggestion was anticipated by a letter which Murray wrote to George Canning as early as September 25, 1807, advising that some means equally popular ought to be adopted to counteract the dangerous tendency of the *Edinburgh*. Murray offered to engage his "arduous exertions to promote its success." As far as we know, Canning did not answer Murray's letter in writing, and it is probable—although it cannot be proved—that in the delay before negotiations were taken up, the plans and suggestions which Stratford Canning and his friends had made were communicated to the minister and to William Gifford. At any rate, it was through Stratford Canning that negotiations were finally opened with Murray. The meeting of Murray and Gifford was in January. It was not until the first of September, evidently, that Canning asked Gifford to take the editorship.

But, during the months before practical steps could be taken,

Walter Scott was enlisted in support of the plan. Formerly a prominent contributor to the *Edinburgh,* he had become alienated from the Scottish publication by a severe review of *Marmion* in April 1808, by the general tone of the political articles, by the injudicious remarks of Constable's partner, Hunter, regarding the contract made with Scott for an edition of Swift, and by Constable's treatment of Weber, Scott's amanuensis. Murray had the astuteness to see that Scott's feelings were hurt, and easily secured him for the Tory *Review.* Thus drawn into the *Quarterly* group, Scott soon became the chief figure. He was not the original suggestor of the *Review* "to some of the men in power," as Southey declared. He was more than that. His letters to Gifford, Murray, Ellis, and his brother, Thomas Scott, indicate that his was the guiding hand during the critical period of its infancy. Southey was nearer the truth when he called Scott the "proprietor." The latter's letters of direction, encouragement, and warning to the men most interested, tell the story. Scott was almost the *creator* of the Tory organ. Many years later he referred with satisfaction to the time when he had "the principal share in erecting this *Review* which has been since so prosperous." How important he was to its success is shown clearly by Gifford's letters to him at this time.

It is clear, then, that the outstanding figure in the group of Tory conspirators, in the later months of 1808, was Scott. Once the *Quarterly* was in progress, and the difficulties and dangers of its birth and infancy largely over, he threw the greater part of his valuable energy into other literary channels, believing it would be comparatively easy to keep the *Review* going. Yet until he was sure of its success, he was the leading spirit in editorial councils, the driving personal force behind the project. Although there was plenty of talent among the others engaged in the venture, he alone had the tact and adroitness to carry through an enterprise which required so much delicacy. Murray felt that the defensive power of the Tories in this conflict "with other principles and doctrines" was undoubted, but without the generalship of Scott it would have been difficult to have drawn them into action at this time.

The two great reviews, the *Edinburgh* and the *Quarterly,* had

much in common politically in the interests of the landed aristocracy; they likewise agreed fundamentally on matters of literary
criticism. Both depended largely upon established standards, and
uttered their verdicts with the same legalistic and all-knowing
finality. Both agreed that critics were persons eminently fitted by
a natural sensibility, as well as reflection and long experience, to
perceive all the beauties that exist and to settle the relative value
of works of literature. "Taste" was thus regarded as in a measure
inherent and to some extent acquired. Both Reviews were generally loyal to Pope, and in them reviewers occasionally defended
classical principles. Yet they were cautious in literary verdicts as
in political. Neither Review desired any great change from the
established order of things, yet neither came out with any great
partiality to the dying classicism of the late eighteenth and early
nineteenth centuries. And both were capable of anarchic individualism upon occasion.

But the *Quarterly* was established to oppose the utterances of
the northern Whigs. So, on questions of literary merit, appreciably diverse positions were found on grounds where they were in
fundamental agreement. One reason for the founding of the
Quarterly was the fact that Scott, Southey, and other Tories were
smarting under the lash of carping Whiggish criticism. This led
inevitably to the expression of critical opinion, the value of
which was modified by political prejudice and favoritism. One of
the most remarkable results of this divergence from the sacred
criteria of the past in search of issues upon which to defend
patrons of Tory favor is manifested in the more liberal attitude
of the *Quarterly* toward novelty, whether it appeared in the
method or the material of literary work. A virtual championship
of the "Lake School" was the result, although the *Quarterly*
always refused to recognize that this term had any value as a
name. In defence of Scott and Southey, this countenance of
novelty was most often expressed; and often these two were the
defenders.

It must be noted that the *Quarterly* was, above all else, the
champion of the Established Church, the palladium of privileged
aristocracy. The *Edinburgh's* critical articles often contained political aspersions, and Jeffrey frequently formed his judgments on

other than literary grounds. But it is true and natural that *Quarterly* reviewers showed a much greater inclination to partiality on matters affecting Church and Crown. Whatever tended to decrease general respect for the established order, the Church, the monarchical form of government, the laws, the King, and the landed aristocracy, was evil. Modified and varied by its applications, this was always the major consideration.

8.

Intellectual Currents:
The New Economics and Utilitarianism

~

ÉLIE HALÉVY

. . . At the opening of the nineteenth century, . . . with the exception of the Scottish universities, the sciences were cultivated by men who belonged to no definite school, who did not conduct their researches on lines previously laid down by a superior authority, who were in the strict sense of the term self-taught. Such were Herschel, Dalton, and Davy. Such was Thomas Young, a London doctor, who varied the routine of his profession by the transformation of optics and the translation of Egyptian hiero-glyphs. Such also was Sir David Brewster, who had just published his work on the polarization of light and who had never taught except as private tutor in the family of a Scottish nobleman. There existed no scientific body, with its professional code of conduct, prescribing to every worker his proper task, to be accom-plished without heed of results, results foreseen for him by oth-ers, to be reaped by others after his death. Spontaneously, there-fore of necessity imperfectly, the study of natural phenomena took shape in the provinces first, later in London. Hence the peculiar character of British science. Detailed researches, mono-graphs, classifications there are few or none. On the other hand,

From Élie Halévy, England in 1815, 2nd rev. ed. (London: Ernest Benn Ltd., 1960); Part III, Chapter 2, "Fine Arts, Literature and Science," pp. 571–587. Selected footnotes renumbered.

there are a small number of important discoveries which give a new direction to the study of detail. The British scientist, like the British manufacturer, is the lucky inventor, the revolutionary.

This is true of the physicists and chemists whose work we have just described. It is even more true of those whose study was humanity. By these we do not mean the historians. Whatever the value of their work, it is impossible to regard the learned researches of Sharon Turner and Linguard, the dogmatic explanations of James Mill, or the sweeping generalizations of Hallam, as marking an epoch in the history of human knowledge. We refer to those daring thinkers, taught only by their own reflection, Malthus, Ricardo, and Bentham. Their powerful genius transformed the social sciences.

Malthus's famous work, the *Essay on the Principle of Population,* had appeared in 1798. The father of Thomas Malthus was a Jacobin, an executor of Rousseau's will, and a disciple of the leveller and anarchist William Godwin. But the son did not share his father's humanitarian optimism, and refused to subscribe the creed of Priestley, Condorcet, and Godwin, the belief in unlimited progress. He held that mankind had grown up in a hostile environment, and is doomed to a never-ending warfare against it—that a life of plenty is not for man. For population tends to increase more rapidly than the means of subsistence. When he came to put in writing his objections to his father's faith, Malthus believed he could enforce his theory by giving it a mathematical form. 'Population has,' he maintained, 'a constant tendency to increase beyond the means of subsistence. . . . Population, when unchecked, increases in a geometrical ratio. . . . The means of subsistence could not possibly be made to increase faster than in an arithmetical ratio.' And 'the necessary effects of these two different rates of increase, when brought together, will be very striking'.

It was a gloomy book. Its conclusions were purely negative. But it appeared during the height of the anti-Jacobin reaction, and the moment was propitious for a refutation of the French Utopias. This amply accounts for the immediate success of the first edition—a small book hastily put together, a mere pamphlet of the moment. But is it a sufficient explanation of the permanent success of the book, of the astounding popularity of the Malthusian doctrine?

To account for it we must first of all remember that the economists of the British school differed from the physiocrats by regarding labour, not the bounty of nature, as the sole source of wealth, from the Continental economists by finding the standard of value in labour, not in utility. But to maintain that labour is the sole source of wealth and the sole standard of value is to maintain that every pleasure is purchased at the cost of an equivalent or almost equivalent pain, that man is not born to plenty, that a parsimonious nature doles out to him in scanty measure the means of subsistence, and that population exercises on its resources an unremitting pressure. Malthus's doctrine was contained implicitly in the doctrine of all the preceding British economists. It can even be found explicitly, if incidentally, enunciated by Hume, Adam Smith, and Stewart. Malthusianism, therefore, confirmed prejudices already dominant in economic science, fitted into the established tradition. This explains a permanent success which survived the accidental popularity enjoyed by the first edition of the *Essay*.

And we must also bear in mind that at the close of the eighteenth century the Poor Law was a source of perpetual anxiety to the English legislator. His object was to obtain from the paupers relieved by the public a due return of labour. But during a period of grave distress he felt himself obliged to permit serious relaxations of principle. A host of pamphlets were published, whose authors, in conformity with the principles of Adam Smith and his followers, maintained that the system of poor relief, as it was administered in Great Britain, was opposed to the laws of nature, put a premium on idleness and incompetence, and encouraged the population to outgrow the means of subsistence. Among these pamphlets was Malthus's work.[1] In 1798, at a

---

[1] To realize how closely the work of Malthus is attached to this entire class of literature, see especially the little treatise of John Townshend, *A Dissertation on the Poor Laws by a Well-wisher to Mankind*, 1786. Townshend is a forerunner of Malthus and even, through Malthus, of Darwin himself. We may also consider the following significant passage (*First Report of the*

moment when the guardians were distributing relief with a reckless extravagance, Malthus endowed the economists with arguments of a novel and striking character to denounce the waste and to pass a wholesale condemnation upon the system of poor relief.

It would, therefore, be a grave error to treat Malthus, as the student might be led to treat him by a consideration of the circumstances in which his work was first published, as a mere pamphleteer of the counter-revolution. Certainly the harsh attitude which it implied towards the proletariat recommended Malthusianism to the middle class. But the English middle class, though it remained sternly opposed to revolution and sentimentality, was increasingly open to the ideas of the Liberal reformers, as the anti-Jacobin panic faded from the public memory. The Tory organ, the *Quarterly Review*, was anti-Malthusian; the *Edinburgh Review*, the organ of the Radical Opposition, erected Malthusianism into a dogma.

No doubt in its author's pseudo-mathematical statement the Malthusian thesis is not easy to maintain; it would be difficult even to give it an intelligible meaning. Nevertheless, Malthus's combination of extreme simplicity and apparent scientific accuracy may well have recommended his book to a middle-class public which, though without any very solid education, prided itself on its scientific temper. It was hard to resist the suggestion made, and refuse to credit the existence of a law stated with such assurance, defined so precisely. In the matter of scientific truth the self-taught man is easily satisfied. Nor is his public more exacting. The historian Hallam would even declare the mathematical formulation of Malthus's principle of population to be as indubitable as the multiplication table. And the day was at hand when Ricardo, more Malthusian than Malthus himself, was going to base on that principle the entire theory of the distribu-

---

Philanthropic Society, 1789, p. 15) : 'So deeply perverted is the whole system of parish government, so defective in execution, as well as wrong in principle, that it falsifies the most substantial maxim in police, that population is the strength and riches of a State. By the creed of an overseer, the number of births is the standard of a nation's decay, and the command to increase and multiply was given as a scourge to mankind.'

tion of wealth, indeed wellnigh the whole of political economy.

The son of a Jewish stockbroker, Ricardo had never received a classical education. In fact his education had scarcely exceeded the standard of what we should now term primary education. Hardly fourteen years of age, he had entered business. In his scanty hours of leisure, and without a teacher, he completed his education as best he could. He studied chemistry and mineralogy, installed a laboratory in his home, was one of the first members of the Geological Society. But his favourite study was political economy. For it was related to the matters which were the subject of his professional work. We have already noticed his share in the controversy occasioned by the depreciation of the banknote, when a series of newspaper articles had revealed his capacity as a thinker. He was already a celebrity, if not yet the head of a school. That position would be his only when another economic question had attracted public attention, and Malthus had distinguished himself by a further discovery.

Since 1805 Malthus had been teaching history and political economy in the college established by the East India Company for the education of its servants. Little by little he had reached an original theory of rent which he regarded as the direct consequence of the *Principle* which he had formulated in 1798. Since population tends to increase more rapidly than the means of subsistence, man is continually obliged to bring under cultivation soils of an inferior quality. Hence of necessity a constant increase in the cost of foodstuffs, which would increase also the reward of labour and of capital spent upon the lands first cultivated, did not both wages and profits tend to the normal level in the manner explained by Adam Smith. In consequence a surplus accrues from the more fertile areas which is the landlord's income—his rent. Thus the increase, nay the very existence of rent, is an effect, not a cause, of the increase in the cost of living. In England economic conditions favoured the acceptance of this theory. On the other hand, the census returns showed a rapid increase of population, and the soil of the United Kingdom was no longer sufficient to feed its inhabitants. On the other hand, rents were continuously rising. Plainly the two phenomena must be related as cause and effect. When the restoration of peace was followed by an agricultural crisis, a parliamentary commission was appointed to investigate its causes. A large proportion of the witnesses before this Commission maintained, almost unconsciously, the theory of Malthus. Buchanan, in his edition of the *Wealth of Nations* published in 1814, and the economist West in an essay published in 1815, maintained theories very similar to his. Malthus decided that, if he were not to lose his property in the theory, he must no longer delay its publication. He therefore published his essay on 'The Nature and Progress of Rent'.

This was the signal for Ricardo to intervene. In a short essay 'On the Influence of a low Price of Corn on the Profits of Stock', he accepted the two laws which Malthus had formulated and of which the latter depended upon the former, his law of population, and his law of rent. But he rejected the protectionist consequences which Malthus deduced from his laws in his essay of 1815. And to prove his own doctrine of Free Trade he built upon both an original system of laws regulating the distribution of wealth.

The law of wages is the first consequence of the law of population. According to this law, the amount of wages received by the labourer, the natural price of his labour, is the amount necessary to enable him to subsist and to perpetuate his species 'without increase or diminution'. For wages cannot decrease without starving the labourer, nor increase without an increase of the population which will re-establish the equilibrium with the means of subsistence.

The law of profits followed. If the amount of wages, as calculated in terms of foodstuffs, remains fixed, that amount, as calculated in terms of money, must constantly increase, since the cost of extracting from the soil an equal amount of nourishment increases constantly, as the growth of population compels the cultivation of inferior soil. But this alteration of wages cannot affect rent which is a fixed quantity. It must therefore affect profits. In this way the law of differential rent and, by implication, the principle of population explain a phenomenon universally verifiable—the progressive decrease of profits. With the natural progress of society the labourer remains at an equal level of bare subsistence, and the capitalist receives a constantly decreasing income. The landowner alone grows continually more wealthy, and this increase of wealth represents neither labour nor risk. Such was the outline of the system which Ricardo now set himself to develop in all its details and applications. Not till 1817 would he publish, as the fruit of two years' labour, his classic, the celebrated *Principles of Political Economy and Taxation*.

This famous work is abstract in its treatment, its style arid. But because Ricardo is a difficult author to read, it does not follow that his work is academic, out of touch with practical life. What indeed was the origin of the principle of population on which the entire edifice is constructed? A pamphlet inspired by the circumstances of the moment, the whim of a publicist, indignant at the maladministration of the Poor Law. What, again, were the books with which in 1809 and in 1815 Ricardo had paved the way for his Political Economy? The reflections of a business man upon a controversy which was occupying Parliament and the Press. The first principles from which Ricardo sets out in his attempt to construct an entire system of economics, were taken practically unaltered from the phenomena of contemporary life. His new theory of the distribution of wealth was an abstract defence of the passions which were exciting the London mob to riot, and were effecting a coalition of Labour and Capital against the landlord. This explains its immediate adoption as their political creed by an entire party, and the ease and rapidity with which it was popularized. In her *Conversations on Political Economy* which appeared in 1816, and whose aim, as the sub-title informs us, was 'to explain in familiar language the elements of that science', Mrs. Marcet explained successfully the entire doctrine of Ricardo without misrepresenting a single point of importance. 'I know not why,' said the hero of a Bulwer Lytton novel, published a few years later, 'this study' (Political Economy) 'has been termed uninteresting. No sooner had I entered upon its consideration, than I could scarcely tear myself from it.'

Thus by 1815 the theories of Malthus had been incorporated by Ricardo into the classical tradition of political economy. But contemporaneously Ricardo's teaching was itself incorporated into an entire system of philosophy whose action upon British

public opinion would be profound and lasting, the philosophy of
Bentham and his school.

Unlike Malthus and Ricardo, Bentham did not achieve an
immediate success. His *Introduction to the Principles of Morals
and Legislation* had been written about 1775, contemporaneously
with the publication of Adam Smith's *Wealth of Nations,* and
had been published in 1788 without attracting any attention.
The countless manuscripts in which he expounded the plan of an
entire system of jurisprudence, wholly different from the established system, emancipated from the domination of metaphysical
fictions and founded on the rational and lucid principle of 'general utility' or 'the greatest happiness of the greatest number',
had been written before the *Introduction* was published. But it
was not until 1802 that Dumont published in France the *Traités
de Legislation Civile et Penale.* And even after their publication
England continued to ignore Bentham, or, if he was known at all,
it was not as a writer but as a philanthropist and, moreover, as an
unsuccessful philanthropist. He had invented a novel type of
prison, a circular prison equipped with a system of central super-
vision, the Panopticon or house where everything is visible. He
had done his best to persuade the British Government to adopt
it, had offered to undertake the financial responsibility and ad-
minister himself the institution he proposed. He had even purchased a site for the future prison out of his private means. But
the passage through Parliament of an Act in favour of the scheme
had borne no fruit. Neither Pitt nor his successors had given
Bentham the support he had been promised. Already sixty years
of age, unknown as a philosopher, impotent as a philanthropist,
his fortune devoured by the Panopticon scheme, he believed his
career at an end, and his life a failure, when in 1808 he made the
acquaintance of James Mill, who had just come up to London
from Edinburgh University, and was laboriously earning a livelihood by hard work with his pen. Bentham converted Mill to his
philosophy. Mill in return restored Bentham's self-confidence,
propagated his ideas, and gathered around him a school of disciples. In the history of social science in Britain during the early
nineteenth century the formation of this Benthamite school was
an event of the first importance. The Benthamites were in the

strictest sense of the term a sect and their influence is comparable in its extent to the influence of the Clapham sect. Possessed by an equal enthusiasm, their inspiration was widely different. Their thoroughgoing rationalism was in striking contrast with the emotionalism of the Evangelicals.

Only seven years had passed since the junction between Bentham and James Mill, only five since Mill had taken a house at Westminster, next door to Bentham's, and already the influence of Benthamism was spreading in every direction. James Mill was expounding its creed in the *Edinburgh Review* and in the *Philanthropist,* the magazine of the Quaker William Allen. In the House of Commons Bentham's lifelong friend, the barrister Romilly, was urging year by year in conformity with his friend's principles a mitigation of the penal code, a reduction in the number of 'capital felonies'. James Mill introduced Bentham to Robert Owen and Lancaster, indeed, to all who were seeking the reform of society in a system of popular education: we have already seen the share taken by Bentham and his friends in the Lancastrian movement. James Mill became the friend of Ricardo and introduced him to his master: without Mill the *Principles of Political Economy and Taxation* would perhaps never have been written. And finally, it was through Mill that Bentham made the acquaintance of Francis Place, the famous electoral agent of the Westminster constituency. We have remarked the formation at Westminster about the person of Bentham of the youthful party of 'Radicals'. Fame had come to Bentham and with fame wealth. In 1813 Parliament had voted him an ample indemnity as compensation for the losses incurred in his Panopticon propaganda. A kindly and eccentric old man, owner of a house in town and a country seat, he commanded an army of disciples. The philosophic and social ideas of the eighteenth century had awoken from a slumber of twenty-five years. What was the common philosophic principle on which the Utilitarians built their jurisprudence, their political economy, and their politics? Man seeks pleasure and avoids pain. This, according to Bentham and his disciples, is the fundamental law of human action. The *summum bonum* is pleasure—not indeed the passing pleasure of the individual, which would render impossible a scientific treatment either of happiness or morality—but 'general utility', 'the greatest happiness of the greatest number'. Hence a rational art of conduct presupposes the knowledge of the conditions which produce pleasure and pain—that the former may be sought, the latter avoided. And this knowledge is in turn to be obtained only by constructing a psychology modelled on the natural sciences already in existence. But these fall into two classes, the sciences which collect facts, and the sciences which explain and construct a system of laws. It was after the pattern of the latter class, the sciences whose objects are elementary and simple phenomena, that the Utilitarians conceived their new science of human nature.

Such was the spirit of their age and country. It is a current belief that the English are cautious observers, with a keen eye for detail, careful to respect the complexity of nature, as opposed to the French, who delight in intellectual constructions and in generalization. This belief, however, is far from the truth. In reality simplification has been the distinctive character of British thought during the nineteenth century. British men of science, for the reasons we have already determined—reasons of a strictly historical character—united the inexperience and the boldness, a boldness often successful, of the self-taught man. They were reasoners who sought and discovered simple laws, men of intuition, who claimed to perceive beneath the manifold of natural phenomena, the outlines of a machine, whose parts are few and whose motions are all sensible.[2] It was because it was at once the simplest hypothesis, and the most easily visualized that Dalton

---

[2] This explains the small progress made by English scientists of this period in higher mathematics. The algorithm of algebra repelled them. They had no liking for this blindfold search of truth. Thomas Young, who cared the most for pure mathematics, avoided symbolic forms of proof, and used as far as possible the language of everyday life, thus making his works more difficult of understanding, by his very attempt to render them more popular (Peacock, *Life of Thomas Young*, pp. 116–7, 183). Similarly, when Berzelius, having accepted the atomic theory, attempted to describe the composition of bodies by formulae in which the atoms were represented by letters to which were appended coefficients showing the number of atoms in a particular combination, Dalton denounced this new algebra, and described Berzelius's symbols as 'horrible'. The student of chemistry, he maintained, could as easily learn Hebrew (W. C. Henry, *Memoirs of John Dalton*, p. 124).

adopted the atomic theory: it rendered the fundamental composition of bodies visible. And the method of Bentham and his school was Dalton's method applied to the moral sciences. In both departments there was the same simplification, the same 'atomism'.

The human soul is a compound of psychical atoms, elementary feelings, agreeable and disagreeable, which differ in intensity, duration, number, and the manner of their mutual combination. And the laws which govern their association are few and simple, the law of association by likeness, and the law of association by contiguity. Possibly even these two laws could be reduced to one, the law of association by likeness being a special case of the law of association by contiguity. Bentham had translated a work of the Swedish chemist Bergmann. James Mill was the intimate friend of Thomas Thomson, a champion of Dalton's atomic theory. Both were conscious imitators of the methods of the new chemistry. Their ideal moralist, educator, and legislator must practise a mental chemistry and learn from the chemist the art of constructing complex psychoses by combining simple elements.

The art of education would thus consist in effecting in the minds of children such an association of ideas that the child could no longer separate his personal happiness from the happiness of his fellows. The art of legislation would consist in producing a similar effect in the mind of the adult. By associating the idea of certain actions with the idea of certain penalties the legislator would intimidate the potential criminal and prevent crime. The scientific analysis both of the crime and its penalty into their constituent elements, their atoms, and the establishment of an accurate proportion between both sets of factors, constituted, for the Utilitarian, the entire science of penology. Evidently a science of calculation and reasoning and nothing beyond. The Utilitarians neglected as useless learned research, knowledge of the historical growth of law. Their method was, as they fully realized, in radical opposition to the historical method which the professors of Germany were bringing into fashion. 'One might,' wrote Bentham in scorn, 'open an historical school *à la mode d'Allemagne*. Der Herr Savigny in Germany could furnish admirable masters. . . . To the army and the navy of a country substitute, for example, a history of the wars waged by that same country . . . to an order on a cook for dinner substitute a fair copy of the housekeeper's book as kept during the appropriate series of years.' These words express the hatred of the reformer for the traditionalist, of the self-educated man for the university scholar.

We may now adopt a slightly different point of view and consider not, as hitherto, the mutual combinations of simple psychoses in the individual consciousness, but the association of individuals to form a society. Bentham and his followers saw in society only an agglomeration of individuals, by nature existing in isolation, and united solely by deliberate acts of choice. A certain proportion of individuals were happy, a certain proportion unhappy. Which side of the account showed a surplus? This was the balance which you must strike whenever you would appraise a law or a custom. Such simple operations of addition and subtraction composed the entire intellectual task of the Utilitarian reformer. And this individualism may be regarded as a kind of sociological 'atomism'. It explains the line of reasoning which led the Utilitarians to political radicalism. And it was the foundation-stone of the entire edifice of the new political economy.

Suppose all the individuals, the atoms, out of which the social body is composed, perfectly selfish, inaccessible to any motive except a self-regarding prudence. Suppose them also perfectly rational, free from any liability to be blinded by passion. And finally, suppose them perfectly free, admitting no external constraint in the pursuit of their economic end. We thus construct a society as unlike any actual human society, as the simplified world of the sciences is unlike the world of sensible experience, but capable of rendering equal service in the explanation of phenomena. In fact, the hypothesis, precisely because of its simplicity, rendered possible an almost mathematically exact description of several economic phenomena such as the circulation of currency, exchange, and banking. It even provided a sufficiently accurate account of the exchange of manufactured goods. And Ricardo believed that, when taken in conjunction with the Malthusian law of population, it made it possible to explain with

equal accuracy the distribution of the profits of labour between
the landlord, the capitalist, and the labourer. No attempt was
made to discover empirical laws by observation. Nor was economic theory controlled by statistics. Political economy, as understood by Ricardo and James Mill, was built up by the series of
hypothetical constructions whose character we have explained
above. And this individualist theory was applied by individualist
practice. The Utilitarians regarded the State as in principle
incapable of controlling economics. It must stand aside and leave
individuals free to regulate their economic interests, whether as
between class and class, or nation and nation.

Thus was erected the finished edifice of Utilitarianism. It was
frankly irreligious. Neither as the explanation of history, nor as
the foundation of ethics or law did it invoke the supernatural, or
any principle transcending sensible experience. Nor is it sufficient
to call Utilitarianism irreligious. It was aggressively anti-reli-
gious, and regarded religion as a whole and Christianity in
particular as the bane of civilization. For religion was of its very
nature a form of asceticism, a perversion of feeling which made
men desire pain and shun pleasure. And asceticism had produced
a taste of slavery of every description, political, legal, and economic. Above all, it was responsible for the notion of punishment
as an 'expiation', which had induced men to regard the infliction
of punishment as a good thing in itself, and had thus led to that
useless severity of the criminal code against which from the
commencement of his literary activity Bentham had never ceased
to protest. It would be impossible, without unduly anticipating
the future, to relate the campaign of anti-Christian propaganda—no longer Deist as in the days of Tom Paine, but frankly
Atheist—to which the Utilitarians would lend their aid. It dates
from the years which followed the conclusion of peace. But even
before 1815 the body of doctrines which composed philosophic
Radicalism exercised in every direction a subversive influence.
Thus with Bentham and his friends we are at the opposite pole
alike to the Toryism of the Government, and to Evangelical
pietism. How then are we to explain the success of the Utilitarian
propaganda in face of the hostility of Government, and the
influence, felt universally, of the Protestant revival?

When the Tories wished to discredit Utilitarianism, they denounced it as an unpatriotic philosophy, inspired by foreign ideas, and especially by French ideas. Were not the political principles of the Benthamites the democratic principles of the Jacobins? Did they not derive their ethics and their jurisprudence from Helvétius and Beccaria, their psychology from Condillac, their philosophy of history and their political economy from Condorcet and Jean-Baptiste Say? Were they not irreligious Voltairians? Had not Bentham composed in French and published at Paris his *Traités de Legislation?* But the Utilitarians could reply with truth that all these so-called French ideas, of whose importation they were accused, were in reality English ideas which had found a temporary home abroad.

Before its appearance in France democracy had been the political theory of the Anglo-Saxon rebels in America, and the Americans had themselves taken the principles which inspired their rebellion from Locke and the English republicans of the seventeenth century. Condillac's psychology had been the psychology of Hartley and Hume before Condillac ever set pen to paper. It was in England that Voltaire had learned to be a Freethinker. Throughout the anti-Jacobin reaction there had been thinkers— Erasmus Darwin, Thomas Day, Edgeworth, the political agitator Horne Tooke, Unitarians of the school of Priestley—who defended what they believed to be the national tradition against the innovations of the Tories. Among the ideas which composed the Utilitarian system, their economic theories tended more and more to take the first place. And, however great the influence of the French physiocratic school, Hume and Adam Smith were undoubtedly the founders of the new political economy, and the action of the latter was influential in circles impervious to the complete Utilitarian system. The English are a nation of traders and can be governed only by men who possess the commercial mentality. Pitt, the leader of the anti-Jacobins, was a disciple of Adam Smith. Burke, at once the orator and the philosopher of the counter-revolution, was as zealous in the defence of economic individualism, as in the denunciation of political. When the Tories became a party of landlords and country squires, they signed their own death warrant. In this way its economic principles obtained for Utilitarianism an entrance into the governing classes.

Twenty-five years of Tory reaction, a reaction, when all is said, only skin deep, had proved insufficient to destroy intellectual traditions so deeply rooted. And moreover, what official body was in existence on which the party in office could rely to combat the ideas of the Benthamites? The Scottish universities? We have seen the empirical spirit which inspired the philosophers of the Scottish school. If they shrank from the conclusions of Hartley and his followers, their hesitation was due only to the extreme simplicity of Hartley's generalizations. For they were men of university training, not self-educated men. But at bottom they differed from the radical empiricists only by their greater caution. Was Cambridge less exposed to the infection of Utilitarianism? We have seen that Cambridge had always professed Whig ideas in political philosophy and in philosophy generally. Locke, Paley, and Hartley were the philosophers studied. A few years hence Benthamism will be the fashion among the Cambridge undergraduates. There remained the impregnable citadel of Oxford. But Oxford was asleep and no one could possibly regard the remnants of Aristotelian scholasticism taught in her schools as a living intellectual tradition.

To be sure, for the past twenty years there had existed on the Continent a new system of philosophy professed by men of genius, capable of attracting the rising generation and counteracting Utilitarianism. But it was not English. And how many Englishmen were able to read Kant, Fichte, and Schelling in the original? The Scottish professors attempted to make acquaintance with the new systems through the channel of French interpreters, Madame de Staël and De Gerando: and what they understood, they disliked. Alone in England the poet Coleridge had been deeply influenced by German thought. He had abandoned verse for prose, and exchanged the naturalistic pantheism of his youth for a transcendental theology inspired by Schelling. But Coleridge, far more than Bentham, was an eccentric and lonely thinker. He belonged to no teaching body, to no national tradition. In 1815 his influence still counted for nothing.

England is a free country in which government pressure plays no part in the formation of public opinion. It is not therefore surprising that the Utilitarian propaganda overcame the opposition of official Conservatism. It is more difficult to understand the influence exercised by Utilitarianism in an environment so impregnated with Evangelical religion as was the England of the early nineteenth century. Was the action of the two forces successive? And was Utilitarianism in 1815 a growing force, Evangelicalism on the verge of decline? Such an explanation would do violence to the complexity of the situation. The fundamental paradox of English society, which it is necessary to explain before we conclude this volume, is precisely the partial junction and combination of these two forces theoretically so hostile.

We have already spoken of the philanthropic activity common to both parties. Utilitarianism was a philosophy wholly practical. Bentham and his friends were ardent advocates of the Panopticon model prison, whose very idea had been conceived by their leader, of Lancaster's model school, and Robert Owen's model factory. They regarded these institutions as 'moral' inventions, akin to the important technical inventions which were transforming industry, as 'moral' machines ingeniously constructed for the automatic production of virtue and happiness. The Christian philanthropists, whatever their repugnance to such a mechanical conception of psychology and ethics, could not be deaf to the appeal of inventions so beneficent as these. Between the Utilitarians and the 'old Dissenters' there existed little short of a permanent alliance. And even the Methodists and Evangelicals sympathized with the Utilitarian philanthropy. As their contribution to the common task the Christians brought their zeal, their missionary spirit, their love for a self-imposed discipline. Nor did the Utilitarians fail to appreciate these qualities. 'Townshend,' wrote Bentham, 'was once what I had liked to have been, a Methodist, and what I should have been, had I not been what I am.' And the Utilitarians contributed their practical sense, their conviction of the possibility of a social technique, an art of employing the right means to obtain the desired end. Many Christian philanthropists, educated in the school of industrialism, shared their convictions on this point. But we may go further and discover closer affinities between Benthamite Utilitarianism and Protestant pietism.

It would be a mistake to establish an irreconcilable opposition between the Utilitarian ethic and the Christian on the ground that the former is founded on pleasure, the latter on sacrifice. For Utilitarian morality cannot be described without qualification as hedonism. It was based simultaneously on two principles. One of these, it is true, was the identification of the good with pleasure; but the other, of equal importance with the former, was the duty incumbent upon man, in virtue of the natural conditions to which his life is subject, to sacrifice present pleasure to the hope of future, and purchase happiness at the cost of labour and suffering. This law of work, implicit in Bentham's moral arithmetic, was the principle explicitly proclaimed by the entire system of the classical political economy, and introduced into Utilitarianism an undeniable element of asceticism. How can we explain the popularity of the Malthusian thesis at the very period when public opinion was apparently attached more closely than ever to the Christian tradition? Undoubtedly it contradicted one of the fundamental doctrines of the Bible. But it also refuted the atheistic humanitarianism of the eighteenth century, and taught that man is destined by his very nature to an unending struggle for existence, to a perpetual condition of hardship. And this appealed to the ascetic and Christian preconceptions of the public. It was in vain that the Benthamites attempted to reconcile the principle of population with the creed of unlimited progress, the pessimism of Malthus with the optimism of Condorcet. Their efforts could not abolish the distinction between the standpoint of the French Utilitarians and that of their English teachers. Benthamism, as its principles were popularized about 1815 by James Mill the Scotsman, was the French philosophy of the eighteenth century adapted to the needs of a nation moulded by a dogmatic and austere religion.

And moreover, the Utilitarians were individualists. The object of their entire ethical teaching was to bring home to the individual that society existed only through him and for his sake, and that it is his personal duty to maintain his rights and pursue his interest. To be sure, this individualism was not that theological individualism of the Protestant, whose character has been described above. And moreover, the new type of Protestantism, which had sprung from Wesley's preaching in the previous century, was in this respect an enfeebled type. The organization of the Methodist sects was more hierarchic than that of the old seventeenth-century sects; and the Evangelicals were Methodists who had refused to break with the Anglican Church. But no Protestant revival could fail to be, in some measure at least, a revival of religious individualism. Between the secular individualism of Bentham and the authoritarian Christianity of the High Churchman, the liberal Protestantism of the Unitarians, Scottish Calvinism, the Methodist sects, the Evangelicalism of the Low Church party, constituted a series of imperceptible transitions. Nor was the individualism of the Utilitarianism radically anti-social. It did not exclude in principle all state intervention. For the Utilitarians looked to the legislature to establish a harmony of interests in the community by imposing obligations sanctioned by penalties. And even where they rejected government interference, they encouraged the formation of voluntary associations whose members would pursue a common end by the free surrender of a portion of their independence. Secular philanthropy and Protestant Dissent stood in equal need of such associations. They were thus among the typical expressions of private initiative in nineteenth-century England. British individualism is a moderate individualism, a mixture whose constituents are often mingled beyond the possibility of analysis, a compound of Evangelicalism and Utilitarianism.

9.

The Curse of Midas

J. L. HAMMOND AND BARBARA HAMMOND

"Two centuries ago not one person in a thousand wore stockings; one century ago not one person in five hundred wore them; now not one person in a thousand is without them." This sentence from *The Results of Machinery* (1831), one of the publications of the Society for the Diffusion of Useful Knowledge, illustrates a feature of the Industrial Revolution that made a profound impression on the imagination of the time. When capital was applied to production on a large scale, it gained its profits by producing in bulk; producing, that is, for mass consumption. Energy and brains were now devoted to satisfying, not the luxurious taste of the classes that were served by the commerce of mediæval Europe, but the needs of the poor consumer.

Man's faculty for creation and self-expression develops when he can diminish the demand that the satisfaction of elementary needs for food and shelter makes upon his intelligence and his strength. Hence this vast improvement in the means for the provision of those needs marked a definite and startling advance in human history. Man, in this sense, became freer than he had ever been; his *jus in naturam,* as Spinoza put it, was infinitely greater. This aspect of the new system struck many contemporary observers as its most important aspect; they were fond of showing that the poor of their time were better off in respect of the

From J. L. Hammond and Barbara Hammond, The Rise of Modern Industry, 7th ed. (London: Methuen & Co. Ltd., 1947); Chapter 13, "The Curse of Midas," pp. 210–223. Selected footnotes renumbered.

conditions of life than the rich of other times; the cottager than the noble.

It was natural for the age that witnessed the first triumphs of the new system to worship production for profit. This great addition to the wealth of the world seemed to follow automatically when men were left to acquire at their pleasure. Swift success is a dazzling spectacle, and the new industrial system provided a new miracle every day. A visitor to a mill in Bolton or Preston watching the inventions of Crompton, Hargreaves, Arkwright and Watt, stood before a power that was conquering the world as no Cæsar or Napoleon had ever conquered it. To the generation that saw on the one hand the small farmer carrying the wool he had woven on his hand-loom at home to Leeds or Halifax on the back of his horse, and on the other the great mills at Blackburn or Rochdale sending out thousands of bales of cotton to be transported by rail and ship to the other ends of the earth, it looked as if progress that had dawdled through so many centuries was, now that man had learnt its simple secret, to follow a rapid and unbroken course; as if the society that surrendered itself to the control of private profit released a force that would regenerate the world. Any people into whose hands this power had fallen would probably have been plunged into the state described by Boulton as "steam-mill mad," just as any people that had first grasped the new wealth of America in the fifteenth century would have been as frantic as the Spaniards for gold and silver.

The English people, from the whole tone and cast of its thought and politics, was specially liable to be swept off its balance by this revolution. The positive enthusiasms of the time were for science and progress: for material development and individual liberty. The restraints of custom, tradition and religion had never been so frail over the classes that held power. In the Middle Ages the Church had laid a controlling or checking hand on manners; the Guilds had hampered individual enterprise by a corporate discipline. But the Church of the eighteenth century was merely part of the civil order, without standards, authority or conscience of its own; the Guilds were dead, and their successors stood not for corporate spirit, but for property and nothing else. Thus neither Church nor Guild survived to offer any obstacle to the view that headlong wealth was the sovereign good for society and for the individual, for cities and for men.

This view was powerfully encouraged by the philosophy of confidence which the eighteenth century had substituted for a religion of awe. Mediæval religion had watched man's instincts with anxious eyes, as instincts needing to be disciplined, coerced, held fast by Pope and priest; the Puritans, though they gave him different masters, were not less suspicious of the natural man. The new philosophy, on the other hand, regarded man's instincts as the best guide to conduct, and taught that left to himself man so acted as to serve rather than injure the society to which he belonged. Capital was a magical power; man was a benevolent creature. Thus so far as an age lives by a system of belief, this age drew its wisdom from a philosophy that found nothing but good in the new force to which it had submitted.

The state of politics was also congenial to this impulse. Neither Conservative nor Radical offered any distracting or competing motive, for while they disagreed about political and administrative reform, they did not disagree about the advantages of a system under which acquisition and profit-making were unimpeded. If it was the manufacturers who promoted the new system in industry, the landowners were equally active in promoting it on their estates. The most important force in making the English an industrial people was the destruction of the village. Nations that kept the peasant could never be completely absorbed in the new industrial system, and it was the landowner, often of course the new landowner, who had come from the world of finance and industry, who pushed the English peasant out.

The quarrel between Conservative and Radical did not raise any issue that was an obstacle to the new system. Their quarrel was political. Reform, both of Parliament and of local government, was long overdue. In a country where all initiative has been gathered, and power has long resided, in the grasp of a class, the instincts of authority and the habits of action enable that class to keep life in a bad system long after it has lost all claim to the support of those whose needs it once served. Such a class ceases in time to be a governing class, and becomes a garrison. Particularly is this true where, as in the case of eighteenth-century England, the governing class possesses the qualities of courage and resolution in a remarkable degree. Thus it came about that Parliament and local government, the administration of justice and of law were full of gross anomalies, and the defence of those anomalies was for a time the chief care of the Conservative party. A party that was engaged in the effort to keep what it held in the way of class privilege, and to protect property rather than custom, a system of inequalities rather than any large design of social harmony, did not offer to the sentiment or the sense of the English people any ideal that could discredit acquisition, as the leading motive of conduct. Lord Hugh Cecil has said of its purpose that it sought to preserve the sanctity of property; property significantly interpreted as the right to the "undisturbed enjoyment of good fortune."

If Conservatism offered no distracting aim, Liberalism gave active encouragement to the new system. In the eighteenth century Liberalism was a crusade against authority based on anything but consent. Its basis was individualism, for it regarded society as existing to enforce respect for rights that man brought with him into society: not as a community whose members and classes served different purposes, and stood in some organic relation to one another. In this sense Liberalism was a revolt from an essential tradition of the Middle Ages. Mediæval society had attempted to preserve what mankind had kept of its inheritance of culture through the havoc of the Dark Ages, by a system that was a sort of caste system. This system was not new in Europe. Diocletian and Constantine had tried to overcome the dangers and difficulties of an exhausted Empire by attaching classes to occupations. By their time the peril of civilization was manifest and the rulers of the Empire had to devise methods for securing that the land should be tilled, the inhabitants of the towns fed, the revenue maintained, and the work of the world carried on. Diocletian had created a class of hereditary seamen to guarantee the transport of corn for Rome; Constantine bound the class of farmers known as the "coloni" to the soil. This caste system included other classes; definite obligations and liabilities, for example, were imposed on the landowners who filled the *curia* in each district, and they were excluded from other careers. This principle was applied to all trades and professions whose members were subject to the capitation tax. There was the same underlying idea in the social system of the Middle Ages. Different classes had different duties. As Chaucer's parson put it, "God has ordained that some folk should be more high in estate and degree, and some folk more low, and that everyone should be served in his estate and his degree."

This view of society would in any case have been obnoxious to Liberals, who refused to believe that a man's place and career should be fixed for him, for all time, by birth and custom. When it was attacked by Liberals in the seventeenth and eighteenth centuries, the system was in decay, and it survived in the main in the form of abuses. The Church, the town, the manor, the guild, represented a philosophy that once had life, meaning and purpose, but, with their decadence into the temper and methods of monopoly, the whole system of regulation to which they belonged had changed its character; instead of an arrangement to serve a rationally ordered and living society, it was become the entrenchment of a class. The mediæval idea, if it kept the poor in their place, gave them some protection and recognized that they had certain rights. In the eighteenth century the system had lost this character of social obligation; it had degenerated for the most part into a mass of idle and unearned privileges. The individualism of Locke, Adam Smith and Bentham in England was directed, like the individualism of Turgot in France, against authority exercised in the interests of the few, no longer seeking its justification in the idea of duty or function, claiming obedience on the ground of divine right.

The Liberals were thus attacking a great body of abuses and an arbitrary system of power. Their vigour and courage enabled them to strike effective blows. They made Parliament less unrepresentative, town government less corrupt, punishment less brutal, justice less unjust. But the philosophy that prompted this campaign did not quarrel merely with the abuses of the feudal society: it combated its underlying principles. It opposed to the idea of mutual obligation the idea of natural rights,[1] and these rights included the right to acquire and use property, as a right subject to no kind of qualification. For these minds one aspect of the Industrial Revolution overshadowed all others. That revolution had made it very much easier for the poor man with courage and intelligence to step out of his surroundings. The door had been thrown open to enterprise and thrift, and men could pass through it without asking leave of ruler or neighbour. The Liberal was chiefly concerned that this door should never be closed: he believed that in a world where exertion and perseverance can carry a man from poverty to riches, injustice will always be kept within tolerable limits.

Thus economic individualism occupied an essential place in Radical theory, and as the right of the capitalist was deduced from a theory, it was treated as a right that was absolute and independent of experience. It belonged for English Radical, as for French, like the right to life, or the right to liberty, to a series of natural rights, which society had no business to limit. It involved the right to take what interest and profit you could get; to buy and sell as you pleased; rights that had been controlled in the Middle Ages. Thus the Radicals tended to substitute for the divine right of kings the divine right of capitalist. They did noble work in abolishing injustices and oppressions, but they acknowledged a new power which was largely to determine the character of a civilization. For a people passing through such changes as those that accompanied the Industrial Revolution, this question, whether and at what point the claim of the capitalist to uncontrolled exercise of his power should be withstood, became the most important question in public life. England was on the eve of a great expansion of resources, numbers, wealth and power. What were the new towns to be like? What their schools, their pleasures, their houses, their standards of a good life, their plans for co-operation and fellowship? What the fate of the mass

[1] Bentham rejected the philosophy of rights, but his Utilitarian philosophy took a direction, from his mistrust of authority, that brought his school to the same practical result. The individual understood his own interest best, and the good of the greatest number would be realized by allowing him complete freedom to pursue it.

of people who did not feel or force their way through the doors thrown open to enterprise? To all these questions the Industrial Revolution gave the same answer: "Ask Capital." And neither Conservative nor Radical, the man defending or the man attacking bad laws and bad customs, thought that answer wrong. But that answer meant that the age had turned aside from making a society in order to make a system of production.

This new power then descended on a society in which the intellectual and political atmosphere inclined the age to give it a free rein. Restraint of every kind on the acquisition and the use of wealth was discredited; the doctrine that the man who seeks his private gain finds the public good was accepted like a discovery of Newton's; progress was regarded as constant, and it was believed that the Industrial Revolution was making the problems of life not more but less complex. For the ascendancy of the mathematical sciences had encouraged abstractions dangerous from their simplicity. The economist dismissed moral and religious impulses, finding in selfishness the driving power of industrial enterprise. The world seemed to be organized in such a way that the capitalist's desire for profit was really the best guarantee that the consumer and the workman would benefit by his activities.[2]

One other circumstance about the place and time of the Industrial Revolution is not without importance. The most famous societies of the past had been made in countries where the physical conditions did not demand a great effort for the maintenance of life. The food and clothing of the Greeks were frugal and simple; the Roman slept naked and wore only a tunic indoors; the legions fought on a diet of spelt. In the English climate the actual needs of life are more exacting, and this, of itself, at a time when a nation was entering on an elaborate economy in which organized production and exchange came to regulate all life, and to make themselves, so to speak, responsible

[2] "The benign and wise Disposer of all things, who obliges men, whether they will or not, in pursuing their own selfish interests, to connect the general good with their own individual success."—Burke, *Thoughts on Scarcity*, Works, Vol. VII, p. 384. Burke went so far as to say that a monopoly of capital was a great benefit, and a benefit particularly to the poor.

for the livelihood of a people, tended to push from men's minds those aspects of civilization that were outside man's immediate necessities. This tendency was encouraged by the calamity that during twenty of these critical years England was engaged in a deadly war, from time to time facing scarcity, fearing famine.

The effect of this concentration is seen in the towns of the age. They were left, like everything else, to the mercy and direction of the spirit of profit. Town planning was not an unknown art; at different times in the world's history it had served the purpose of defence, of religion, of display, of commerce. Rulers with their eyes on the needs of war had planned towns like Stockholm; others, thinking of their personal glory, had planned great reconstructions in Paris or Rome. The English town of this period, which looked like the product of a tired age that had lost its stride, was really the product of an age full of energy, that had no care for order, space or plan. Public beauty seemed to have been banished by the new science. The England of the first industrial age was richer than most ages in painters and poets, but the great achievements of its literature, the galleries of its private mansions, the elegant taste of its aristocracy, all these served to emphasize the significance of the deliberate exclusion of beauty from its common life. The humanism of Shelley, the passion of Byron, the piety of Wordsworth, the imagination of Scott, were all in a sense protests against the industrial spirit; the mind that had any feeling for the large spaces of fancy or of history turned away from it. What there is of beauty in the age belongs either to the lingering charm of an aristocratic culture with its agreeable ease and self-satisfaction, or to the desire to picture a past or future as unlike the present as dreams could make it. All that belongs to the new life of the nation bears a character as unmistakable as the character given to a mediæval town by its handsome buildings. The chimneys of Lancashire represented energy, initiative, ambition: qualities that had given to Manchester the grasp of a larger and richer world than that from which Tyre or Venice, Antwerp or Amsterdam had drawn their lavish wealth. The random and squalid buildings of the new Manchester where 200,000 people lived without a single public garden, were not less eloquent; they spoke for the discredit into which man's life outside this system of production had fallen, the poverty that had stricken the social consciousness of the race.

Mankind did not admire wealth for the first time; but the rich merchant of Bruges, Genoa or Norwich, like the rich Pope or the rich noble of the Middle Ages, or the rich Senator of the Roman Empire, had regarded the beauty and culture of his town as a sign of his own importance and success. Vespasian, frugal as he was, did not hesitate to begin the restoration of the Capitol, though he had inherited a debt of over three hundred million pounds. The private citizen who gave Bordeaux an aqueduct costing £160,000, or the benefactor who spent £80,000 on the walls of Marseilles, the soldier who provided free baths for slave girls at Suessa Senonum, the civic dignitaries who gave temples and theatres, these typical figures of the early Roman Empire would have been astonished to learn that in the districts of South Wales, where men had risen in a few years to such wealth as would have rivalled the wealth of Atticus or Herodes, the poorer classes had to go a mile for water, waiting in a queue a great part of the night; that the chief town of this rich district had neither public lighting nor drainage.

Yet the Industrial Revolution which had given these men their fortunes had made it much easier to supply the needs of the towns that sprang up beside their great establishments. One of the products of that revolution was gas lighting; the Soho Works were lighted with gas in 1802 to celebrate the Peace of Amiens. Great factories at Manchester and Leeds soon followed the example of Boulton and Watt. Another product was the cheap water-pipe. At the end of the American War English ironmasters were exporting water-pipes to Paris and New York. The Romans had no cheap water-pipes made by the help of mechanical power, but they could supply their towns with clean water, whereas the people of Merthyr Tydfil, their streets echoing by day and night with the clamour of forge and furnace, had to drink whatever the river brought them. Augustus' Rome, with its undeveloped mechanical arts, would not have looked more primitive to the Lancashire of Arkwright or Crompton than nineteenth-century Manchester, with its random and formless streets, would have looked to the Rome of Vitruvius, the architect of the first century

B.C. who set the classical tradition, to whom the task of deciding where a town should place its temples, its circus, its forum, its amphitheatre, and how it should organize its water supply and its drainage seemed the most urgent of the tasks of a civilized society. Great wealth has been prized for different reasons at different times. It has been coveted by men who liked power or display, who sought to satisfy the generous impulses of their religion, or to lay to rest its haunting fears. Perhaps the most comprehensive account of the attractions of wealth was that given by a man of religious temperament, who believed himself to have been guided by Providence to the discovery of the new World, and did not foresee the havoc its prizes would play with the finer impulses that had inspired his courage. It occurs in the letters of Columbus.

> "Gold constitutes treasure, and he who possesses it has all he needs in this world, as also the means of rescuing souls from purgatory, and restoring them to the enjoyment of Paradise."

Columbus himself wished this new wealth to be used for another crusade, for the recovery of the Holy Sepulchre, and he spent long hours with the Bible and the early Fathers seeking for light on this project. The eager world of which he was one of the founders would have deplored such dissipation of time and energy. In the new industrial age, more emphatically than in any other, wealth was prized as an end in itself: the rich spinner or the rich ironmaster believed that the way to save your soul was to become richer.

An original and interesting writer, discussing the significance of different types of architecture, remarked that "only what can be got out of life can be put into art." Thus he traced definition and the sense of ideas in Greek art, energy and passion in Gothic art, the recovery of the balance and order of intellectual composure in the art of the Renaissance. The town of the industrial age, without beauty or method, marked the spirit of this age just as truly as St. Paul's Cathedral marked the spirit of the Renaissance, or the cathedral of Durham the spirit of the Crusades. It expressed a concentration in which religion, beauty, leisure, the life of the spirit, or the life of the senses, were all held to be rivals to the stern life of selfish duty. The purpose of man's life was not to fight or to pray, to contemplate or to create, to enjoy or to become, but to make profits, profits for himself, if a master, profits for another, if a servant. This was man's duty, and it was the duty of society to put no obstacle in his way. The Greek view of life, as the expression and exercise of many faculties, has been threatened by the asceticism of the seeker after salvation, and by the asceticism of the seeker after profits; of the cotton spinner, who lived and worked like a slave, and ruled like a slave driver, it was as true as it was of St. Simon Stylites on his pillar that he sacrificed the whole to the part of a man's life. The rage for production had swept England, as the rage for piety had swept the age of the monachists. And production had taken a form that was intensely isolating; the successful man kept his secrets, tried to find his neighbours' secrets, strove for personal gain, took personal risks, made his way by personal initiative and personal enterprise.

This concentration led to the complete neglect of the most urgent of the tasks of the age. In the first twenty years of the nineteenth century the population of Manchester increased from 94,000 to 160,000; of Bolton from 29,000 to 50,000; Leeds more than doubled its population between 1801 and 1831; Bradford, which had 23,000 inhabitants in 1831, grew grass in its streets at the end of the eighteenth century. Oldham, which had 38,000 inhabitants in 1821, had three or four hundred in 1760. In the twenty years from 1801 to 1821 the population of Lancashire grew from 672,000 to 1,052,000; in the next twenty years it grew to 1,701,000. The population of Merthyr increased from 7,700 to 35,000 between 1801 and 1841, and that of the two counties of Glamorgan and Monmouth from 126,000 to 305,000. Industry was accumulating dense masses of people into particular districts, where the workman was shut up in melancholy streets, without gardens or orchards. England was passing from a country to a town life, as she passed from a peasant to an industrial civilization. What this meant is clear if we compare the state of the towns as revealed in the health statistics, with that of the country districts. In 1757 Dr. Percival put the death-rate for Manchester at 1 in 25, for Liverpool at 1 in 27. In Monton, a few miles from

Manchester, the ratio was at that time 1 in 68, at Horwich, between Bolton and Chorley, 1 in 66, at Darwen, three miles from Blackburn, 1 in 56. The Industrial Revolution was to spread the conditions of town life over places like Monton, Horwich and Darwen.

10.

Post-Napoleonic Agitation
for Reform: Peterloo

~

R. J. WHITE

As the summer of 1819 advanced, the political reform movement not only increased in *tempo;* it reverted to the temper, the
tactics, and even the *personnel* of the vigorous and confident days
before the fiasco of the winter of 1816–17. With the removal of
the ban on public meetings, which had had the disastrous effect
of driving agitation into the dark ways of underground conspiracy, meetings were held once more in the open air: sometimes
monster meetings which, it was suspected, were intended to teach
the people "to estimate their own numerical force . . ." Meetings
which had been intended for no political purpose might be
invaded and turned to political ends by the parliamentary reformers. For example, when forty thousand poor weavers met at
Glasgow on June 16th in order to petition the Prince Regent for
passage-money to Canada for the hopelessly unemployed, an
amendment was moved that no good was to be expected from
anything but annual parliaments, universal suffrage and a reduction of taxation. It was carried, after speeches denouncing emigration and petitioning—although it was said that its supporters
knocked down the hands of those who opposed it. At these
meetings, the old "politicals" who had regarded Luddism, hun-

From R. J. White, Waterloo to Peterloo *(New York: The Macmillan Co.,
1957)* ; *Chapter 15, "Peterloo," pp. 179–187. Footnotes omitted.*

ger-marching and the adventures of Jeremiah Brandreth as futile irrelevancies, were now to be observed in their element. Some of them, like Joseph Harrison and Sir Charles Wolseley, were veterans of the nineties. Others, like Samuel Bamford and his friend "Doctor" Healey, the Falstaff of the movement, were the children of Cartwright's Clubs. The Major himself was out and about again, snuffing the fresh breeze from the north with the zest of the old war-horse. And, of course, Orator Hunt, the idol of the open-air meeting, was furbishing up the famous white topper to serve once more as the beacon of reform, from Westminster to Manchester. Other signs and symbols, too, were showing themselves again, after the long winter of Radical discomfiture, notably the Tricolour Banner and the Cap of Liberty. The very name "Radical" came into common use in this year.

More important than the revival of the old paraphernalia was the recourse to the old tactics. Conventions, anti-parliaments, mock-elections, these devices for the discomfiture of the corrupt institution at Westminster had a history that went back to the days of Wilkes and Middlesex, and to the great campaign for Economical Reform in 1780. Nothing, indeed, short of statutory treason itself, was so calculated to affront the susceptibilities of England's governors as the implied challenge to the sovereignty of Parliament which lay in a mock-election. It had been bad enough when, in the winter of 1816–17, the delegates of the Hampden Clubs had assembled at the *Crown and Anchor Tavern*. Now, in 1819, the old game began again, with renewed insolence and even greater menace, at the hands of gentlemen like Sir Charles Wolseley. On June 28th, this gentleman-Radical, of the Burdett tradition, presided at a meeting at Stockport, where, beneath a Cap of Liberty, he swore eternal faith in annual parliaments and universal suffrage. Sir Charles, like Lord Liverpool, had been present at the taking of the Bastille. Unlike Lord Liverpool, he was fond of declaring that this qualified him to take part in the attack on the Bastilles of his native land. When, a fortnight later, this aristocratic fire-brand was elected "Legislative Attorney and Representative of the People of Birmingham", the Government thought the joke—never in very good taste—had gone far enough. Sir Charles was sent to prison for

eighteen months for seditious words uttered at Stockport. Some
ten days later, the *Manchester Observer* printed an advertisement
for a meeting to be held in St. Peter's Fields in that town on
August 9th, for the purpose of adopting Major Cartwright's plan
of parliamentary reform and to elect a "representative" for Manchester. Henry Hunt was billed to play Sir Charles' role at
Manchester.

Such was the inception of the Manchester Meeting, known to
history as "Peterloo". Legend has diminished its singularity at
the behest of outraged feelings, thereby obscuring its significance
in the larger story to which it belongs. Peterloo was no ordinary
meeting of "distressed persons" hounded down by a heartless
magistracy. It was no culmination of a ruthless government's
rough-handling of a long-standing menace from the "mobility".
On the part of the people, it was the culmination of many years
of political education at the hands of the Cartwright-Cobbett-
Hunt group of Radicals: the point at which Parliamentary Reform came of age as a popular programme. On the part of the
governors, it was the death-bed of an outmoded conception of
"The People"—that multitude which, according to Burke, remained when the politically effective half-million (The Public)
had been abstracted: "the rest who, when feeble, are the objects
of protection, when strong, the means of force". At Peterloo, "the
rest" were obviously—frighteningly—"strong", and therefore the
object of force. They were the more strong, and the more alarming, because they were organized. Not until the watching magistrates observed "the beautiful order" of the contingents arriving
at St. Peter's Fields did they feel alarm. They mistook not disor-
ganization, but its opposite, for sedition.

For, after all, the thing was unbelievable. Here were fifty,
perhaps sixty, thousand men and women who belonged, by every
tradition of the older English society, to the vast, politically
excluded world of the workshop and the loom, the coal-seam and
the shovel. They had come dressed in their Sunday clothes, wives
and children included, trooping into Manchester in orderly
array, unarmed and cheerful, at the command of Mr. Hunt who
had required them to bring "no other weapon than that of an
approving conscience". They were peaceable, they were orderly,

and they knew what they wanted. Their banners bore such devices as: UNITY AND STRENGTH, LIBERTY AND FRATERNITY, PARLIAMENTS ANNUAL, SUFFRAGE UNIVERSAL. True, there were Caps of Liberty, in crimson velvet, and "Doctor" Healey's contingent, the Lees and Saddleworth Union, bore a pitch-black banner with staring white words—EQUAL REPRESENTATION OR DEATH; but even this was accompanied by a heart and two clasped hands adorned with the word LOVE. No pains had been spared to show the world that working-class reformers knew how to conduct themselves with order and sobriety. Many of them had spent the summer evenings, for weeks past, out on the moors, learning how to march in rank and wheel in column, at the instruction of old soldiers; a species of rehearsal which had greatly alarmed the authorities. It was intended, as Bamford put it, to disarm criticism "by a display of cleanliness, sobriety and decorum such as we had never before exhibited". To the gentlemen who watched the fruit of all this painstaking preparation, as it showed itself at eleven o'clock on the morning of August 16th, from the high windows of a house overlooking St. Peter's Fields, such "beautiful order" was in itself a symptom of untold menace. They could not know that they were watching the arrival of a new era no less certainly than their brethren of Paris, who, exactly thirty years earlier, had watched the Third Estate walking to Versailles. For them, these marching feet held only the echo of the mob; and the gaily decorated hustings in the middle of St. Peter's Fields gave up the thin, ghostly shadow of a guillotine.

For the greatest demagogue in England was on his way to the heart of this vast assembly. Cheering swelled up from the far side of the Fields, as a barouche appeared, covered with blue and white flags, drawn along by the people. It came through a lane in the crowd, and presently Henry Hunt stepped forth and ascended the hustings, the famous white top hat gleaming in the sunshine, the focal point of fifty thousand pairs of eyes. Then the band played "God save the King", and many of the people took off their hats, in imitation—it is to be hoped—of the white topper. Then Mr. Hunt began to speak.

The lane down which Henry Hunt had come now disappeared. But another lane, long prepared, and leading from the hustings to the house at the corner of Mount Street, remained open. It was lined by special constables, and it was to be used for the purpose of arresting Mr. Hunt, if and when such a proceeding seemed necessary to the watching magistrates. The fact that this decision had been left in abeyance has sometimes been supposed to indicate a certain irresolution on the part of the authorities. Why, if Mr. Hunt's presence was calculated to produce a breach of the peace—and it was upon that ground that his arrest was finally based—did not the magistrates arrest him at once, or—better still—before he could arrive at St. Peter's Fields? These questions were asked at the time, and they have often been asked since, notably by those who contrive to combine criticism of the authorities for their "continental" habits of preventive action with condemnation of those same authorities for not acting upon them. The fact is, however, that the Manchester Meeting was perfectly legal and was concerned with a perfectly respectable purpose. Its sponsors had taken legal advice, after issuing their original advertisement announcing that it would proceed to elect a "representative" for Manchester. They were informed that "the intention of choosing representatives, contrary to existing law, tends greatly to render the proposed meeting seditious". In consequence, the date was postponed to August 16th, and the purpose was declared to be that of considering "the propriety of adopting the most *legal* and *effectual* means of obtaining Reform of the Commons House of Parliament". It would be difficult to imagine a milder or less tendentious expression of a political purpose. As for Mr. Hunt, he could, of course, have been arrested on his way to the meeting if anyone had been prepared to swear an affidavit that his presence there was likely to cause a breach of the peace. Plenty of people could have been found prepared to do this. The Rev. Edward Stanley, a sympathetic observer who watched the whole of the proceedings from a window immediately above the room where the magistrates were stationed, afterwards stated upon his oath that any crowd under the control of Henry Hunt must have been a dangerous crowd. The necessary affidavit was sworn, indeed, and the warrant for Hunt's arrest was ready long before he arrived on the scene. The fact that no attempt was made to arrest him until the proceedings had already begun can only be attributed to the desire of Mr. Hulton and his fellow magistrates to wait and see—as Hulton put it—what the complexion of the meeting might be: a peculiarly English attitude on the part of the representatives of a peculiarly English government, who fully shared the dislike of the Prime Minister himself for "coming to extremes".

The fact is that the magistrates at Peterloo were precisely those "gentlemen of the parish" in whom Lord Liverpool—even against the advice of less complacent friends, like Lord Grenville—delighted to put his trust. Three months after Peterloo, the Prime Minister was still content to limit public meetings to "parochial meetings" which, he predicted, "would generally be flat", and where "the gentlemen who live in the parish would have influence enough to check those with whom they are so intimately connected and whose actions in this respect could not be concealed from them". Lord Grenville was willing to agree that this might do for the country, but he inquired rather pertinently: "How will it apply to the metropolis and the great towns which are at present the chief seat of this evil? The real inhabitants of a single parish may amount to many thousands or tens of thousands, and are so little known to each other that no person could discriminate. . . ." In fact, Grenville pointed out, the existing system of peace-keeping was "originally adapted to a state of our society to which the present bears no resemblance". It would be rash, indeed, to assume that Mr. Hulton and his colleagues at Peterloo had ever seen one man in a thousand of those who assembled in St. Peter's Fields. As for the peace-keeping machinery of the town of Manchester, it was a feudal relic: it consisted of a Court Leet, a Deputy Constable, and reeves. It possessed no regular police-force. The forces available on this occasion, for dealing with a crowd of some fifty or sixty thousand people, were the special constables who now formed a ring round the hustings and a lane from the hustings to the house where the magistrates sat, and a body of local civilians dressed in regimentals and known as "The Manchester and Salford Yeomanry". In reserve and out of sight, like a secret confession of the absurdity of the situation, there were standing by six troops of the 15th Hussars, nearly the whole of the 31st Regiment, several companies of the 88th, and a troop of Horse Artillery: the whole under the command of Colonel Guy L'Estrange. As usual, in Regency England, the regular forces of the Crown were likely to be called upon to perform the duties of a police force.

It would have been better for everyone concerned if the magistrates had placed the duty of arresting Mr. Hunt and dispersing the crowd, once these measures had been decided upon, in the hands of the regular troops. Correct formation and skilful handling of horses will suffice to break up any unarmed assembly without the use of sabres and with the minimum of bodily injury. It may be assumed that the 15th Hussars, who were wearing their Waterloo medals, were not thirsting for the blood of the unarmed weavers of Lancashire, their wives and their children. The straight-forward, humane and manly account of their behaviour which has been handed down to us by one of their officers, Lieutenant Jolliffe, would alone serve as good evidence for that. But the 15th Hussars were not called upon until a tragic overture had been performed by the Manchester and Salford Yeomanry. "The stupid boobies of yeomanry cavalry," the *Manchester Observer* called them, "fawning dependents of the great, with a few fools and a greater proportion of coxcombs, who imagine they acquire considerable importance by wearing regimentals." Perhaps there was always something a trifle ridiculous about the Yeomanry. It really depended upon who composed it. On the one hand, there were the gentlemen and farmers of the Home Counties, where Lords Sidmouth and Liverpool had led respectable levies in the nineties, and where Edward Gibbon claimed to have learnt something of the discipline of the Legions. On the other hand, there were the small masters, inn-keepers and tradesmen of Manchester: the butcher, the baker and the candlestick-maker on horseback. The Manchester and Salford Yeomanry consisted almost exclusively of cheesemongers, ironmongers and newly enriched manufacturers, and the people of Manchester and district thought them a joke, and a not very good joke. It was to their very great disadvantage that they were on their native heath, the only people in all that populous scene who really belonged to the place and to whom the place belonged. They were defending their own property. Unfortunately, they had not properly learnt how to control their horses.

It was upon these gentlemen that the magistrates called for assistance when Deputy Constable Nadin protested that he was unable to execute the warrant for the arrest of Mr. Hunt without military assistance. They came charging into the Field, knocking down a woman and killing her child on the way, and when they appeared Mr. Hunt pointed at them and said something which "excited a shout from those immediately about him, which was re-echoed with fearful animation by the rest of the multitude." Halting in disorder, they then proceeded to advance into the crowd, converging upon the hustings. The crowd stood fast. There was little opportunity for flight in that densely packed multitude. For a moment it looked as if the people were to triumph by their very physical inability to retreat. However, some of the Yeomanry reached the hustings, and Mr. Hunt was hustled along the lane of special constables to the magistrates' house. Then it became apparent to the watching magistrates that the Yeomanry were stuck. There they sat, stranded on their horses, all over the Field, hemmed in by the jeering, pressing crowd, unable either to advance or to retire, and no doubt looking extremely foolish.

It was at this point that the 15th Hussars were summoned to the scene. Here is Lieutenant Jolliffe's description of what he saw:

"It was then for the first time that I saw the Manchester troop of Yeomanry; they were scattered singly or in small groups over the greater part of the Field, literally hemmed up and hedged into the mob so that they were powerless either to make an impression or to escape; in fact, they were in the power of those whom they were designed to overawe, and it required only a glance to discover their helpless position, and the necessity of our being brought to their rescue."

Jolliffe thought the Manchester Yeomanry, "and the manner in which they were made use of (to say the least) greatly aggravated the disasters of the day". They lacked the knowledge of a trained military body, and "they were placed, most unwisely, as it appeared, under the immediate command and order of the civil authority".

Colonel Guy L'Estrange, halting his Hussars on the edge of this ludicrous scene, looked up to the magistrates' window for his orders.

"Good God, sir," Mr. Hulton called down to the Colonel, "do you not see how they are attacking the Yeomanry? Disperse the crowd."

The Hussars advanced with drawn swords, and Mr. Hulton turned away from the window because he "would rather not see any advance of the military".

The Hussars, Lieutenant Jolliffe records, drove the people forward with the flat of their swords: "but sometimes, as is almost inevitably the case when men are placed in such situations, the edge was used." He also asserts that

"although nine out of ten of the sabre wounds were caused by the Hussars, it redounds to the humane forebearance of the men of the 15th that more wounds were not received, when the vast numbers are taken into consideration with whom they were brought into hostile collision; beyond all doubt, however, the far greater amount of injuries were from the pressure of the routed multitude".

It was all over in a few minutes. The crowd was fleeing along the streets towards the open country, and St. Peter's Fields was littered with hats, bonnets, shawls, shoes, musical instruments, and the bodies of the dead and injured. In the midst stood the hustings with its broken flag-staffs and tattered banners. A group of Yeomanry loosened their horses' girths, adjusted their accoutrements, and wiped their sabres. Over all, the hot August sunshine filtered down through a cloud of dust. It was a battle-field. It was Peterloo.

11.

The Poaching War

~

E. W. BOVILL

The unhappy but short-lived consequences that flowed from
the invention of the threshing-machine paled before the long-
drawn misery that the invention of the flint-lock gun brought to
rural England. For more than half a century much of the countryside was wracked by a bitter war, costly in human life and
happiness, provoked by the sporting gun having given to wild
game an importance it had not known before. There is no greater
proof of the stability of the social structure of the English countryside than its having survived unscathed a merciless struggle in
which an infinitesimal privileged minority fought to retain an
exclusive right to what the whole of the rest of the community
were convinced was a gift from God to be enjoyed by all.

'The great business of life, in the country,' wrote Cobbett,
'appertains, in some way or other, to the *game* . . . and, as to the
anger, the satisfaction, the scolding, the commendation, the cha-
grin, the exultation, the envy, the emulation, when are there any
of these in the country, unconnected with *the* game?' That, one
of the very few understatements that ever came from Cobbett's
uncurbed and venomous pen, was written in 1825. It would have
been equally true over half a century before that.

Under an Act of 1671 the killing of game was prohibited, in

From E. W. Bovill, English Country Life, 1780-1830 (London: Oxford
University Press, 1962); Chapter 12, "The Poaching War," pp. 174-183,
191-196. Selected footnotes renumbered.

general terms, to all except owners of land worth £100 a year,[1] lessees of land worth £150 a year, the eldest sons of esquires or of persons of higher degree, and the owners of franchises. A curious anomaly was that if an esquire or a person of higher degree had not the necessary qualifications to kill game, his eldest son was not debarred from doing so. Another was that although a lord of a manor might grant the right to kill game to his gamekeeper, he might not do so to his younger sons. This led to younger sons sometimes engaging themselves as keepers in order to secure the right to shoot. Thus owners of only a few acres could not enjoy the game their fields harboured, and which destroyed their crops, unless they could persuade a qualified neighbour to shoot it for them. In practice qualified neighbours usually treated the small man's game as if it were their own, to be shot and disposed of as they chose. The small man had his remedy in an action for trespass, but it was one he seldom dared to use.

The sale of game was altogether prohibited, and any unqualified person found in possession of it was liable to a fine of £5 per head of game. Rabbits, woodcock, snipe, quails, and landrails, however, although they had the legal status of game so far as shooting was concerned, might be sold. The occupier of land might kill the rabbits on it, but the law forbade him to lift a finger against the hares which, in those days of few rabbits and many hares, did far greater damage. The penalty for taking or wilfully destroying pheasant and partridge eggs was £1 for each egg. No unqualified person might own a sporting dog, including greyhound and lurcher (farmers sometimes got round this restriction by cutting off a lurcher's tail and passing him off as a sheepdog), nor might he take with him any sort of dog when he was accompanying a qualified friend out shooting. A servant might 'beat bushes etc. for his master', and so might a stockbroker, attorney, surgeon, 'or other inferior person' if invited to do so by a qualified sportsman, but they might not take part in the actual killing of game. Such, in brief outline, was the penal

---

[1] *The Black Book* of 1831 pertinently noted that fifty times more property was required to enable a person to kill a partridge than to vote for a knight of the shire or, as someone else pointed out, to qualify him as a juror to kill a man.

code which sought to preserve for the privileged few the game of the countryside.

An early advocate for the reform of the Game Laws pointed out in *The Farmer's Magazine* of 1800 that as they stood they failed altogether in their object. 'In fact, since all these laws', he wrote, 'instead of preserving the game for the rightful owner, have been fabricated in the genuine spirit of a grasping monopoly, the present property in the game is completely vested in the hands of the nocturnal poacher, who has, in most manors, even the *undisputed* possession: Indeed it is a necessary consequence of all unjust laws, to create the very thing they are intended to prevent.'

With the killing of game so closely restricted and its sale prohibited, game could legally come to the table only as a gift from the few the law permitted to shoot it. This gave it a high prestige value which greatly enhanced its price in the black market. In the shooting season no dinner party with any pretensions to smartness was complete without a game course. None was more aware of this than the *nouveaux riches* whose inability to acquire game legally was matched by their determination to appear as if they could. They got it with what came to be called the silver gun, by paying for it. 'A waddling fat fellow', wrote Cobbett, 'that does not know how to prime and load, will in this way, beat the best shot in the country.' The same silver gun placed game on the menu of every good eating-house in London.

These were the circumstances in which the farming community became resentfully opposed to shooting, and poaching first became a serious menace to rural peace.

The bitter hostility of farmers to game preservation, for bitter it soon became, was not entirely due to the unjust and discriminating Game Laws. A contributory cause was the value which their landlords attached to hedgerows as covert for game. Many landlords forbade the cutting and trimming of hedges more than once in seven years; some went so far as to prohibit them altogether. At the same time that the hedgerow was finding increasing favour with the landlord it was falling into greater disrepute with his tenants. To begin with the hedgerows of the Enclosure Acts had been too small to interfere with agriculture; they occu-

pied little ground and were too low to shade crops. As they grew
to maturity, spreading far out at the base and towering high
above the crops, farmers began to resent having to pay rent for so
large an area of unproductive and often harmful land. When,
with the new craze for shooting and game preservation, they were
required to leave the hedges alone in the interests of the hares
that ate their crops but which they might not kill, their resentment became bitter, and many a poacher found stout allies
among them.

One of the first to realize that the unjust Game Laws were
defeating their own ends by antagonizing the farmers and encouraging the poachers was Joseph Chitty who, in 1770, wrote:
'Those vagabonds are rather encouraged than prevented by the
present Laws: For if the Farmers who live upon the lands, and
visit their fields every day, are not allowed to sport themselves, or
to be game-keepers of their own farms, or licensed to kill Game
upon them, for their own use; they will either destroy the Game
out of resentment, or allow the poacher to do it for them; neither
will their servants prevent, or inform against a Poacher, who can
perhaps afford to make them a small present, which most of them
would accept of, rather than a share of a large fine, accompanied
with the detested name of an informer. . . . Many farmers have
told me . . . that they would allow their Dogs to destroy every
Hare, and every Bird in the breeding time, which is certainly in
their power. . . . Others have acknowledged that they often had
entertained Poachers in their houses, and in return for the hospi-
tality, have had a Hare, or a brace of Birds, to send to a friend in
town.' Joseph Chitty, it was clear, saw that the surest way to
protect game was to secure the good will of the farmers by
granting them some right to the game on their land. But nobody
liked the idea of 'a new legion of Nimrods . . . in the farmers
and their sons'. It took over sixty years for Chitty's view to win
sufficient support to secure the abolition of the archaic restrictions on the killing of game.

In the meanwhile the trend was markedly away from any
relaxation of the restrictions. As shooting gained in popularity so
did the demand for more repressive legislation. As prices in the

black market rose so did poaching increase. Clearly game must be given greater protection than the laws of Charles II afforded, and during the reign of George III thirty-two new Game Laws were passed.

Landowners endeavoured to curb the poachers by employing more keepers and watchers, which forced the poachers to confine their raids to hours of darkness. This was countered by the passing of an Act in 1770 under which anyone convicted of poaching between sunset and sunrise was to be punished with imprisonment up to six months; for a second offence the punishment was doubled with a public whipping added. This had little deterrent effect and two years later William Taplin, following Chitty's example, began advocating the relaxation of restrictions. 'Till the present Act is repealed', he wrote, 'there will be almost double the Quantity killed yearly, more than there would be were there no restraint, and every Person had an unlimited power to kill. . . . It is most certain if there were more Shooters, there would be more Birds. . . . I have in the Sporting Season, visited many Farmers, and never saw one that could not take me into his Pantry, and produce a Hare or more, and two or three Brace of Birds.' Taplin also perceived that the worst of all poachers were the gamekeepers themselves. Those who, he truly said, 'are known by all but their Employers to be the greatest Poachers, are the *pretended Preservers* Deputies, called game-keepers. . . . The extensive Game Trade that is carried on by these plush-coated, black-capp'd Gentry with the Road Waggoners, would, to those unacquainted with it, surpass Belief.' He knew of one waggoner who had bought in a small Hampshire inn as many as twenty-one hares at a time from a gamekeeper for half-a-crown apiece and sold them for 3*s.* 6*d.* each to a London poulterer. So long as keepers were paid only £20 a year, more keepers meant less game.

The blind confidence of the landowners in the integrity of their servants seems to have continued, for in 1802 W. B. Daniel, writing in much the same sense as Taplin, said that game poached by keepers 'readily finds its way to market, through the medium of the *Coachmen* and *Guards* to *Mail* and other coaches;

(the *Higlers*[2] generally deal with the Poachers themselves). The Gentlemen, in conjunction with the *Porters* of the different inns where they arrive at, carry on almost a *public traffic* in this article of Game, and at prices which render it astonishing how *purchasers* are to be met with, viz. *four* and *five* shillings (and sometimes as high as *eight*,) a brace for *Partridges; twelve* to *sixteen* for Pheasants, and from *five* to *seven shillings and six pence* for a Hare.'

Before the end of the previous century rising prices and the employment of more keepers and watchers had combined to bring about an alarming change in the poaching business. Poachers had begun forming themselves into gangs, the better to deal with the keepers, and were taking much greater risks. In 1781 a gang, eleven strong, raided the Duke of Cumberland's coverts in Windsor Park, and shot two keepers, but, on running out of ammunition, were pursued and taken by the Duke's servants armed with cutlasses. A few years later, in 1795, in an affray in the Bishop of Winchester's park at Farnham Castle, one of his servants was killed, but his keeper 'then fired his remaining barrel, which was loaded with ball, and killed one of them'. Gangs such as these were becoming a terror to the countryside and leading to grave disturbances of the peace. In 1800 Parliament sought to stop them by passing an Act by which if two or more persons were found poaching together they were to be treated as rogues and vagabonds and punished with hard labour; for a second offence they were to be treated as incorrigible rogues, imprisoned and whipped, or alternatively they could be made to serve in the army of navy. The severer penalties, far from achieving their object, only encouraged resistance to arrest and the formation of bigger and more determined gangs. So in 1803 Parliament passed the Ellenborough Act by which anyone who offered armed resistance to lawful arrest was to be hanged as a felon. This terrible Act seems to have served its purpose, but only for a time.

The control of poaching was made especially difficult by the conviction of most country people that there was nothing morally

[2] Higglers were dealers who travelled round the country, from farm to farm, buying poultry and eggs.

wrong in it. 'It is utterly impossible to teach the common people', wrote Sydney Smith, 'to respect property in animals bred the possessor knows not where—which he cannot recognise by any mark, which may leave him the next moment, which are kept, not for his profit, but for his amusement. . . . It is in vain to increase the severity of the protecting laws. They make the case weaker, instead of stronger; and are more resisted and worse executed, exactly in proportion as they are contrary to public opinion.' 'The same man who would respect an orchard, a garden, or a hen-roost', he wrote on another occasion, 'scarcely thinks he is committing any fault at all in invading the game covers of his richer neighbour.' In consequence no one had 'the slightest shame at violating a law which everybody feels to be absurd and unjust'. Moreover, they would protest, it was contrary to the teaching of Holy Writ. 'A wonderful lot of working men', said an old labourer, dictating his autobiography to Eleanor Eden, 'don't believe as there's any harm in poaching. We never read that in the Testament, nor yet in the Bible. We always read there, that the wild birds is sent for the poor man as well as the quality.'

That attitude of mind, which still sometimes persists, has always ensured to the habitual poacher more sympathy than a common thief would be accorded. Among the educated the poacher has often also enjoyed the respect that love of sport commands. 'Some are incorrigible poachers', wrote Howitt, 'from the love of the pursuit of wild creatures, of strolling about in solitary glens and woods, of night-watching, and adventure.' The man who insists on indulging his love of sport, and of wandering at will over the countryside, in defiance of the law, is often regarded by those who know him least as a romantic and engaging character. Alas, he usually, but not always, proves to be the least estimable character in the parish, the ne'er-do-well of the village who has taken to poaching in preference to honest toil, and who spends his money in the pub rather than on the home. Moreover, poaching has unfortunately far too often led to a career of crime extending far beyond the illicit killing of game.

Only by bearing this in mind can we understand the bitterness with which poachers were execrated a century and a half ago.

Surtees described them as 'the very scum and scourings of the
country, men whose least crime is that of poaching'. Surtees,
though eminently fair-minded and not a shooting man, was a
squire and therefore his testimony is suspect. But Sydney Smith,
who railed against the injustice of the Game Laws and the
selfishness of the gentry, confirmed every word that Surtees wrote.
The poacher, he wrote, 'proceeds from one infringement of law
and property to another, till he becomes a thoroughly bad and
corrupted member of society'.

   Nevertheless, the greatest disservice poaching did the country
was the corrupting of so many honest men. It was too easy and
too profitable. 'What we say in regard to poaching', declared
Eleanor Eden's friend, 'is this: "Poachers' money, it ain't worth
fourpence a bushel; it comes light and it goes light." ' But he had
one friend who turned it to good account. With a stool as the
only bit of furniture in their house and nothing but straw to lie
on, this man and his wife decided to invest all the cash they had,
four pennies, in poaching. He bought 'four-penn'orth of wire,
and set off a-poaching, and he done very well. He soon laid £5 on
one side, for fear he might get ketched, and in a few years he had
got £40 worth of household goods in his house.' Another observer, of a slightly earlier period, noted that 'where wastes and
commons are most extensive, there I have perceived the Cottagers
are the most wretched and worthless . . . for cottagers of this
description the game is preserved, and by them destroyed; they
are mostly beneath the law and out of reach of detection; and
while they can earn four or five shillings, and sometimes more, in
a night, by poaching they will not be satisfied with 10d., or 1s. a
day for honest labour.' 'The village poacher', wrote W. H. Hud-
son, 'as a rule is an idle, dissolute fellow.'

   The conclusion that the habitual country poachers were nearly
always drawn from the lowest ranks of village life is inescapable.
Many of them, corrupted by easy money, had become, as Sydney
Smith said, 'thoroughly bad and corrupted members of society'.
Closely associated with them, and perhaps often the major partners in their trade, were many desperate men from London and
other towns, mostly fugitives from justice, who had been attracted into poaching by the large profits it yielded and the

comparative security of life in the open country from the arm of the law. Thus, through the creation of a black market for game by archaic and absurdly restrictive laws, had poaching become the refuge and main support of a large part of the criminal classes.

When the Napoleonic wars ended and rural England was plunged into the misery of an acute agricultural depression, with half the farm workers dependent on parish relief on which it was often impossible for married men to live, the savage Ellenborough Act began to lose some of its terrors. For many a labourer poaching became the only means of keeping alive a starving family. Poachers multiplied, and the gangs became more desperate. In the early days of 1816 one of Lord Fitzhardinge's keepers was 'killed by a gang of miscreants, who', according to a contemporary chronicler, 'with blackened faces, and armed with guns, had taken an oath, administered by one of them . . . not to 'peach on each other. Scarcely ever did any criminal trial excite more interest. . . . Eleven young men . . . led on, in the unlawful pursuit of game, to the destruction of human life, and consequently making their own lives dependent on the decision of a court of justice, could not fail to create an interest of the highest degree in the feelings of the public.' All were found guilty, but only two were hanged. In the same year poaching convictions more than doubled.

Clearly an even greater deterrent was required than the Ellenborough Act. Therefore in 1817 Parliament passed an Act, almost without debate, under which anyone poaching at night with no more than a net was to be transported for seven years even if he were unarmed. From the moment of the passing of that Act the long-drawn poaching war assumed a bitterness it had never known before. This was because, as we saw in an earlier chapter, transportation, for no matter how short a term, was virtually a life sentence because return from Australia was impossible for all but a very few. It was the terror of transportation, the parting for ever from wife and children and all that made a hard life endurable, that drove the poacher to risk his life by resisting arrest. 'The preposterous punishment of transportation', wrote Sydney Smith, 'makes him desperate, not timid. Single poachers are gathered into large companies, for their mutual protection; and go out, not only with the intention of taking game, but of defending that they take with their lives.' It was a theme to which he returned a few months later: 'If the question concerned the payment of five pounds, a poacher would hardly risk his life rather than be taken; but when he is to go to Botany Bay for seven years, he summons together his brother poachers—they get brave from rum, numbers, and despair—and a bloody battle ensues.'

In the poacher's eyes the gallows were only slightly more terrible than transportation. This explains the fierce resentment the new Act provoked, but it only partly explains the tragic tale of murders and hangings that followed. These were largely due to the enforcement of the Game Laws depending on the corrupting influence of informers. Not only was the informer offered a substantial reward but he was also 'entitled to it, even though he should have been an accomplice, and will, by *turning evidence, escape* all *penalties*'. Now that poachers had been forced to work in gangs, so great an inducement to treachery as escape from gallows or transportation added immeasurably to the fierce resentment the new Act provoked. Its 'first and most palpable effect', wrote someone in 1818, 'has naturally been an exaltation of all the savage and desperate features in the poacher's character. . . . A marauder may hesitate perhaps at killing his fellow-man, when the alternative is only six months' imprisonment in the county gaol; but when the alternative is to overcome the keeper, or to be torn from his family and connections, and sent to hard labour at the Antipodes, we cannot be much surprised that murders and midnight combats have considerably increased this season.'

At about the same time a Bath newspaper quoted an anonymous letter, which was being circulated amongst local landowners, reading: 'We have lately heard and seen that there is an act passed, and whatever poacher is caught destroying the game, is to be transported for seven years—*This is English Liberty.*'. . .

Poaching could not have been carried on in the face of so many difficulties and on so large a scale without assured facilities for getting it to market, which usually meant Leadenhall Market, and for selling it at high prices. Leadenhall Market was supplied through two channels. The more important was the coachmen and guards of the mail and stage coaches—hence the greater prevalence of poaching on the main trunk roads. 'Almost any poulterer, waiter or book-keeper of the different coach and waggon inns', wrote Daniel at the beginning of the century, 'can give ample information where game of any kind can be procured with one hand provided money is carried in the other.' The innkeepers on the main roads, who of necessity had to keep on good terms with the coaches, provided a ready market for anything the local poachers had to offer.

The other source of supply, especially from districts off the coach routes, was the higglers, who travelled round the country buying poultry and eggs. In the season they probably handled game more readily than their legitimate trade, for it was more profitable. In 1802 it was recorded that two of these higglers 'in *two* seasons shared upwards of *fifteen hundred* pounds (after deducting all expenses) for Game purchased at very inferior prices from the *Poachers,* who caught it in the country, by forwarding and selling it to the London Poulterers, who again supply the taverns, coffee-houses, & where it is a regular article in the bill of fare'. The higglers arranged with the poachers where game was to be left, to be picked up on their rounds. They fed the London market from as far afield as Scotland, forwarding the game in the same packages as their poultry. As the result of hot competition from the coaches the higglers found it necessary to associate themselves more closely with poachers. In 1812 Daniel wrote that the illicit game trade had become so profitable 'that there now exists in several Places, an *Association* of *Poachers,* and the *Abettors* of them, who are ready to advance Money, for the Purpose of paying Penalties, or otherwise assisting any of the suffering *Brethren*'. The higglers were also doing a good trade with dishonest gamekeepers who, once in their clutches, found escape very difficult, for, as Daniel said, 'the Gamekeeper (after having sold them one Partridge) is placed, with *these Purveyors* of Game, in the same predicament as a Revenue-Officer after having once touched a bribe from a Smuggler; both are completely in the power of the *buyer* and *briber,* and must proceed, under the dread of being reported to their different employers if they hesitate or refuse'.

Leadenhall Market, besides being the centre of the trade in dead and live pheasants, was also that of the trade in the eggs of both partridges and pheasants of which, with the growing popularity of shooting and the clamorous demand for bigger bags, game preservers, to their own undoing, were avid buyers. Many a landowner stocked his shoot with birds and eggs stolen from his own ground. The prices game eggs fetched in London in 1822 reflect the comparative scarcity of pheasants and the abundance of partridges. Pheasant eggs were 8s. a dozen against 2s. for partridge eggs.

Parliament sought to curb the illicit game trade, which was carried on as freely as if the laws against it did not exist, by making the purchase of game also illegal, and subject to the same penalties as its sale, but, of course, to no effect. The trade was quite unaffected. Sydney Smith saw the futility of all such legislation and was convinced, as William Taplin had been in the previous century, that the remedy was to legalize the sale of game. 'The foundation on which the propriety of allowing this partly rests', he wrote, 'is the impossibility of preventing it. There exists, and has sprung up since the Game Laws, an enormous mass of wealth, which has nothing to do with land. Do the country gentlemen imagine, that it is in the power of human laws to deprive the Three-per-cents of pheasants?—that there is upon earth, air, or sea, a single flavour (cost what crime it may to procure it), that mercantile opulence will not procure? Increase the difficulty, and you enlist vanity on the side of luxury; and make that be sought for as a display of wealth, which was before valued only for the gratification of appetite. The law may multiply penalties by reams. Squires may fret and justices commit, and gamekeepers and poachers continue their nocturnal wars. There must be game on Lord Mayor's day, do what you will. You may multiply the crimes by which it is procured; but nothing can arrest its inevitable progress from the wood of the esquire to the spit of the citizen.'

The humble countryman's deep conviction that there was morally nothing wrong in stealing the rich man's game naturally

influenced the attitude of the higglers and poulterers. Respectable London tradesmen who would never have wittingly touched
stolen goods felt no pang of conscience in regularly dealing in
game. In 1823 a Committee of the House of Commons on the
Game Laws reported that no poulterer could afford not to deal in
game because if he did not he would lose all his regular custom-
ers for poultry. It was also virtually impossible to prosecute a
poulterer for he had only to report an unpopular customer, a
higgler with whom he had quarrelled, a keeper who had let him
down, or even one of his competitors, for some breach of the
Game Laws to secure the informer's reward, a part of the fine,
and the acquittal of himself.

No one who bought or sold game was ever safe from black-
mail. One Christmas the ingenious wife of a well-known Penrith
poacher called on the townspeople her husband was in the habit
of supplying with game, and told them that he had been caught
and fined, but if each of them would contribute 5s. he would be
able to pay the fine 'without his being under the necessity of
informing against them'. The story that her husband had been
caught was a lie.

The report of the Commons Committee emphasized the immense scale of this illicit traffic. One of the smaller London
poulterers, asked the quantity of game he handled a year, answered 'perhaps 10,000 head; mine is a limited trade . . . I only
supply private families'. Asked whether he could obtain a thousand pheasants a week if he had an order for them, he said he
could get 10,000 a week if he wanted to, and he explained how he
would set about it. 'I should, of course, request the persons with
whom I am in the habit of dealing, to use their influence to bring
me what they could by a certain day; I should speak to the
dealers and the mail-guards, and coachmen, to produce a quantity; and I should send to my own connections in one or two
manors where I have the privilege of selling for those gentlemen.
. . . Being but a petty salesman, I sell a very small quantity; but I
have had about 4,000 direct from one man'. *The Black Book*
gives one explanation of this dealer's sinister reference to his
'privilege of selling' for certain gentlemen. After pointing out
that 'the poor labourer, mason, or weaver, who imperilled his

life, his limbs, and his health, in the covert attempt to catch a hare or partridge, could not possibly be adequate to support a commerce like this', with waggon loads of game pouring into London, the report continues: 'No, it was not done by poaching exactly; the *wholesale* dealers are the lawmakers themselves— those who had interdicted the traffic—NOBLE LORDS and MEN OF TITLE, who had condescended to supply the London poulterers and salesmen with game, on commission, as a means of augmenting their territorial revenues.'

The illicit sale or bartering of game by owners of shoots had long been carried on. A writer to *The Sporting Magazine* in 1804 inquired: 'What shall we say of those who send venison, hares, pheasants, partridges, and all other game to their poulterer in London, to receive an equivalent in poultry and fish in winter, when they are in town. Though these sportsmen do not truck their commodities for money, they are nothing less than higlers, hucksters, dealers, and chapmen, in the proper sense of the words; for an exchange was never denied to be a sale, although it is affirmed to be no robbery?'

It is not surprising to learn that at times there was such a glut of game that the surplus was 'either thrown away or disposed of by Irish hawkers to the common people at very inferior prices'. In 1823 there was one of these gluts, with pheasants retailing at 7*s*. a brace, and partridges at not more than half-a-crown. But the normal prices are not easy to determine. In 1817 the poacher had got 7*s*. a brace for pheasants, for which the London poulterer paid 15*s*. and the consumer two guineas. It is improbable that such high prices returned after the slump of 1823, but they were attractive enough for poaching to continue to flourish and expand.

Parliament was at last beginning to find that the Game Laws, far from checking poaching, were in fact encouraging it by their very severity. So strong had public hatred of these laws become, so convinced was everyone that they were absurd and unjust, such odium attached to anyone who aided their enforcement, that even common informers, 'too well aware of the coldness of pump and pond', were refusing to come forward. Juries, wiser and more humane than Parliament, were countering the savagery of the laws by refusing to convict. Thus were the Lords and Commons at last compelled at least to consider a new approach to the problem and a reform of the Game Laws. The proposals, which had been urged on Parliament for long years past, and which till now it would not even consider, were three: The abolition of the qualifications which restricted the killing of game to a privileged few; the making of game the property of the owner of the land on which it was found; and the legalizing of the sale and purchase of game.

These proposals were widely debated, in and out of Parliament, for many months during which hardly any objection to them was raised that does not today seem ridiculous. The general feeling was that such revolutionary measures would quickly result in the total destruction of game throughout the country, 'and if there is no game, there will be no country gentlemen'. To legalize the sale of game would inevitably provoke a price-cutting war between gentry and poachers without any certainty that the former would win. Lord Londonderry particularly disliked the idea because 'it would deprive the sportsman of his highest gratification—the pleasure of furnishing his friends with presents of game: nobody would care for a present which every body could give'.

Meanwhile, the dreadful war continued. In June 1829, when rural England was sunk in the misery that culminated in the Swing Riots, there were ninety-six prisoners for trial in Bedford gaol of whom, wrote Potter MacQueen to Lord Grey, 'seventy-six were able-bodied men in the prime of life, and chiefly of general good character, who were driven to crime by sheer want, and who would have been valuable subjects, had they been placed in a situation, where by the exercise of their health and strength they could have earned a subsistence. There were in this number eighteen poachers, awaiting trial for the capital offence of using arms in self-defence, when attacked by gamekeepers; of these eighteen men, one only was not a parish pauper, he was the agent of the London poulterers, who, passing under the apparent vocation of a rat catcher, paid these poor creatures more in one night than they could obtain from the overseer for a whole week's labour.' These poachers included two brothers. One, aged twenty-eight, had a pregnant wife and two children, but could not get work; he was, he said, 'allowed 7s. a week for all; I was expected to work on the roads from light to dark, and to pay £3–3–0 a year for the hovel that sheltered us'. His brother, aged twenty-two and unmarried, received 6d. a day. Both were hanged.

At last, in 1831, when nearly one sixth of the total number of convictions in the country were for offences against the Game Laws, the archaic qualifications were abolished and the sale and purchase of game were made legal.

12.

The Regency Style

~

DONALD PILCHER

The "Man of Taste" might well congratulate himself as he saw the Regency house beginning to take shape in conformity with his theories. For, quite apart from its aesthetic merits, it was, as a pleasant and workable "home," something far in advance of the standards set by its Georgian predecessor. For this achievement he may be allowed to take much of the credit. He should certainly not be allowed to take it all. Quite as much is due to the technician, whose conscientious study of materials and building technique contributed almost as much towards the Regency Style as did the theories of the "Man of Taste."

Regency architecture is, more than anything, the product of these, often conflicting, influences. In it theory had to be reconciled with practice, taste with technique. The tax on windows and the glimpse of a Picturesque prospect were considerations of almost equal weight in determining the form of the house. The repeal of the Laws of Apprenticeship had almost as far-reaching an effect on its decoration as Denon's travels in Egypt or Daniell's in India. Sometimes practical considerations even suggested the direction in which taste was to develop. An instance of this is the design of balconies in town houses. At one time a law forbidding their projection over the pavement threatened to eliminate balco-

From Donald Pilcher, The Regency Style, 1800 to 1830 *(London: B. T. Batsford Ltd., 1947); Chapter 3, "Taste and Technique," pp. 47–50, and Chapter 5, "Town and Countryside," pp. 85–86, 91–92. Footnotes omitted.*

nies altogether in the town house. They were, however, generally permitted by local surveyors on condition that they were designed with a sufficient appearance of lightness, and this necessity became the mother of Regency architects' inventiveness in devising light decorative balcony forms.

There was one practical consideration above all which affected the trend of contemporary taste. It was one which was implicit in the early nineteenth-century background of England's rapid commercial expansion, and, as an influence on architectural appearances, it took the form of a changeover from craftsmanship to factory production. For industry was not only producing new building materials. It was also producing them in a new way, which, whether they liked it or not, architects had to take some account of. Architects whose traditions of practice had been built up on the limited range of materials available were now faced with the use of new materials, with no traditional precedent for applying them. For these were materials whose final appearance was no longer decided by the individual touch of a craftsman, but by the standardising stamp of the machine. How was this new factor of "mass-production" to be reconciled with the canons of contemporary "Taste"? This was one of the most important of the questions which contemporary conditions forced the Regency architect to answer.

To the majority of them the reply seemed obvious enough. The machine was a heaven-sent answer to the demand for taste. It was not only sent so that they might have taste, but that they might have it more abundantly. By means of it, "works of the most refined and delicate character, which, executed in the usual expensive materials, could have exercised a refining influence over the minds of the few only, have been, and may be, so generally disseminated, as to enter into the household existence and daily associations of the larger portion of the educated community." Such at least was the opinion of the manufacturers of "Jackson's Papier Mâché Ornaments," whose pattern books show a typical use of machinery to imitate the craftsman's ornament. But more important even than the "general dissemination" of taste which these products made possible was their ability to do so cheaply. As Jackson's pattern book points out, they were

". . . ready for immediate application at a defined and economical cost, which the tedious process of designing and modelling
prevents, as well as the great saving of time that results from
employing those products that are ready, or that can be supplied
at a speed equal to any requirement."

These were arguments which were particularly telling at a time
when skilled labour was hard to come by owing to the increasing
number of men employed on government work, such as barrack
building, and when war conditions had sent the cost of building
materials soaring. As a means of eliminating "the tedious process
of designing and modelling" these materials were therefore welcomed, not only by speculative builders but by many of the most
reputable architects of the Regency. . . .

The success of the papier-mâché ornament is typical of the
advance of "mass-production" at the expense of craftsmanship,
an advance which is symbolised by the repeal of the "Laws of
Apprenticeship" in 1813. The machine and its idiosyncrasies
could no longer be denied as a factor in architecture. Many of its
effects were deplorable, but in some cases it was made to contribute handsomely to architectural design. The highly standardised
types of balcony railing, which were distributed all over England
and often abroad, represent, for example, a notable contribution
made by "mass-production" to Regency architecture.

There is one particular accompaniment to this "mass-production" of building materials which had an important bearing on
Regency design, and that is the immense development of communications at the time: the large-scale road-making which was
fostered by Macadam's legislation and made effective by Telford's improved methods of construction, also the hectic cutting
of canals to keep pace with the expansion of industry. These, in
themselves, encouraged significant adventures in structural engineering. They also made possible a rapid and widespread distribution of materials, and with them, of ideas as to how they should
be used. The new roads and canals brought to the remote countryside materials, such as cast-iron balconies from Bersham and
stock bricks from London, which foreshadowed the end of local
building traditions. They also brought sophisticated notions of
the Picturesque and a townsman's version of rural architecture

which sprinkled the countryside with villas and ornamental cottages.

With Regency architecture there starts the period of a rapid levelling of architectural ideas. In remote quarters "local traditions" may have held their own, but a great part of the countryside fell before the advance of artificial standards of taste. The loudest praise for the use of "local materials" did not come from the places in which such materials still fostered special building styles: it came from the city offices of architects intent on exploiting the countryside as a playground for the "Man of Taste." Symbolical of the levelling of ideas which followed improved communications is the indiscriminate use of stucco, a material which was first used to solve a special architectural problem. For stucco, as Repton relates in the *Theory and Practice of Landscape Gardening,* was essentially a product of the seaside town. As a protection against strong winds and salt sea air it was a material of special value. But, once successfully used in this way, it soon began to spread a standardising veneer over the architecture of town and countryside: and, as was so often the case in Regency architecture, the essentially practical idea which first suggested its use came to be of less account than its associations with "correct taste," and particularly its aptitude for Picturesque design. In this connection it is important to realise that, like Jackson's "papier mâché" and so many of the building materials of the period, stucco was a substitute material. Its chief recommendation was that it could be used to imitate stone. Busby made the suggestion in connection with his design for an entrance lodge that "the whole should be stuccoed in imitation of stone" and this was the point of view from which most enthusiasts for the material came to consider it.

An appearance of "richness" was generally considered to be a necessary accompaniment to the Picturesque, and stone was thought to be the ideal material for producing such an effect. Brick was conveniently out of favour among Regency architects for its alleged poverty of appearance, but with a stucco coating "in imitation of stone," it easily acquired some measure of respectability. . . .

That stucco was a material with a quality of its own and one with particular pitfalls and possibilities inherent in its use seems to have struck architects less than its value as a short cut to Picturesque effect. But, although it does not seem to have been consciously aimed at, an individual quality does show through many of the stucco subterfuges of Regency architects. The effects they were after in stucco design can be seen particularly clearly in the case of the many fine buildings in Cheltenham, where there is a free use of both stucco and stone. Papworth's "Landsdowne Terrace" represents the ideal of the elaborate stone "terrace," well provided as it is with the "richness," "elaboration" and "tints variously broken and blended" which accompanied Picturesque design. Other Cheltenham terraces have been faced with stucco as a measure of economy, and, although they have set out to look like stone buildings, they have acquired, willy-nilly, a certain individual quality from the material they use.

Living, as we are, at a time in which new materials and the type of design they suggest have been studied to such immediate architectural effect, we may feel inclined to regret that Regency architects did not inquire more deeply into the individual qualities of their materials. But, although it may not have been a conscious one, there does exist a recognisable relationship between the design of the Regency façade and the use of stucco as a facing for it. And this indebtedness of design to material is, to some extent, a reciprocal one. Stucco was welcomed because it provided a pliable and cheap medium in which to realise the intricacies of the Picturesque. At the same time it is quite possible that its use helped to suggest the actual "style" of façades. For smooth, unbroken surfaces, although they are responsible for many delightful effects in Regency buildings, are apt to encourage staining and general deterioration of the walls. Experience of this taught architects to reserve the use of such surfaces for brick buildings. Carried out in stucco, the flutings, string courses and imitation stone joints of the "Grecian" style, or the all-over elaboration of the Gothic, made for a more effective "weathering" of surfaces, and the increasing reverence for the "Styles" during the Regency period may have been in some measure due to this fact.

Whatever the reasons, and there are no doubt many others

beside the ones already suggested, stucco established itself as the fashionable material of the day. It was the one to which the villa and the terrace house looked alike for their crockets and their capitals. As evidence of the social standing associated with it there are numerous cases in which one house in a brick-built terrace has had its front stuccoed as a means of asserting its superiority over its neighbours. . . .

The questions of taste with which the Regency was most occupied were those concerned with the landscape and of the architecture which formed a part of it. In fact it might be said that taste was initially a country product. Its manifestations appeared on the country estate long before they reached the town. The former was at least its particular province during the eighteenth century. Architects and their patrons thought of taste in terms of the country house, while the town was more often than not left at the mercy of the speculator and the builder. This, however, can no longer be said of the Regency. The attention he gave to "improving" his country property did not prevent the landowner from discovering the town and from bringing his taste to bear on its appearance. And, in doing so, he evolved an idea of town architecture which was highly individual and appropriate, one which produced a fitting frame for his own culture and which is by no means without significance for our own times.

The English town had always remained close to nature. Its conscious planning had been something of an elaboration of the village, whose layout is freely adapted to the contours of the countryside. Those external considerations of military strategy and the geometrical frenzy of cultured princes which together produced the much-admired continental "town-plans," these had played negligible parts in the making of the English town. Such a limited feeling for order and architectural layout as appeared in it came from more domestic sources, among them the monastic courtyard and the quadrangle of the university town. A town laid out as a town hardly existed until eighteenth-century Bath. And this in spite of its geometrical framework, is a town whose plan interprets many of the characteristics of the village and the university quadrangle in terms of a sophisticated taste. Regency architects did not overlook this remarkable precedent (Nash's

Regents Park layout owes a great deal to the circuses and cres-
cents of Bath), but they had much of their own to add to the
forms it established.

Theirs was above all an effort to break down the barrier
between town and countryside, and a wider application of the
principles of taste to this end. Kent, who "leaped the fence and
saw that all nature was a garden," was in the Regency followed
by Nash, who leaped the outer circle of town houses and discovered that the whole town could be a landscape. It was perhaps
less of an athletic achievement than Kent's, because others had
already partly demolished the barrier. The aristocrat who came
to town bringing his taste with him, had ridden rough-shod over
it, while his city-bred imitator had bridged it from the other side
when he emulated a "rural" character in his town house. It was
from this two-way traffic that there resulted the architectural
congestion, which is appropriately seen on the main roads leading out of London, on the Wandsworth Road and the Brixton
Road particularly, where terraces and villas in all shades of
conformity with the precepts of "Taste" commemorate this dem-
olition of the fence that Nash leaped. Cruikshank's cartoon of
Regency "ribbon development" shows the first steps in this
"march of bricks and mortar." Its final effort is recorded with
equal distaste by Coleman, who contemplates the scene:

> Stretching round England's chief Emporium far,
> No rage for Building quench'd by raging War,
> What would-be villas, ranged in dapper pride,
> Usurp the fields, and choke the highway side!
> Peace to each swain, who rural rapture owns,
> As soon as past a toll, or off the stones.

Loudon for one had already subscribed to the depressing philosophy which is implied in the idea that "the very purpose for
which we engage in commerce is that we may one day be enabled
to retire to the country."

But while Brixton was the furthest that many Londoners got
in their pursuit of the pleasures of "retirement," those who had
indulged more successfully in commerce were able to invade the
precincts of the country estate itself with their villas and *Cottages*

Ornées. During the Regency period the break-up of the country
estates had already begun, and the landscaped estate was being
split up into plots for these "country cottages" designed according to the townsman's second-hand idea of landscaped
architecture. . . .

. . . Bringing the country into the town in general involved
some form of compromise with existing ideas of an ordered
community. The Georgian tradition was an extremely rigid one
so far as the town house was concerned and the separation of
houses into different "rates" according to their superficial area
had crystallised their design into what must be the most extreme
form of "standardisation" known in the history of English architecture. In their layout there did, however, persist a sufficient reflection of the forms of village layout and the monastic plan to
suggest a point of departure for Regency architects.

This was particularly so in the case of the London squares.
The idea may have been partly a foreign one, derived as it was
from Inigo Jones's layout of Covent Garden in imitation of a
fashionable continental "piazza." The squares which followed it
in the eighteenth century nevertheless acquired something of a
characteristic native air. The very acts under which many of
them were laid out hint at a monastic sense of community. The
Regency development of Brunswick and Mecklenburg Squares
round the Foundling Hospital still placed many obligations on
the tenants in the form of contributions to the upkeep of the
neighbourhood. The layout of the central garden, and its maintenance particularly, were the concern of a board of Commissioners
representing the residents in the squares and the governors of the
Foundling Hospital. Rates "up to one shilling in the pound"
were levied on the residents for this purpose. This idea of laying
out a central garden in a residential square to be used by the
residents and maintained by them is a democratic feature of
Georgian planning which is very far removed from the paved
promenade of the continental piazza. More than that it provided
a point of departure for architects developing the idea of the
"garden city."

James Burton, when he laid out his housing estate round
Bloomsbury Square in the early nineteenth century, planned it in

the form of regular blocks of houses forming open squares and enclosed gardens, with Repton making his contribution to the layout in the form of a project for the planting of Russell Square. But here, as on most of the occasions on which he was consulted in the layout of squares, Repton himself had little of value to contribute to the idea of the landscaped housing estate. His eye for architecture as an element in the landscape was reliable enough when it was free to rove in the country park. It was less so when confined within the framework of city streets. In the case of Russell Square, the leveling of the site before he was consulted admittedly deprived him of those natural undulations which were the foundations on which he built his park layouts. All the same, more might have been expected of him than the mere encirclement of the garden by a "belt" of trees and shrubs; a feature which he carefully avoided in the planting of parks. The idea that the planting of a square should be considered in relation to the surrounding architecture, not obscuring it but making a Picturesque composition of the whole, was one which simply does not seem to have occurred to him. It was left for others, and particularly for his former collaborator, John Nash, to develop the Regency "garden city" in conformity with more architectural principles.

The Regency ideal of transplanting the countryside in the town raised problems both for the landscape gardener and for the architect. The two might be solved by one man, as they were by J. B. Papworth, who gave evidence of his prowess in both capacities when he laid out the Cheltenham estates. Alternatively, members of the two professions might work in collaboration, as they did in the syndicate composed of Nash, the young Reptons and the former head gardener at Kew, William Townsend Aiton. The latter's expert hand can be detected in the layout of St. James's Park, Regent's Park and the Brighton Pavilion Garden. By whatever means it might be brought about, the builder's idea of the Picturesque had to be reconciled with the planter's view of it before any positive results could be expected in town planning. To ignore the builder, as Repton did, ruled out the possibility of obtaining any such results. For ideas of Picturesque design were now changing the appearance of the city street scarcely less than they had affected the appearance of the country house, and "escape from Georgian plainness" was recognised by at least one commentator on the town house as being a necessary counterpart to the emulation of *rus in urbe*.

13.

Turner:
Imagination and Reality

~

LAWRENCE GOWING

There is a special reason for looking at Turner. We are aware that in his painting something singular and incomparable happened. It astounded and bewildered his contemporaries and it is still not altogether comprehensible today. In the pictures that Turner showed—and concealed—in the last two decades of his life a change was evidently taking place of a kind that is disturbing to an artist's public. The critic who wrote in 1839 of imagination and reality striving for mastery in Turner's works was in no doubt that reality was suffering a lamentable defeat. It is evident that both the kind of reality and the order of imagination that painting had traditionally offered were changing in Turner's hands. Since his time such transformations have recurred with increasing frequency. We are now familiar with the disturbance that they make. We are far from familiar with Turner.

We cannot show the whole of Turner. It is not certain that we are yet prepared to see him whole. . . . Of course, one cannot separate an artist's late works from the rest; his meaning unfolds throughout his life. To understand the direction of Turner's development, it is necessary to look first at his starting point and

---

From Lawrence Gowing, Turner: Imagination and Reality *(New York: The Museum of Modern Art, 1966)* , *pp. 7–10.*

at some of the studies and drawings of subsequent years that
prepared the way for his ultimate achievement.

In Turner's first pictures imagination and reality seem like
opposite alternatives. *Buttermere Lake,* which he exhibited when
he was twenty-three, is real. We are hardly aware of the picturesque arrangement of the scene. The banks of shadow have the
gentle breadth of tone that Turner had learned copying watercolours by J. R. Cozens, in the company of Girtin, but the picture
seems almost styleless. To a contemporary it looked merely dull.
Hoppner, the fashionable portraitist, went to Turner's studio to
see it and pronounced him 'a timid man afraid to venture'. To us
the stillness has a different meaning. It gives a sense of awe, as if
the painter and subject were both subdued by the unearthly
majesty of light.

Turner's vision of the rainbow over Buttermere was poetic,
and he knew it. It was one of the pictures to which he attached
lines of poetry in the Academy catalogue, for the first time. For
Buttermere he strung together fragments of Thomson's *Spring,* as
if forcing them to compose a poem of his own. Significantly, he
avoided the lines in which 'the showery prism' unfolded the
colours of Newton's spectrum. His poem was different, and colour still had little part in it. Light and the grandeur that it gave
the place excluded everything else. But as the light fell it scattered shining flecks, sprinklings of incandescent pigment. They
suggest that one other thing was as real to him, the paint itself.

Turner soon corrected the impression of timidity. *The Fifth
Plague of Egypt,* exhibited two years later, is a grand imaginative
invention . . . Yet its origin was similar. Impressions of a storm
in the mountains of North Wales were grafted onto the style of
Poussin to make a formidable manifestation of the Sublime—the
representation, in Burke's words, of 'whatever is in any sort
terrible'. Turner's natural sense of awe had become linked with
his ambition and his sense of style. We do not think of sheer
ambition as a particularly creative or sympathetic quality in an
artist, but in Turner it was surely both. He wrote in one of his
sketchbooks an invocation:

> O Heaven avert the impending care,
> O make my future prospects fair.

The Fifth Plague, which actually represented the Seventh, for
Turner had no particular interest in any part of the Bible but
the Apocalypse, was the first of his great gestures of emulation.
The equation of the weather of North Wales with the thunder
and hail and the fire that ran along the ground was the beginning of a long engrossment in the force of nature. In the years
that followed, Turner was, in fact, compiling a collection both of
overwhelming natural effects and of compelling artistic styles.
The hostile power of nature provided a series of subjects that
culminated in *Hannibal Crossing the Alps,* in which the giant
stride of a storm across a Yorkshire moor inspired a picture as
styleless and original as *Buttermere.* But he gave an equal force
to his other theme, the pictures of fair prospects. In combination
the two were irresistible. Light and the elements were not only
Turner's subjects; they were his as allies in carrying everything
before him. He was never again accused of timidity and in a year
or two we hear that Hoppner 'reprobated the presumptive manner in which he paints.'

Turner's presumption was certainly enormous. The historic
styles were engrossing painters everywhere, but the vigour and
resource with which he seized on them were quite exceptional.
He took the past by storm, and his pictures were soon being
'compared . . . and rather preferred to the greatest masters'. But
the extravagance of what followed placed him beyond the pale of
tradition. In 1801 a critic already detected in the first of his
sea-pieces in the Dutch manner an affectation of carelessness. Sir
George Beaumont, the magisterial connoisseur, pronounced
against him. 'Turner', he said, 'is perpetually aiming to be extraordinary, but rather produces works that are capricious and
singular than great.'

Beaumont became the leader of the opposition to Turner, and
the diarist Farington, who wrote down everyone's opinion in the
hope of developing his own, recorded the hostile judgments year
by year. Turner painted 'strong skies and parts not corresponding
to them'; he made nothing out; he had no power of execution;
his foregrounds were 'comparative blots'. The word is interesting, and it recurs in the comments. Turner's figures, someone
said, were 'left like blots'. Fuseli told Northcote that the *Holy*

Family was 'like the embryo or blot of a great master of colour-
ing'. Alexander Cozens's 'new method' of generating landscapes
from random blots was common knowledge. Turner's effects look
to us far from haphazard. But to his contemporaries they evidently recalled the tradition of random suggestion that goes back
to Leonardo and his famous recommendation to assist invention
by looking at the stains on old walls or the veins of stones.
Indeed, Hoppner told Farington that Turner 'left so much to be
imagined that it was like looking into a coal fire or upon an old
wall'. Beaumont said that the water in *Calais Pier* was 'like the
veins in a marble slab'.

It was clear that the consistency of representation had altered;
the intention had shifted. The purpose was no longer to deploy
an accepted vocabulary of representation. Water, for example,
was expected to be sea-green and transparent. Turner was care-
less of the convention. He required a ruder and more real substance, which appeared outrageously incongruous. In 1802 his
waves were said to be chalky; in 1803 his sea looked like soap and
chalk; in 1804 the water in his picture reminded Opie of a
turnpike road over the sea and in 1805 Benjamin West said it was
like stone.

It was not only a conventional code of figuration that was
breaking down under Turner's relentless pressure. The whole
condition of painting was in question. It had been founded on an
axiom derived from classical sources, the axiom, as Fuseli put it,
'that the less the traces appear of the means by which a work has
been produced, the more it resembles the operations of nature'.
The traces of Turner's means were unconcealed. In 1805 he was
applying paint freely and visibly with the palette knife. Wilkie,
who had just arrived in London with an admiration for Teniers,
thought it the most abominable workmanship he ever saw; only
the effect was natural. By the next year there was a host of young
painters working in the new manner. 'It is the scribbling of
painting,' a critic remarked, 'so much of the trowel—so mortary.'
Painting was now required to resemble itself before anything
else; the operations portrayed were first and foremost the
painter's. The change was a lasting one and twenty years later a
writer described what had happened. 'It is evident that Mr

Constable's landscapes are like nature; it is still more evident that they are like paint.' It is the fact that this became the new condition of painting that makes the old criticisms now read like praise.

A Chronology of
the Romantic Period, 1789-1832

~

Listings of events of political, social, and literary history are followed by publications or exhibitions of that year. Where a question mark follows the title of a work probable date of composition, not publication or exhibition, is indicated.

1789

French Revolution; Three Estates convene; fall of Bastille. Wordsworth at Cambridge; Coleridge at Christ's Hospital; Scott studying law; Turner's first exhibition of watercolors at Royal Academy.

Bentham, *Introduction to Principles of Morals and Legislation.*
Blake, *Songs of Innocence; Book of Thel.*
Bligh, *Narrative of the Mutiny on board The Bounty.*
Bowles, *Sonnets.*
E. Darwin, *The Loves of the Plants.*
Radcliffe, *The Castles of Athlin and Dunbayne.*
Wordsworth, *Evening Walk* (?) .

1790

Famine and unemployment create more unrest in France. Pitt forces Spain to recognize British rights in Vancouver. Wordsworth on walking tour on Continent.

Alison, *Essays on the Nature and Principles of Taste.*
Austen, *Love and Friendship* (?) .
Blake, *Marriage of Heaven and Hell.*
Bruce, *Travels to Discover the Source of the Nile.*
Burke, *Reflections on the French Revolution.*
Radcliffe, *A Sicilian Romance.*

1791

King of France flees Paris, is captured; death of Mirabeau. Priestley's home destroyed by mob. Wordsworth in France; Coleridge at Cambridge.

Bartram, *Travels Through North and South Carolina.* . . .
Blake, *The French Revolution.*
Burns, *Tam O'Shanter.*
Cowper, translations of *Iliad* and *Odyssey.*
Inchbald, *A Simple Story.*
Malone, edition of Shakespeare.
Paine, *The Rights of Man.*
Priestley, *Letters to Mr. Burke.*
Radcliffe, *The Romance of the Forest.*
Wordsworth, *Guilt and Sorrow* (?).

1792

Allies invade France; imprisonment of French royal family. Wordsworth's friendship with Beaupuy in France. Sir Joshua Reynolds dies; West president of Royal Academy. Soane's Bank Stock Office. Shelley born.

Bage, *Man As He Is.*
Blake, *Song of Liberty.*
Gilpin, *Essays on Picturesque Beauty.*
Holcroft, *Anna St. Ives.*
Rogers, *The Pleasures of Memory.*
Wollstonecraft, *Vindication of the Rights of Women.*
Young, *Travels in France.*

1793

Trial and execution of Louis XVI and Marie Antoinette; the Terror; fall of Girondins; murder of Marat; Robespierre in power; France declares war on Britain; British troops to West Indies. John Clare born.

Blake, *A Vision of the Daughters of Albion; America; Gates of Paradise.*
Dalton, *Meteorological Observations.*
Godwin, *Political Justice.*

Wordsworth, *Descriptive Sketches; An Evening Walk; Letter to the Bishop of Llandaff* (?) .

1794

Danton executed; Robespierre executed; establishment of the Directorate and end of Terror. Trial for sedition and acquittal of Tooke, Holcroft, Thelwall. Gibbon dies. Coleridge and Southey meet, plan Pantisocracy.

Austen, *Lady Susan* (?) .
Blake, *Songs of Innocence and Experience; Europe; The Book of Urizen.*
Coleridge, *Monody on the Death of Chatterton;* (with Southey) , *Fall of Robespierre.*
Godwin, *Caleb Williams.*
Holcroft, *Hugh Trevor.*
Paine, *The Age of Reason.*
Paley, *Evidences of Christianity.*
Payne Knight, *The Landscape.*
Radcliffe, *The Mysteries of Udolpho.*
Uvedale Price, *Essay on the Picturesque.*

1795

Napoleon's victories in Italy. Speenhamland procedures (wages supplemented from parish funds) initiated. Wordsworth meets Coleridge and Southey, receives legacy from Calvert. Coleridge and Southey marry. Beddoes, Carlyle, Keats born.

Austen, *Elinor and Marianne* (early form of *Sense and Sensibility*) (?) .
Blake, *Book of Los; Song of Los; Book of Ahania.*
Landor, *Poems.*
Lewis, *Ambrosio, or The Monk.*
Paine, *First Principles of Government.*
Smith, *Montalbert.*

1796

Spain declares war on England. French invasion of Ireland fails. Burns dies; Macpherson dies. Mary Lamb kills her mother. Hartley Coleridge born. Coleridge's periodical, *The Watchman.*

Bage, *Hermsprong.*
Burney, *Camilla.*
Cobbett, *Life and Adventures of Peter Porcupine.*
Coleridge, *Ode on the Departing Year; Poems on Various Subjects.*
Edgeworth, *The Parent's Assistant.*
Scott, translations from Bürger.
Southey, *Joan of Arc.*
Wordsworth, *The Borderers* (?).
Turner's first oil-painting exhibition, *Fishermen at Sea; Moonlight, a Study at Millbank.*

1797

Treaty of Campo Formio. Naval mutinies at Spithead and the Nore. Battles of Cape St. Vincent, Camperdown. Bank crisis. Burke dies, Mary Wollstonecraft Godwin dies. Scott marries. Close association of Wordsworth and Coleridge. *Anti-Jacobin* founded.

Austen, *First Impressions* (early version of *Pride and Prejudice*) (?).
Blake, begins *Vala* (?) ; illustrations for Young's *Night Thoughts.*
Coleridge, *Poems; The Ancient Mariner* (?) ; *Christabel I* (?).
Godwin, *The Inquirer.*
Radcliffe, *The Italian.*
Southey, *Poems.*
Wordsworth, *The Pedlar* (Book I, *Excursion*) (?).

1798

French invasion of Egypt, Battle of the Nile. Irish rebellion. Newspaper Publication Act. Davy superintendent of Pneumatic Institute. Wordsworth and Coleridge in Germany. Turner's drawing of Norham Castle, other pictures, popular at Royal Academy exhibition.

Austen, *Northanger Abbey* (?).
Coleridge, *Fears in Solitude; France, An Ode; Frost at Midnight; Kubla Khan* (?).
Gilpin, *Picturesque Remarks on the West of England.*
Godwin, *Memoirs of Mary Wollstonecraft.*

Inchbald, *Lovers' Vows* (translation from Kotzebue; see Austen's
   Mansfield Park).
Lamb, *The Tale of Rosamund Gray.*
Landor, *Gebir.*
Malthus, *Principles of Population.*
Vancouver, *A Voyage of Discovery to the North Pacific.*
Wordsworth, *Peter Bell* (?) ; beginning of *Prelude* (?).
Wordsworth and Coleridge, *Lyrical Ballads.*
Turner, *Buttermere Lake.*

1799

Napoleon returns from Egypt, overthrows Directorate. Formation of second coalition against Napoleon. Corresponding Society
and similar associations suppressed, Combination Acts. Royal
Institution founded. Wordsworths at Dove Cottage, Coleridge in
London. Thomas Hood born.

Campbell, *The Pleasures of Hope.*
Godwin, *St. Leon.*
Lewis, *Tales of Terror.*
Park, *Travels in the Interior of Africa.*
Scott, translation of Goethe's *Götz von Berlichingen.*
Blake, *The Last Supper.*
Fuseli's Milton Gallery (40 paintings).

1800

Battles of Alexandria, Hohenlinden, Marengo. Act of Union
with Ireland. Royal College of Surgeons founded. Volta reports
invention of the battery. Watt's steam-engine patent expires.
Beckford's Fonthill begun. Cowper dies.

Coleridge, *Poems; Christabel* II (?) ; translations of Schiller's
   Piccolomini, Death of Wallenstein.
Edgeworth, *Castle Rackrent.*
Gifford, *Epistle to Peter Pindar.*
Moore, *Mordaunt.*
Wordsworth, *The Recluse* I (?).
Wordsworth and Coleridge, *Lyrical Ballads,* second edition.
Turner, *Fifth Plague of Egypt.*

1801

Assassination of Czar Paul of Russia. King George III opposed to Catholic emancipation, Pitt resigns, Addington becomes Prime Minister. British naval victory at Copenhagen. Britain seizes Cape of Good Hope, Ceylon. First census: England's population 8,330,000; British Isles, 10,900,000 (France approx. 24 millions). Davy director of chemical laboratory, Royal Institution. Bage dies. Bonington born.

Edgeworth, *Moral Tales; Belinda.*
Hogg, *Scottish Pastorals.*
Hunt, *Juvenilia.*
Mackenzie, *Voyage . . . to the Frozen and Pacific Oceans.*
Moore, *Poems by Thomas Little.*
Southey, *Thalaba the Destroyer.*
Turner, *The Army of the Medes Destroyed.*

1802

Peace of Amiens. Reoccupation of Switzerland by the French. Royal Military College founded. *The Edinburgh Review* founded. Cobbett's *Political Register.* Wordsworth marries. Davy, *Discourse Introductory to a Course of Lectures on Chemistry.*

Coleridge, *Dejection, An Ode* (first version) (?).
Lamb, *John Woodvil.*
Landor, *Poetry by the Author of Gebir.*
Scott, *Minstrelsy of the Scottish Border.*
Wordsworth, first four stanzas of *Ode: Intimations of Immortality* (?).
Turner, *Calais Pier.*

1803

French-British war renewed. Napoleon prepares for invasion of England. Capture of Delhi. Sale of Louisiana territory to U.S.

Bentham, *A Plea for the Constitution.*
Campbell, *Collected Poems.*
Coleridge, *The Pains of Sleep* (?).

Porter, *Thaddeus of Warsaw.*
Repton, *Theory and Practice of Landscape Gardening.*

1804

Addington resigns, Pitt Prime Minister again. Napoleon proclaimed Emperor. Fuseli appointed Keeper of Royal Academy. Blake acquitted of charge of sedition. Coleridge travels to Malta.

Barrow, *Travels in China.*
Blake, begins *Jerusalem* (?) ; *Milton* (?) .
Edgeworth, *The Modern Griselda.*
Lewis, *The Bravo of Venice.*

1805

British naval victory at Trafalgar, death of Nelson. Battles of Ulm and Austerlitz. Samuel Palmer born. Wordsworth's brother drowns. Dalton publishes first table of atomic weights.

Cary, translation of Dante's *Inferno.*
Godwin, *Fleetwood.*
Knight, *Principles of Taste.*
Scott, *The Lay of the Last Minstrel.*
Southey, *Madoc.*
Wordsworth, first version of *Prelude* completed (?) ; *The Waggoner* (?) ; *Elegiac Stanzas* (?) .
Turner, *The Shipwreck.*

1806

Death of Pitt, Grenville Prime Minister of "Ministry of All the Talents." Death of Fox. Napoleon's Berlin and Milan decrees, neutrals forbidden to trade with Britain. Coleridge returns to England.

Byron, *Fugitive Pieces.*
Moore, *Epistles, Odes, and other Poems.*
Peacock, *Palmyra.*
David Wilkie, *The Politicians.*

1807

Russians defeat French at Preuss-Eylau, are defeated at Friedland. Treaty of Tilsit; Alexander of Russia becomes Napoleon's ally. French invasion of Spain and Portugal. Abolition of slave trade. Orders in Council, blockade of Napoleonic Europe. Geological Society founded. Thomson, *System of Chemistry.*

Byron, *Hours of Idleness; Poems on Several Occasions.*
Crabbe, *Poems.*
Godwin, *Faulkner.*
Hogg, *The Mountain Bard.*
Maturin, *The Fatal Revenge.*
Moore, *Irish Melodies.*
Wordsworth, *Poems* (including *Ode: Intimations of Immortality, Resolution and Independence*).
Turner, *Liber Studiorum* I.

1808

Spanish rise against the French. British land in Portugal, military successes there vitiated by Convention of Cintra allowing French withdrawal. Byron sails to Mediterranean. Coleridge lectures on Shakespeare and Milton at Royal Institution. Hunt editor of *Examiner.* Dalton, *A New System of Chemical Philosophy.*

Hunt, *Critical Essays on . . . the London Theatres.*
Lewis, *Romantic Tales.*
Maturin, *The Wild Irish Boy.*
Scott, *Marmion.*
Blake's illustrations for Blair's *Grave.*
Turner, *The Battle of Trafalgar.*

1809

Death of Sir John Moore, Arthur Wellesley (Wellington) in Portugal. Peace of Schönbrunn. Perceval becomes Prime Minister. Bentham's Parliamentary Reform Catechism circulated (published 1817). Coleridge's periodical *The Friend. Quarterly Review* founded. Coleridge-Wordsworth quarrel. Blake's unsuccessful exhibition. Paine dies. Tennyson, Charles Darwin, Gladstone, Elizabeth Barrett (Browning) born.

Byron, *English Bards and Scotch Reviewers.*
Campbell, *Gertrude of Wyoming.*
Edgeworth, *Tales of Fashionable Life.*

Hobhouse, *Travels through Albania.*
Wordsworth, *The Convention of Cintra* (?) .

1810

Arrest of Sir Francis Burdett; persecution of Cobbett. Increasing financial crisis. Coleridge lectures on Shakespeare.

Crabbe, *The Borough.*
Hogg, *The Forest Minstrel.*
Porter, *The Scottish Chiefs.*
Rogers, *The Voyage of Columbus.*
Scott, *The Lady of the Lake.*
Shelley, *Original Poetry by Victor and Cazire; Posthumous Fragments of Margaret Nicholson; Zastrozzi.*
Southey, *The Curse of Kehama.*
Wordsworth, *Topographical Description of the Country of the Lakes; Essay on Epitaphs.*

1811

George III declared insane; beginning of Regency. Trade crisis, Luddite riots. Prosecution of John and Leigh Hunt. Nash intrusted with design of Regent's Park. Soane's Dulwich Art Gallery. Shelley expelled from Oxford, marries. Byron returns from Mediterranean. Keats leaves school, apprenticed to apothecary.

Austen, *Sense and Sensibility.*
Hunt, *The Feast of the Poets.*
Lamb, *On the Tragedies of Shakespeare.*
Ricardo, *On the High Price of Bullion.*
Scott, *The Vision of Don Roderick.*
Shelley, *The Necessity of Atheism.*

1812

Frame-breaking bill. Perceval assassinated; Liverpool becomes Prime Minister. British successes in Portugal and Spain. British-American war begins. Napoleon invades Russia, retreats from Moscow with loss of army. National Light and Heat Company (gas) formed. Shelley in Ireland. Browning, Dickens born.

Byron, *Childe Harold* I and II; *The Curse of Minerva*.
Cary, translation of *Purgatorio* and *Paradiso*.
Combe, *Tour of Dr. Syntax in Search of the Picturesque*.
Crabbe, *Tales in Verse*.
Landor, *Count Julian*.
Maturin, *The Milesian Chief*.
Montgomery, *The World Before the Flood*.
H. and J. Smith, *Rejected Addresses*.
Turner, *Snowstorm, Hannibal Crossing the Alps*.

1813

Defeat of Napoleon at Leipzig. Southey made poet laureate.
Leigh Hunt imprisoned. Wordsworth appointed Stamp Distributor. Nash, Carlton House.

Austen, *Pride and Prejudice*.
Byron, *The Bride of Abydos; The Giaour; The Waltz*.
Coleridge, *Remorse*.
Owen, *A New View of Society*.
Scott, *Rokeby; The Bridal of Triermain*.
Shelley, *Queen Mab*.
Southey, *Life of Nelson*.
Turner, *Frosty Morning; The Deluge*.

1814

Fall of Paris, abdication of Napoleon. End of war with America.
Repeal of statute of apprentices. Stephenson's first locomotive.
Shelley on continent with Mary Godwin. Nash plans St. James
Park.

Austen, *Mansfield Park*.
Byron, *The Corsair; Lara; Ode to Napoleon*.
Malthus, *Observations on the Effect of the Corn Laws*.
Scott, *Waverley*.
Shelley, *The Refutation of Deism*.
Southey, *Roderick*.
Wordsworth, *The Excursion*.

1815

Napoleon returns from Elba, Battle of Waterloo; restoration of Louis XVIII of France. Holy Alliance. New Corn Law. Nash, Royal Pavilion at Brighton (finished 1823). Gillray dies; Byron marries; Trollope born.

Black's translation of Schlegel's *Lectures on Dramatic Art and Literature.*
Byron, *Hebrew Melodies.*
Hunt, *The Descent of Liberty.*
Lloyd's translation of *The Tragedies of Alfieri.*
Malthus, *An Inquiry into Rent.*
Scott, *The Lord of the Isles; Guy Mannering.*
Wordsworth, *The White Doe of Rylestone; Poems.*
Turner, *Crossing the Brook.*

1816

Repeal of income tax. Spa Fields riot. Spreading economic distress and social unrest. Cobbett reduces price of his *Weekly Political Register,* increasing its circulation. Elgin marbles publicly exhibited. Harriet Westbrook commits suicide; Shelley marries Mary Godwin. Byron leaves England. Keats receives Apothecaries' Certificate. C. Brontë born. W. Smith, *Map of the Strata of England and Wales.*

Austen, *Emma.*
Byron, *The Prisoner of Chillon; Childe Harold* III; *The Siege of Corinth.*
Coleridge, *The Pains of Sleep; Christabel; Kubla Khan; The Statesman's Manual.*
Galt, *The Majolo.*
Hunt, *The Story of Rimini.*
Keats, *On First Looking Into Chapman's Homer.*
Lady Caroline Lamb, *Glenarvon.*
John Martin, *Joshua.*
Maturin, *Bertram.*
Peacock, *Headlong Hall.*
Scott, *The Antiquary; The Black Dwarf; Old Mortality.*

Shelley, *Alastor.*
Wordsworth, *Thanksgiving Ode.*

1817

Death of Princess Charlotte. Habeas Corpus Act suspended again.
Trial of Hone. Young applies principle of interference to light.
Blackwood's *Edinburgh Magazine* founded. Jane Austen dies.

Austen, *Sanditon* (?).
Byron, *Manfred; The Lament of Tasso.*
Coleridge, *Sibylline Leaves; Zapolya; Biographia Literaria.*
Godwin, *Mandeville.*
Hazlitt, *The Characters of Shakespeare's Plays.*
Keats, *Poems* (including *I Stood Tip-toe* and *Sleep and Poetry*);
    Endymion (?).
Moore, *Lalla Rookh.*
Peacock, *Melincourt.*
Ricardo, *Principles of Political Economy.*
Scott, *Harold the Dauntless.*
Shelley, *Hymn to Intellectual Beauty; Mont Blanc.*
Southey's edition of Malory.
West, *Death on a Pale Horse.*

1818

Imprisonment of Carlisle. Agreement between Britain and U.S.
on Canadian boundary. Institution of Civil Engineers founded.
Blake meets Linnell. Shelley leaves England. Keats meets Fanny
Brawne; his brother dies. "Monk" Lewis dies. E. Brontë born.

Austen, *Northanger Abbey; Persuasion.*
Byron, *Childe Harold IV; Beppo.*
Ferrier, *Marriage.*
Hazlitt, *Lectures on the English Poets; A View of the English
    Stage.*
Hunt, *Foliage.*
Keats, *Endymion; Isabella* (?).
Lamb, *Works.*
Peacock, *Rododaphne; Nightmare Abbey.*
Scott, *Rob Roy; The Heart of Midlothian.*

Shelley, *Prometheus Unbound* (?) ; *The Revolt of Islam.*
Mary Shelley, *Frankenstein.*
Howard, *The Climate of London* (influenced Constable) .

1819

Peterloo. The Six Acts. Bentham, *Radical Reform Bill.* Ruskin
and George Eliot born.

Byron, *Mazeppa; Don Juan* I–II.
Crabbe, *Tales of the Hall.*
Hazlitt, *Lectures on the English Comic Writers.*
Hunt, *Hero and Leander; Bacchus and Ariadne.*
Keats, *Eve of St. Agnes* (?) ; *La Belle Dame Sans Merci* (?) ; Ode
    to a Nightingale.
Reynolds, *Peter Bell; Benjamin the Waggoner.*
Scott, *The Bride of Lammermoor; Legend of Montrose.*
Shelley, *Prometheus Unbound* II–IV (?) ; *Lines Written Among
    the Euganean Hills; The Cenci; Peter Bell the Third* (?) .
Wordsworth, *Peter Bell; The Waggoner.*
Constable, *The White Horse.*

1820

Death of George III, accession of George IV, Trial of Queen
Caroline. Cato Street Conspiracy. Davy president of Royal
Society. *London Magazine* founded. Keats seriously ill, sails to
Italy. West dies. A. Brontë born.

Bulwer-Lytton, *Ismael.*
Clare, *Poems Descriptive of Rural Life and Scenery.*
Godwin, *Of Population.*
Hazlitt, *Lectures on the Dramatic Literature of the Age of Eliza-
    beth.*
Keats, *Lamia, Isabella, Eve of St. Agnes, and Other Poems* (in-
    cluding *Hyperion*) ; *Ode on a Grecian Urn.*
Lamb, *Essays of Elia.*
Malthus, *Principles of Political Economy.*
Maturin, *Melmoth the Wanderer.*
Peacock, *The Four Ages of Poetry.*
Scott, *Miscellaneous Poems; Ivanhoe; The Monastery; The
    Abbot.*

Shelley, *Swellfoot the Tyrant; Prometheus Unbound; Ode to the West Wind; The Sensitive Plant.*
Wordsworth, *The River Duddon.*
Blake illustrations for Thornton's *Virgil* (?).

1821

Death of Queen Caroline. Greek War of Independence begins. Stockton-Darlington railway authorized. Keats dies.

Beddoes, *The Improvisatore.*
Byron, *Marino Faliero; The Prophecy of Dante; Don Juan III–V; Sardanapalus; The Two Foscari; Cain.*
Clare, *The Village Minstrel.*
DeQuincey, *Confessions of an English Opium Eater.*
Galt, *Annals of the Parish.*
James Mill, *Elements of Political Economy.*
Scott, *Kenilworth.*
Shelley, *Adonais; Epipsychidion.*
Southey, *A Vision of Judgment.*
Constable, *The Hay Wain.*

1822

Suicide of Castlereagh. Canning Foreign Secretary and leader in Commons. Hydrographic Department makes Admiralty charts publicly available. *The Liberal* (1822–23) founded. Shelley dies. Arnold born.

Beddoes, *The Bride's Tragedy.*
Byron, *The Vision of Judgment.*
Darley, *The Errors of Ecstasie.*
Peacock, *Maid Marian.*
Rogers, *Italy.*
Scott, *Halidon Hill; The Pirate; The Fortunes of Nigel; Peveril of the Peak.*
Shelley, *Hellas.*
Wordsworth, *Ecclesiastical Sonnets.*

1823

War between France and Spain. O'Connell forms Catholic Association. Anne Radcliffe dies.

Byron, *Don Juan* VI–XIV; *The Age of Bronze; The Island; Werner.*
Franklin, *Narrative of a Journey to the Polar Seas.*
Galt, *The Entail.*
Hazlitt, *Liber Amoris; Characteristics.*
Praed, *Australaisia.*
Scott, *Quentin Durward.*
Shelley, *Poetical Pieces.*
Mary Shelley, *Valperga.*
Blake begins engravings for *Book of Job* (?).
Constable, *Salisbury Cathedral.*

1824

Combination Laws repealed. London Institute opens. National Gallery opens. Exhibition of Constable's paintings in Paris. *Westminster Review* founded. Byron dies. Wilkie Collins born.

Byron, *Don Juan* XV–XVI; *The Deformed Transformed.*
Campbell, *Theodoric and Other Poems.*
Carlyle, translation of *Wilhelm Meister.*
Ferrier, *The Inheritance.*
Hogg, *Memoirs of a Justified Sinner.*
Landor, *Imaginary Conversations* I–II.
Medwin, *Conversations with Lord Byron.*
Morier, *Adventures of Hajii Baba.*
Scott, *St. Ronan's Well; Redgauntlet.*
Shelley, *Posthumous Poems.*
Blake begins Dante illustrations (?).

1825

Financial panic. Further agitation for Catholic Emancipation. Faraday director of chemical laboratory at Royal Institution. Fuseli dies. Nash, Buckingham Palace (to 1830).

Brougham, *Practical Observations upon the Education of the People.*
Carlyle, *Life of Schiller.*
Coleridge, *Aids to Reflection.*
Hazlitt, *Table-talk; The Spirit of the Age.*

Hood and Reynolds, *Odes and Addresses to Great People.*
Scott, *The Betrothed; The Talisman.*
Southey, *A Tale of Paraguay.*
Wade, *Tasso.*
Constable, *The Leaping Horse.*

1826

Liverpool Ministry ends. Election. Joint-stock banks authorized. Liverpool-Manchester railway authorized. Ballantyne, Scott's publisher, fails.

Elizabeth Barrett (Browning), *Essay on Mind.*
Disraeli, *Vivian Grey.*
Hood, *Whims and Oddities.*
Scott, *Woodstock.*
Mary Shelley, *The Last Man.*
Constable, *The Cornfield.*

1827

Canning dies. Greek War of Independence won at Navarino. Rowlandson dies; Blake dies. Holman Hunt born.

Bulwer-Lytton, *Falkland.*
Carlyle, *German Romance.*
Clare, *The Shepherd's Calendar.*
Darley, *Sylvia.*
Hood, *The Plea of the Midsummer Fairies.*
Scott, *The Chronicles of Cannongate.*
Tennyson, *Poems by Two Brothers.*

1828

Wellington Prime Minister. Repeal of Test and Corporation Acts. O'Connell defeats Fitzgerald in Irish by-election. University of London founded. Bonington dies. Meredith, Rossetti born.

Bulwer-Lytton, *Pelham.*
Hunt, *Lord Byron and Some of his Contemporaries.*
Landor, *Imaginary Conversations* III.
Lockhart, *Life of Burns.*
Rogers, *Italy* II.

Scott, *The Fair Maid of Perth.*
Constable, *Dedham Vale.*

1829

Catholic Emancipation. O'Connell excluded from Parliament. Metropolitan Police Act. Royal Observatory at Cape of Good Hope opened. Constable elected to Royal Academy.

Bulwer-Lytton, *The Disowned; Devereux.*
Hogg, *The Shepherd's Calendar.*
Hood, *The Epping Hunt; Eugene Aram.*
Marryat, *The Naval Officer.*
James Mill, *Analysis of the Human Mind.*
Peacock, *The Misfortunes of Elphin.*
Scott, *Anne of Geierstein; The House of Aspen.*
Tennyson, *Timbuctoo.*
Constable, *Hadleigh Castle* (?).
Turner, *Ulysses Deriding Polyphemus.*

1830

Death of George IV, accession of William IV. Fall of Wellington's Ministry, Grey Prime Minister. Increasing agitation for reform, agrarian disturbances. Revolution in France. Huskisson killed at opening of Liverpool-Manchester railway. Hood's *Comic Annual* founded. Hazlitt dies.

Bentham, *The Rationale of Punishment.*
Bulwer-Lytton, *Paul Clifford.*
Cobbett, *Rural Rides.*
Godwin, *Cloudesley.*
Lyell, *Principles of Geology* (completed, 1833).
Moore, *Letters and Journals of Lord Byron: with Notices of his Life.*
Scott, *Tales of a Grandfather.*
Tennyson, *Poems, Chiefly Lyrical.*
Turner, *The Evening Star; The Lake, Petworth* (?).

1831

Separation of Belgium and Holland. First Reform Bill. Dissolution of Parliament; general election. Final Reform Bill introduced. Faraday begins investigations into magneto-electricity. Darwin sails on *Beagle*.

Disraeli, *The Young Duke.*
Elliott, *Corn-Law Rhymes.*
Ferrier, *Destiny.*
Peacock, *Crotchet Castle.*
Wordsworth, *Yarrow Revisited.*

1832

Wellington fails to form a ministry. Grey secures passage of Reform Bill. First geological survey at state expense. Bentham, Crabbe, Scott die.

Bulwer-Lytton, *Eugene Aram.*
DeQuincey, *Klosterheim.*
Disraeli, *Contarini Fleming.*
Martineau, *Illustrations of Political Economy.*
Scott, *Count Robert of Paris; Castle Dangerous.*
Shelley, *The Masque of Anarchy.*
Tennyson, *Poems.*
Constable, *Waterloo Bridge.*

Selected Bibliography

~

Only a few works of special interest or of convenience to students of literature are included here; comprehensive listings can be found in most of the works cited in the first section, and in the other sections I call attention to those books with specially useful bibliographies. Place of publication is London unless otherwise indicated.

1. Literary References

The *Cambridge Bibliography of English Literature*, Vol. III, ed. F. W. Bateson, (Cambridge, England, 1940), covers the nineteenth century and is supplemented by Vol. V, ed. G. Watson, 1957. The *Dictionary of National Biography*, founded 1882, reprinted in 22 volumes, 1908–1909, gives biographical data on major and minor figures alike. *Annals of English Literature, 1475–1950*, 2nd ed., 1961, lists books published each year. C. R. L. Fletcher's and Emery Walker's *Historical Portraits 1700–1850* (1919) is the easiest place to see what leading historical figures looked like.

The annual bibliography published by the Modern Language Association of America is up-to-date, accurate, and remarkably complete. *The Year's Work in English Studies* is published annually by the English Association, and the Modern Humanities Research Association publishes the *Annual Bibliography of English Language and Literature,* now very nearly up to date. David Erdman edits for the Modern Language Association a *Bibliography of Romanticism,* appearing each year as a supplement to *English Language Notes,* formerly in *Philological Quarterly* and before that in *Journal of English Literary History.* The *Keats-Shelley Journal* publishes, besides articles on Keats, Shelley, Byron and their associates, an excellent bibliography and book reviews. *Studies in Romanticism* is a journal devoted to the publication of essays on all aspects of Romanticism.

The English Romantic Poets: A Review of Research, ed.
Thomas M. Raysor, rev. ed. (New York, 1956) and *The English
Romantic Poets and Essayists: A Review of Research and Criticism,* ed. C. W. and L. H. Houtchens, 2nd rev. ed. (1966) provide
judicious guidance for the fifteen most important authors of the
period. Vols. IX and X of the Oxford History of English Literature are the best recent histories: W. L. Renwick's *English Literature 1789–1815* (1963) is a useful survey with a good bibliography, and Ian Jack's *English Literature 1815–1832* is an excellent
survey with a fine bibliography. Vols. III and IV of Allardyce
Nicoll's *A History of English Drama* (1955) contain indispensable bibliographies. Only a small portion of the same author's *The
Development of the Theatre,* 5th rev. ed. (1966), treats of the
Romantic era, but both pictures and text convey vividly the most
significant characteristics of the Romantic theatre.

2. *The Nature and Significance of Romanticism*

There are innumerable books and essays about literary Romanticism. Probably the best book for the beginner is *Romanticism Reconsidered,* ed. Northrop Frye, Selected Papers from the
English Institute (New York, 1963). This volume contains essays
by Frye, Meyer Abrams, Lionel Trilling, and René Wellek, each
lucid, original, and sensible. Wellek, both as a theoretician and as
a historian, is in my view the most important student of Romanticism of the past quarter of a century. One of his primary
theoretical statements is to be found in two articles published in
Comparative Literature: "The Term 'Romantic' and its Deriva-
tives," Vol. I, No. 1 (Winter, 1949), pp. 1–23; and "The Unity of
European Romanticism," Vol. I, No. 2 (Spring, 1949), pp.
147–172. An interesting reply to these articles by the distinguished Chicago critic R. S. Crane is to be found in *Philological
Quarterly,* XXIX, No. 3 (July, 1950), pp. 257–59. One of Wellek's major historical contributions is his monumental *History of
Modern Criticism 1750–1950,* Vol. II (1955) and Vol. III (1965),
both New Haven, covering the chief Romantic critics. One of
Wellek's persistent concerns is the refutation of A. O. Lovejoy,
whose famous denial of Romantic unity, "On the Discrimina-
tions of Romanticisms" (*PMLA* XXXIX, No. 2, June, 1924, pp.

229–53) is reprinted in *Essays in the History of Ideas* (Baltimore, 1948), along with some related articles. Lovejoy implicitly reaffirms his position in *The Reason, The Understanding, and Time* (Baltimore, 1961).

Another significant theorist is Morse Peckham. His most important statements will be found in "Toward a Theory of Romanticism," *PMLA,* LXIV, No. 2 (March, 1951), pp. 5–23; "Toward a Theory of Romanticism. Reconsiderations," *Studies in Romanticism,* I, No. 1 (Autumn, 1961), pp. 1–8; and *Beyond the Tragic Vision* (New York, 1962). Peckham, however, has been less influential than Meyer H. Abrams, whose *The Mirror and the Lamp* (New York, 1953) has provided the fundamental terminology of most discussions of Romanticism during the past decade. More interested in patterns of poetic practice than in theory is Albert Gérard, whose *L'idée romantique de la poésie en Angleterre* (Paris, 1956) is undoubtedly the best French book on the subject. Of the many German studies of Romanticism Max Deutschbein's *Das Wesen des Romantischen* (1921) will perhaps be the most congenial to students of English literature. The best of the modern Italian scholars of the early nineteenth century is Mario Fubini, who, unfortunately, has written little on English Romanticism, though there is much of value to students of other literatures in his *Romanticismo Italiano* (Bari, 1953), for example. Probably the most interesting application of Benedetto Croce's theories to British Romantic literature is still Annie E. Powell's (Mrs. Dodd's) *The Romantic Theory of Poetry, An Examination in the Light of Croce's Aesthetic* (1926).

There are many specialized studies which either explicitly or implicitly define significant aspects of literary Romanticism. Among these I should single out for special notice the first chapter of Robert Langbaum's *The Poetry of Experience* (1957), Earl Wasserman's *The Subtler Language* (Baltimore, 1959), G. Wilson Knight's *The Starlit Dome: Studies in the Poetry of Vision,* rev. ed. (1959), Paul de Man's "Structure intentionelle de l'image romantique," *Revue internationale de philosophie,* No. 51 (1960), pp. 68–84; and Geoffrey Hartman's "Romanticism and 'Antiself-consciousness,' " *The Centennial Review,* VI, No. 3 (Fall, 1962), pp. 553–65.

Good collections of essays which attack the problem of Romanticism through the elucidation of particular trends or works are *The English Romantic Poets,* ed. Meyer Abrams (New York, 1960), *The Major English Romantic Poets,* ed. Clarence D. Thorpe et al. (Carbondale, 1957), and *From Sensibility to Romanticism: Essays Presented to Frederick A. Pottle,* ed. F. W. Hilles and Harold Bloom (New York, 1965). When wearied by too much theory one can turn to the factual tabulation of F. Baldensperger, " 'Romantique,' ses analogues et ses équivalents: tableau synoptique de 1650 à 1810" in *Harvard Studies and Notes in Philology and Literature,* XIX (1937), pp. 13–105; or to Ernest Bernbaum's now somewhat antiquated *Guide Through the Romantic Movement,* rev. ed. (New York, 1948). Refreshed, one can tackle "The Romantic Reaction," Chapter 5 of Alfred N. Whitehead's *Science and the Modern World* (Cambridge, 1925), the best treatment of the subject by a major twentieth-century philosopher.

3. Social, Political, and Intellectual History

Adamson, J. W. *English Education, 1789–1902* (1930). Sensible and informative; useful bibliography.

Altick, Richard D. *The English Common Reader: A Social History of the Mass Reading Public, 1800–1900* (Chicago, 1957). Good survey of an important topic.

Aspinall, A. *Politics and the Press, 1780–1850* (1949). The best general treatment of the subject.

Bovill, E. W. *The England of Nimrod and Surtees, 1815–1854* (1959). Similar to *English Country Life.*

Briggs, Asa. *The Age of Improvement* (1959). Original and judicious.

Brown, F. K. *Fathers of the Victorians: The Age of Wilberforce* (1961). For an understanding of the Evangelicals.

Bryant, Sir Arthur. *The Years of Endurance* (1942). *Years of Victory* (1944). *The Age of Elegance* (1950). Popular account of Napoleonic wars; good guys clearly distinguished from bad guys. The first volume is the best, but the last includes a vivid narrative of the Czar's visit to England.

Clark, G. S. R. *The English Inheritance* (1950). The Romantic era occupies only a portion of this excellent discussion of the influence of religion on English culture.

Coupland, R. *The British Anti-Slavery Movement* (1933). Good study of an important issue.

Court, W. H. B. *A Concise Economic History of Britain from 1750 to Recent Times* (Cambridge, England, 1954). Excellent on the industrial revolution.

Darvall, F. O. *Popular Disturbances and Public Order in Regency England* (1934). Helps to make sense of many confused events.

Davidson, W. L. *Political Thought in England: The Utilitarians From Bentham to Mill* (1915). Less valuable than Halévy's work but brief and readable.

Feiling, K. *Sketches in Nineteenth Century Biography* (1930). Vivid and amusing portraits of many of the leading figures of the Romantic period.

Halévy, Élie. *The Growth of Philosophical Radicalism* (English translation, 1928). Still the most thorough account of this movement.

————. *The Liberal Awakening, 1815–1830.* (English translation, 1926.) Another volume in Halévy's monumental series, *Histoire du peuple anglais au XIXe siècle.*

Hammond, J. L., and Barbara Hammond. *The Village Labourer, 1760–1832* (1911). *The Town Labourer, 1760–1832* (1917). *The Skilled Labourer, 1760–1832* (1919). Detailed but fascinating volumes by committed writers.

Palmer, R. R. *The Age of Democratic Revolution: A Political History of Europe and America, 1760–1800;* Part I, *The Challenge* (1959); Part II, *The Struggle* (1964). Palmer is broader in scope and more concerned with intellectual history than Lefebvre.

Seton-Watson, R. W. *Britain in Europe, 1789–1914: a Survey of Foreign Policy* (Cambridge, England, 1937). The best study of this topic.

Thompson, E. P. *The Making of the English Working Class* (1963). Excellent social history including intelligent commentaries on some of the poets.

Trevelyan, G. M. *British History in the Nineteenth Century and After*, 2nd ed. (1937).

——. *Illustrated English Social History: The Nineteenth Century* (1952). Both brilliantly succinct.

Watson, J. Steven. *The Reign of George III, 1760–1815* (1960). Vol. 12 of the Oxford History of England (Woodward's book noted below is Vol. 13); thorough and well-balanced.

Wearmouth, R. F. *Methodism and the History of the Working Class Movements of England, 1800–1850* (1937). Interesting for both social and religious history.

Willey, Basil. *The Eighteenth Century Background* (1940). *The Nineteenth Century Background* (1949). Some essays from each book treat matters of importance to Romanticism.

Woodward, Sir Llewellyn. *The Age of Reform, 1815–1870*, 2nd ed. (1962). Because this book is organized topically, the student interested in the Romantic era must skip around. The skipping is richly rewarded. Fine bibliography.

4. Science and Exploration

Baker, J. N. L. *History of Geographical Discovery and Exploration* (1931). Succinct if somewhat drab descriptions of all the principal expeditions.

Beaglehole, J. C. *The Exploration of the Pacific* (1934). Best scholarly study of the subject.

Eiseley, Loren. *Darwin's Century: Evolution and the Men Who Discovered It* (1960). Highly readable survey.

Gillispie, C. C. *The Edge of Objectivity* (Princeton, 1960). The first part of this fine book is especially relevant to Romanticism.

Moorehead, Alan. *The Fatal Impact: An Account of the Invasion of the South Pacific 1767–1840* (New York, 1966). Brilliantly written, popular but accurate, with handy bibliography.

Singer, C. *A Short History of Science in the Nineteenth Century* (1941). Good general survey.

Von Hagen, Victor W. *South America Called Them* (New York, 1945). Treats the major explorers of the New World.

5. The Arts

Badt, Kurt. *John Constable's Clouds* (English translation, 1950). Relates Constable's art to the practice of contemporaneous poets and the intellectual-scientific movements of his day.

Boase, T. S. R. *English Art 1800–1870* (1959). A useful compendium with a good bibliography.

Bradbury, R. *The Romantic Theories of Architecture of the Nineteenth Century in Germany, England, and France* (New York, 1934). One of the few works focusing on Romantic architecture as a distinctive style.

Butlin, Martin. *The Watercolours of J. M. W. Turner* (1951). Fullest study of one phase of Turner's art.

Clark, H. F. *The English Landscape Garden* (1948). Sensible general account.

Clark, Sir Kenneth. *Landscape Into Art* (1948). One of the most stimulating of modern art historians has much to say of relevance to Romantic art.

———. *On the Painting of English Landscape.* British Academy Lecture (1935).

George, M. Dorothy. *English Political Caricature 1793–1832* (1959). A fascinating study which illuminates both the art and the political-social history of the period.

Gillray, James. *Fashionable Contrasts.* Introduction and annotations by Draper Hill (1966). Splendid illustrations.

Hoskins, W. G. *The Making of the English Landscape* (1955). Describes how social and technological developments transformed the countryside.

Hussey, Christopher. *The Picturesque* (1927). An important book, though the definition of "the picturesque" is unduly narrow.

Klingender, F. D. *Art and the Industrial Revolution* (1947). Somewhat disappointing but the best book on a significant topic.

Lemaitre, Henri. *Le paysage anglais à l'aquarelle 1760–1851* (Paris, 1955). Perceptive survey.

Newton, Ric. *The Romantic Rebellion* (1962). Original and stimulating.

Rothenstein, Sir John, and Martin Butlin. *Turner* (1964). Deals only with the oil paintings.

Summerson, Sir John. *Architecture in Britain 1530–1830* (1953). Sound general history.

————. *John Nash, Architect to King George IV* (1935). Still the best book on the leading architect of the Regency period.

Whitley, W. T. *Artists and Their Friends in England 1790–1799* (1925). *Art in England 1800–1820* (1928). *Art in England 1821–1837* (1930). The three volumes are a mine of detailed information.

6. Selections Included in This Volume

Ashton, T. S. *The Industrial Revolution, 1760–1830* (New York, Galaxy Book Edition, 1964 [1st ed., 1948]); Chapter 1, "Introduction," pp. 3–17.

Bovill, E. W. *English Country Life, 1780–1830* (1962); from Chapter 12, "The Poaching War," pp. 174–183 and pp. 191–196.

Forbes, R. J. "Power to 1850," Chapter 5, Vol. IV of Charles Singer et al., eds., *A History of Technology*, 5 vols. (Oxford, 1958); pp. 148–164.

Gowing Lawrence. *Turner: Imagination and Reality* (New York, 1966); pp. 7–10.

Graham, Walter. *English Literary Periodicals* (New York, 1930); from Chapter 8, "The *Edinburgh, Quarterly,* and *Westminster* Reviews," pp. 230–237 and 238–245.

Halévy, Élie. *England in 1815,* Vol. I of *A History of the English People in the 19th Century,* 2nd rev. ed., translated by E. I. Watkin (1960 [first published in French, 1913]); from Part III, Chapter 2, "Fine Arts, Literature and Science," pp. 571–587.

Hammond, J. L., and Barbara Hammond. *The Rise of Modern Industry,* 7th ed. (1947 [1st ed., 1925]); from Chapter 13, "The Curse of Midas," pp. 210–223.

Lefebvre, Georges. *The French Revolution from 1793 to 1799,* translated from the 2nd ed. in French (1957) by John Hall Stewart and James Friguglietti (New York, 1964); from Chapter 15, "Revolutionary Expansion and its Effects," pp. 318–324, and from Chapter 17, "The Results of the War," pp. 347–355.

Pilcher, Donald. *The Regency Style, 1800 to 1830* (1947); from

Chapter 3, "Taste and Technique," pp. 47–50, and from Chapter 5, "Town and Countryside," pp. 85–86, 91–92.

Singer, Charles. See Forbes, R. J., above.

Smith, Bernard. *European Vision and the South Pacific, 1769–1850* (Oxford, 1960) ; Chapter 1, "Introductory: The European and the Pacific," pp. 1–7.

Somervell, D. C. *English Thought in the Nineteenth Century* (1929) ; from Chapter 1, "The Old Tory Orthodoxy," pp. 3–8, and from Chapter 2, "Religion and Philanthropy," pp. 16–27.

Trevelyan, G. M. *History of England*, 3rd ed. (1952 reissue, with minor corrections [1st ed., 1926]) ; from Chapter 5 of Book V, pp. 571–587.

White, Reginald James. *Waterloo to Peterloo* (New York, 1957) ; from Chapter 15, "Peterloo," pp. 179–187.